Judaism, Christianity, and Islam

 Global Connections

School of Modern Languages and Cultures
The University of Hong Kong

Series General Editor: Dixon H. W. Wong

The Global Connections series explores the movement of ideas, people, technologies, capital and goods across national and regional borders. Books in the series reveal how these interconnections have the power to produce new global forms of cultures, politics, identities, and economies. Seeking to explore the dynamics of change, the series includes both historical and contemporary topics. It focuses on interactions between the world's diverse cultures through the production of new interdisciplinary knowledge.

Also in the Global Connections series:

Narratives of Free Trade: The Commercial Cultures of Early US-China Relations
Edited by Kendall Johnson

Europe and China: Strategic Partners or Rivals?
Edited by Roland Vogt

Harbin to Hanoi: The Colonial Built Environment in Asia, 1840 to 1940
Edited by Laura Victoir and Victor Zatsepine

Drawing New Color Lines: Transnational Asian American Graphic Narratives
Edited by Monica Chiu

Judaism, Christianity, and Islam

Collaboration and Conflict in the Age of Diaspora

Edited by Sander L. Gilman

HKU
PRESS
香港大學出版社

Hong Kong University Press
The University of Hong Kong
Pokfulam Road
Hong Kong
www.hkupress.org

© 2014 Hong Kong University Press

ISBN 978-988-8208-27-2 *(Hardback)*

British Library Cataloguing-in-Publication Data
A catalogue record for this book is available from the British Library.

10 9 8 7 6 5 4 3 2 1

Printed and bound by Paramount Printing Co., Ltd. in Hong Kong, China

Contents

Contributors

Mehnaz M. Afridi is assistant professor of religious studies and director of the Holocaust, Genocide, and Interfaith Education Center at Manhattan College. She is committed to interfaith, and Holocaust education. Her expertise is in contemporary Islam and the Holocaust. She teaches Islam, Judaism, world religions and genocide studies.

Wayne Cristaudo is professor of politics at Charles Darwin University, NT Australia. He has written and edited various books, journals articles and chapters on the philosophical history of ideas and institutions. His latest books are *Religion, Redemption and Revolution: The New Speech Thinking of Franz Rosenzweig and Eugen Rosenstock-Huessy* (2012) and *A Philosophical History of Love* (2012).

Yulia Egorova is senior lecturer in anthropology at Durham University. Her research interests include anthropology of Jewish communities and anthropology of science. She is a co-author of *The Jews of Andhra Pradesh: Contesting Caste and Religion in South Asia* (2013).

David Feldman is professor of history and director of the Pears Institute for the Study of Antisemitism at Birkbeck, University of London. He has written on the history of Jews in Britain as well as on migrants and immigrants. He is currently working on a book to be titled *The Meanings of Anti-Semitism*.

Katja Garloff is professor of German and humanities at Reed College, where she specializes in German Jewish culture, critical theory, and contemporary German literature. She is the author of *Words from Abroad: Trauma and Displacement in Postwar German Jewish Writers* (2005).

Jane Garnett is fellow and tutor in history at Wadham College, Oxford. She has published widely on religious, intellectual and cultural history. She is working with Michael Keith on the Oxford Diasporas Programme, funded by the Leverhulme Trust from 2011 to 2015.

Sander L. Gilman is a distinguished professor of the liberal arts and sciences as well as professor of psychiatry at Emory University. He was a visiting research professor at The University of Hong Kong from 2010 to 2013. A cultural and literary historian, he is the author or editor of over eighty books. His *Obesity: The Biography* appeared in 2010; his most recent edited volume, *The Third Reich Sourcebook* (with Anson Rabinbach), was published in 2013.

Benjamin Hary is a professor of Hebrew, Arabic, and linguistics and the director of the Program in Linguistics at Emory University. He is interested in Judeo-Arabic language and linguistics in the framework of the Jewish linguistic spectrum, Jews in the Islamic world, Religion and Language and sociolinguistics and dialectology. Hary is the author of *Multiglossia in Judeo-Arabic* (1992); *Translating Religion* (2009) and the forthcoming *Sacred Texts in Judeo-Arabic*. He has also edited *Corpus Linguistics and Modern Hebrew* (2003) and co-edited *Judaism and Islam—Boundaries, Communication, and Interaction* (2000) and *Esoteric and Exoteric Aspects in Judeo-Arabic Culture* (2006). He is currently working on *The Jewish Languages—An International Handbook* (2016).

Michael Keith has a personal chair in the School of Anthropology at the University of Oxford and has been the director of Centre on Migration, Policy and Society (COMPAS), core funded by the Economic and Social Research Council, since 2008. He is working on projects on labor markets, citizenship and belonging, and urban change and settlement.

Martin J. Wein was born in Frankfurt am Main, Germany. He holds an MA in Jewish studies from Emory University and a PhD in Jewish history from Ben Gurion University. His research specialization includes Czech-Israeli relations, modern Central European–Middle Eastern ties, Czechoslovak multilingual and interreligious history, history of sacred text translation, Bible translation, and theory of nationalism.

Zhou Xun is lecturer in modern history at the University of Essex. Born in Sichuan province, China, Dr. Zhou received her PhD from the University of London in 1998. In the past twenty years, she has lived in London, Jerusalem, Beijing, and Hong Kong. She has authored or co-authored a number of ground-breaking books including *Chinese Perceptions of the 'Jews' and Judaism: A History of the Youtai* (2001). Between 2007 and 2012, she worked on a project on the Great Famine in China under Mao. *The Great Famine in China, 1957–1962: A Documentary History (2012)* and *Forgotten Voices of Mao's Great Famine, 1958–1961: An Oral History* (2013) are the labor of her research. Dr. Zhou has also a long track record of media activities. Her most recent media appearance include the new French documentary film *Mao's Great Famine* (2012) and BBC Radio 4 program *As History Is My Witness* (October 2012).

Introduction

The Abrahamic Religions in an Age of Diaspora

Sander L. Gilman

In his 1922 explanation of what constitutes "ethnicity," the German sociologist Max Weber claimed that "the belief in group affinity, regardless of whether it has any objective foundation, can have important consequences especially for the formation of a political community" (Weber 1922, 56). Today we understand that the key word here for Weber is "belief." If you believe that you are part of a community, there is an affective aspect to your identification that then defines the group itself. Neither history, nor biology, nor national boundaries is primary; belief is central. One can add to this statement that this is equally true in constituting the religious communities of others. Non-Jews have regularly constituted the image and nature of the "Jew" as seen from their perspectives and needs (as Jean-Paul Sartre admirably illustrated in his *Anti-Semite and Jew* [1995]). The image of the Christian, seen from the perspective of secular society, which is itself grounded on Christian presuppositions, is as compromised as that of the Jew: Are Christians perpetrators or victims passive or active? Are they Protestant or Catholic or otherwise defined? After 9/11 the very image of the Muslim and of Islam is also fractured: not only do the older fissures of theological differences within Islam, such as Shia, Sunni, Alawite, Druse, etc., take on new meaning, but they also are read along newer national and political lines, as well as along reformist and neo-conservative ones. From the standpoint of non-Muslims in the West the schism seems between "terrorists" and benign Muslims (if such a dichotomy is even permitted to exist). Never mind the complexity when we begin to tease out how each of the fragmented views of Jew, Christian, and Muslim are understood from the multiple perspectives of the various segments of the other religious communities. And indeed can we even claim that individual identities as Jew, Christian, or Muslim are only the concretization of the more generalized if complex image of the religious community? Can you be a Jew, Christian, or Muslim outside of or beyond a religious practice?

Sigmund Freud argued, shortly after World War I, that all such community images were constituted out of antithesis. He wrote in "Group Psychology and the Analysis of the Ego" (1921) that:

Every time two families become connected by a marriage, each of them thinks itself superior to or of better birth than the other. Of two neighbouring towns each is the other's most jealous rival; every little canton looks down upon the others with contempt. Closely related races keep one another at arm's length; the South German cannot endure the North German, the Englishman casts every kind of aspersion upon the Scot, the Spaniard despises the Portuguese. We are no longer astonished that greater differences should lead to an almost insuperable repugnance, such as the Gallic people feel for the German, the Aryan for the Semite, and the white races for the coloured. (Freud 1921, SE 18:100)

This idea of conflict becomes commonplace in the 1920s, echoed by thinkers such as Carl Schmitt in his dichotomy of "friend and foe" in his *The Concept of the Political* (1927), in which, like Freud's view, the potential of conflict did not foreclose the potential of collaboration (Beattie 2010).

It should be of little surprise that the Abrahamic religions today—with multiple national, cultural, linguistic, class, gender identities—desire to imagine that what constitutes their own religious identity is seemingly independent of such a world of complex images. Yet it is very clear that today, at least within diasporic culture, those images are often framed by the debates about multiculturalism within the context of the Abrahamic religions and are defined by multiple potentials of conflict but also by collaboration. Judaism, Christianity, and Islam constitute their own, multifaceted self-images as well as images of the other "related" religions as forms of ritual practice, historical antecedents, or ethnic or national identities. Today such images shape both conflicts among as well as collaboration between the Abrahamic religions, often in odd forms. Thus, the positive representation of Jews in evangelical Christianity is as those who will trigger the second coming, while Islam has assumed, at least according to preachers such as the American Evangelical preacher Franklin Graham, the negative image long associated with Jewish conspiracies against Christians. Graham stated that the "persecution or elimination of non-Muslims has been a cornerstone of Islamic conquests and rule for centuries" and referred to Islam as "a very evil and wicked religion" (Niebuhr 2001). These images come to be free-floating signifiers moving from one Abrahamic religion to another based on the dynamics of the inter-relationship among them.

Theodor Adorno claimed in *Minima Moralia* that "dwelling, in the proper sense, is now impossible. The traditional residences we grew up in have grown intolerable . . . the house is past . . . it is part of morality not to be home in one's home" (Adorno 1951, 87). And yet the claims of a new Abrahamic multiculturalism beginning with the twenty-first century are that this rupture has been healed. Jews, Christians, and Muslims are equally "at home" in national cultures as well as "global citizens." In his insightful study *Cosmopolitanism*, the Princeton philosopher Kwame Anthony Appiah points out that the new globalization is both constrained and furthered by the new nationalism (Appiah 2007). He quotes what is perhaps the ultimate colonial, cosmopolitan text, the Victorian explorer Sir Richard Burton's 1880 "translation" of the Sufi *Kasidah of Haji Abdu El-Yezi*:

> All Faith is false, all faith is true:
> Truth is the shattered mirror strown
> In Myriad bits: while each believes
> His little bit the whole to own. (Appiah 2007, 296)

Burton's version of G. E. Lessing's (Christian) Enlightenment promise of the Abrahamic religions as identical in their revelation mirrored in the "Parable of the Three Rings" in his drama *Nathan the Wise* still holds out the fantasy that even if the other two rings are perfect copies, there is an original, true ring among the three. But are the cultures in which the Abrahamic religions are to be found neutral about this new sense of globalized religious identity? Are they today more tolerant of seeing their bit of the mirror as one part of a whole or do they continue to compete, so that conflict rather than collaboration defines the Abrahamic religions in the twenty-first century?

The Abrahamic religious cultures existing in the Western world and beyond during the last two centuries have been and continue to be read as hyphenated phenomena within a specific national context, such as German-Jewish or American-Muslim culture. Even where the new nationalism reflects the creation of a state defined by one of the Abrahamic religions the answer is never simple. The creation of the State of Israel as a Jewish State has led to classifications within Israeli society (from the ultra orthodox to the secular, from the "Arab" [Mizrachi] to the "European" [Ashkenazi]) to the radical secular *but* nevertheless Jewish Israeli. In addition the status of Christians and Muslims is often defined by their political rather than their religious identity. Added to this, the extensive Israeli Diaspora ("Israeli-Americans") and the complexity of Jewish identity in the twentieth century have become more rather than less contested. States founded to make Sharia law the defining moment of the national state, such as Iran after the "Islamic Revolution" in 1979, make clear differences between modes of religious belief that would globally be called "Muslim." The differences between Shia and Sunni define Iranian political acceptability while offshoots of Islam, such as the members of the Baha'i faith, are simply labeled heretics by law and fall completely beyond the boundaries of traditional (if in Iran marginal) toleration for Jews and Christians as fellow members of the Abrahamic tradition. But twenty-first-century Christianity, too, has its own complex relationship to national states that have become more and more secular. In Great Britain, where the monarch remains the head of the Church of England, the Archbishop of Canterbury complained in 2013 of the anti-Christian views of her majesty's government (supported by political parties on the right and the left) on issues such as gay marriage, and the British population has shown a marked collapse in the belief that being "British" has anything at all to do with being "Christian," even in historical or ethical contexts.

Even historically, such constructs are undermined by the histories of Abrahamic expulsion and migration, which were accompanied by the migration of languages and cultural-religious expressions that were written out of the cultural paradigms of particular nation states and the dominant religious communities within. The Enlightenment's demand that all human beings be understood as equal was paralleled by the nation-states' understanding of the need for such universality to be defined in terms of national identity. Immanuel Kant's claim that Christianity, Judaism, and Islam are all underpinned by a rational religious belief differing only in the nature of their claims about revelation as the source of the internal coherence is typical (Kleingeld 2011, 120). This conflict, which in the West subsumed religious identity with personal or national identity shaped religious identity of all forms in modernity. It is, of course, specious, as Kant's idea of rationality is Christian in its underpinnings. Christian thinkers since at least the Renaissance have imagined Jewish thought, specifically that of the "pilpul," the mode of Talmudic argument, as inherently irrational because it violates the premises of Western logic, specifically the syllogism.

Yet to what extent do such nationalized constructs of Abrahamic culture and identity still dominate religious self-expressions, as well as the discourses about them, in the rapidly globalizing world of the twenty-first century? In a world in which diaspora societies have begun to reshape themselves as part of a super-or non-national identity, the virtual Ummah of contemporary Islam, for example, what has happened to religious identity? How are the Abrahamic religions now understood as transcending the old boundaries and ideologies of nation states or their continental reconfigurations, such as Europe or North America, but also as crossing the fragmentation of internal distinctions, as well as the confines of national states, such as Israel and Iran, and the diasporic communities that result from them? In a cosmopolitan world where the newest and most substantial diaspora communities are defined by a mix of religious, political, and ethnic identities in a new globalized culture, is "being religious" suddenly something that can reach beyond the older models of diasporic integration or nationalism? Which new paradigms of Abrahamic self-location within the evolving and conflicting global discourses about the nation, race, history, anti-religious feeling, colonialism and post-colonialism, gender and sexual identity does the globalization of the Abrahamic cultures open up, and to what extent might transnational notions of religious identity create new discursive margins and centers?

The terms themselves are constituent of the compromise formations necessary to comprehend "religious" culture in a self-consciously multicultural world. Let me use one example: The term "Arab" (and "Persian") Jews has its own history. "Jewish

Arabian" tribes were defeated by Islam in the 620s and early 630s and their medieval relics were the Jews of Khaibar or refugees such as those from the city of Dar'a in Transjordan and perhaps the city of Hit in Mesopotamia. To modern Iraqi Jews, the terms "Hitis" and "Jews of Khaibar" refer to the Karaites, which perhaps confirms Samuel Goitein's general hypothesis about proto-Karaism among Arabian Jews. Iraqi Jews fiercely dislike Hiti Jews, or more exactly, the Karaite community that lived in Hit until 1950. "Hiti" is considered synonymous, to modern Iraqi Jews, with the despised "Yehud Khebar," i.e., the "Yahud Khaibar" of northern Arabia who are identified as those who went to Hit. Yet medieval Jews from the Khaibar region had resorted to the Gaonate. When Yassir Arafat's brother held a Kuwaiti-funded chair in the United Kingdom, he focused his research on the Jewish tribes defeated in Arabia, as this provided a history of "Arab"–"Jewish" conflict as though it was perennial. The "Bachutzim" communities of Tunisia were "Arabs," as perceived by the other Tunisian Jews, i.e., the regular Twansa, and the Gorna (the latter being of Leghorn extraction). "Arab Jews" are one of the two self-perceived subdivisions of Jews in Hilla, Iraq, in modern times. A brief experimentation with "Arab Jewish" identity in the 1920s and 1930s was undertaken to accommodate Arab sovereign states. Yet to both Jews and Muslims, it was artificial. Jews felt Iraqi, or Egyptian, and so forth, but not Arab, and Arabs in turn used to be bound to what in Europe was an either premodern or a far-right notion, by which nations are defined by religion, and vice versa (e.g., Arabs and Turks are Muslims, and to this very day, in secularist but nationalist Turkey, informal prejudice blocking promotion is based on that belief, whereas in Ottoman Constantinople Jews could attain high ranks from the 1870s, e.g. as medical officers in the army). Today if you find yourself in Los Angeles, you might find within an American Conservative religious congregation, such as Sinai Temple, 107 years old, now with a large "Persian" Jewish community, a split between the older immigrants from Iran and their newly Americanized children over the issue of gay marriage, a question inconceivable in today's Iran (Nagourney 2013). Who are the "Arab" Jews and how do they relate to the other Abrahamic religions and cultures? The answer is historically dynamic and culturally fraught.

We are focusing in this volume on Abrahamic cultures and identities as minoritized ethnic and cultural groups in a diaspora that may be majority Muslim, Christian, Jewish or self-consciously secular. It is clear that if one of the major foci of any project on globalized religion is the interface of the "Abrahamic" religions, then this arena demands further and more comprehensive study. It is the seeming closeness of "Abrahamic" religions and their joint histories that draws attention to their real or imagined differences in relation to the majority religion and its new form: secular society. Even our key term is complicated. "The 'Abrahamic' religions" is the newest politically correct phrase: the "Judeo-Christian tradition" was the catchphrase for common aspects shared between Judaism and Christianity after the Holocaust made this an acceptable notion; "the Abrahamic religions" is the new buzzword, which has become current only after 9/11, that incorporates Islam into the Judeo-Christian fold. Both phases attempt to defuse the clearly Christian aspects of modern Western secular society by expanding it, but, of course, in doing so only re-emphasize it. Here Jonathan Sacks's notion of difference is helpful: in creating categories that elide difference, that stress superficial similarities one believes that one is bridging "differences" (Sacks 2002, 53). Actually one is submerging them.

The historic acknowledgment, for good or for ill, of the closeness of Judaism, Christianity, and Islam results in what Sigmund Freud called the "narcissism of minor differences." Those differences are heightened in a secular society, which is rooted in the mindset and often the attitudes, beliefs, social mores, and civic practices of the majority religious community, which in Western Europe is Christianity. Thus, in Western Europe there was a radical secularization of religious institutions throughout the course of the nineteenth century. The new minority was promised a wide range of civil rights (relabeled by the twentieth century as "human" or "natural" rights)—including those of freedom of religion—if only they adhered to the standards of civilized behavior as defined by the secular society. This is rooted in the desire to make sure that that society with its masked religious assumptions redefines a minorities' religious practice or "secularizes" a religious minority into an "ethnic" one. The standards of "civilized behavior" are, for the most part, secularized versions of the claims of Christianity (either in its Catholic or Protestant forms) for appropriate behavior. Here, the claims are little different from those of the colonial belief in a civilizing mission. Secularization may be opposed to "religion," but when this opposition is examined, we find that it is usually cast in terms of the warfare between "theology" and "science" (also the title of a major book of 1896 by the former American Ambassador in Berlin, Andrew Dickson White). "Theology" is a specific religious claim or structure rather than a religious belief itself. Thus Jewish and Islamic claims as well as those from certain directions of Christian belief (Catholic or Puritan from the perspective of the liberal Andrew Dickson White) are seen as in need of modification. What that modification is and how it is to be accomplished is at the core of our question.

Can we now look at the experiences within the various strands of Jewish religious (and therefore social) ritual practice from the late eighteenth century (which marked the beginning of the civil emancipation of the Jews and the claim of a "human right" to one's own religious belief and practice) that parallel those now confronting diaspora Islam in "secular" (read "Christian") Western Europe. Here the trope of "foe and friend" needs to be sharpened based on the potential for collaboration around common interests in states that see their secular identity as separate from their own Christian history. The similarities between Western European attitudes toward Islamic practice and Jewish ritual in the twenty-first century are striking:

a religious minority enters into a self-described secular (or secularizing) society which is Christian in its rhetoric and presuppositions and which perceives a "special relationship" with this minority. The co-territorial society sees this entry as an act of aggression. The minority speaks a different secular language and also has a different religious language. This may be seen as odd in countries that have a national language and (in some) a religious language but not a secular language spoken by a religious minority. Religious schools that teach in the languages associated with the religious group are seen as sources of corruption and illness. Religious rites are practiced that seem an abomination to the majority "host" culture: unlike the secular majority these religious communities practice the mutilation of children's bodies (infant male circumcision and, for some Muslims, infant female genital cutting); the suppression of the rights of women (lack of women's traditional education; a secondary role in religious practice; arranged marriages; honor killings); barbaric torture of animals (the cutting of the throats of unstunned animals allowing them to bleed to death); disrespect for the dead through too rapid burial; ritual excess (drunkenness at Purim in the case of the Jews; feasting during Ramadan in the case of the Muslims); ostentatious clothing that signals religious affiliation and has ritual significance (from women's hair covering such as the Muslim hijab or Jewish sheitels to men's hats such as the Eastern European Jewish shtremil or the Arab kafiyya); and, centrally relating all of these practices: a belief in the divine "chosen-ness" of the group in contrast to all others. The demonization of aspects of religious practice has its roots in what civil society will tolerate and what it will not, what it considers to be decorous and what is unacceptable as a social practice. Why it will not tolerate something is, of course, central to the story. Thus, Alan Dundes argued almost twenty-five years ago that the anxiety about meanings associated with the consumption of the body and blood of Christ in the Christian Mass shaped the fantasy of the Jews as slaughtering Christian children for their blood (Dundes 1991, 336–345). This image lies at the core of both Jewish and Muslim fantasies about Christians, fantasies that both shaped and were shaped by community responses to Christian religious practices. But it is equally present in the anger in secular Europe today still directed at Jewish and Islamic ritual practices such as ritual slaughter with its obligatory bloodletting.

One of the most striking similarities of the process of integration into Western secular society is the gradual elision of the national differences among the various groups. Muslims in Western Europe represent multiple national traditions (South Asian in the UK, North African in France and Spain, Moroccan and "Moluccan" (Indonesian) in the Netherlands, Turkish in Germany). But so did the Jews in Western Europe who came out of ghettos in France and the Rhineland, from the rural reaches of Bavaria and Hungary, who moved from those parts of "Eastern Europe"—Poland, the eastern Marches of the Austro-Hungarian Empire—which became part of the West, and from the fringes of Empire to the center. To this diverse population one can add the Sephardi Jews from the Iberian Peninsula who settled in areas from Britain (introducing fish and chips) to the fringes of the Austrian Empire. The standard image of the Jews in eighteenth-century British caricature was the Maltese Jew in his oriental turban. By the nineteenth century, it was that of Lord Rothschild in formal wear receiving the Prince of Wales at his daughter's wedding in a London synagogue (Nissan 2008, 129–190). Religious identity (as the Jew or the Muslim) replaced national identity—by then few (except the anti-Semites) remembered that the Rothschilds were a Frankfurt family that escaped the Yiddish-speaking ghetto. The Jews are seen to be everywhere and all alike; Muslims are seen to be everywhere and are becoming all alike. Even ritual differences and theological antagonism become diminished in the Diaspora where the notion of a Muslim *Ummah* (or community) seems to be realized. It is the ideal state, to quote Talal Asad, of "being able to live as autonomous individuals in a collective life that exists beyond national borders" (2003, 180). But this too has its pitfalls, as the Jewish template shows.

Now for Jews in those lands that will become Germany, in the Austro-Hungarian Empire, in France, and in those lands that will become Great Britain, the stories will all be different as they encounter different forms of Christianity and different expectations as to the meaning of citizenship. Never mind if we now factor in the colonial world and its postcolonial manifestation. Different notions of secularization all present slightly different variations on the theme of what one must give up to become a true citizen. Do you merely have to give up your secular language (Western and Eastern Yiddish, Ladino, Turkish, Urdu, colloquial Arabic)? Today there has been a strong suggestion in Germany and the United Kingdom that preaching in the mosques be done only in English—for security reasons. Do you have to abandon the most evident and egregious practices or, as the German philosopher Johann Gottlieb Fichte (1762–1814) states (echoing debates about Jewish emancipation during the French revolution), do you have to "cut off their Jewish heads and replace them with German ones"? And that was not meant as a metaphor, but as a statement of the impossibility of Jewish transformation into Germans.

All of these changes deal in general with question of Jewish "identity" but in a complex and often contradictory manner. For the history of the Jews in the European Diaspora the late eighteenth century called forth three great "reformers" who took on different reforms in the light of the diaspora status of the Jews: Moses Mendelssohn (1729–1786) and the followers of the Jewish Enlightenment in Germany (and their predecessors in Holland) who confronted a secularizing world. Rabbi Eliyahu of Vilnius—the Vilna Gaon (1720–1797)—in the Baltic who desired to reform Orthodox tradition to make it more able to function in a self-contained Jewish world. The first modern Jewish mystics, the Hasidim, typified by Rabbi Yisrael—the Baal Shem Tov (1698–1760) (the Master of the Good Name)—who fought, like their contemporaries in Berlin and Vilnius, against what they saw as the stultifying practices and worldview of contemporary Judaism. All lived roughly simultaneously. In their wake came radical changes in what it meant to be a Jew in belief and practice. For contemporary Islam, all can serve as answers to the pressures found throughout the Diaspora. All offer parallels to the dilemmas faced by Islam in the West today. Thus the list of "abominations" that secular Europe saw in Jewish ritual practices became the earmark for the question of what Jews were willing to change in order to better fit the various national assumptions about citizenship.

Now we know that there are also vast differences between Jews in the eighteenth and nineteenth centuries and Muslims today. There are many more Muslims today in Western Europe than there were Jews in the earlier period. The Jews historically never formed more than 1 percent of the population of any Western European nation. Muslim populations form a considerable minority today. While there is no Western European city with a Muslim majority, many recent news stories predict that Marseilles or Rotterdam will become the first European city to have one. In France today there are 600,000 Jews while there are between 5 and 6 million Muslims, who make up about 10 percent of the population. In Germany, with a tiny Jewish population of slightly over 100,000 almost 4 percent of the population is Muslim (more than 3 million people). In Britain about 2.5 percent of the total population (1.48 million people) is Muslim. Demographics (and birthrate) aside, there are salient differences in the experiences of the Jews and Muslims in the past and today. Indeed in all of these nations the so-called Christian majority is also collapsing: not because of the increase of Muslims or Jews but because of the gradual dissolution of state Christianity into ever more irreligious (not secular) forms. The Roman Catholic Church as well as the various state Protestant Churches have become aware of this problem, perhaps best indicated by the radical decline in the number of individuals entering into religious life as priests, nuns, or ministers.

Unlike Muslims today and their Christian compatriots, the Jews had no national "homeland"—and, indeed, were so defined as nomads or a pariah people (pace Max Weber and Hannah Arendt). They lived only in the *goles* (or *galut*, exile)—for even traditional Jews living in the Holy Land considered themselves to be in an exilic condition—within the Diaspora and seemed thus inherently different from any other people in Western Europe (except perhaps the Roma). Most Muslims in the West come out of a national tradition often formed by colonialism in which their homelands had long histories disturbed but not destroyed by colonial rule. And last but not least the Israel-Palestinian conflict over the past century (well before the creation of the state of Israel), the Holocaust, and the establishment of a Jewish homeland seem to place the two groups—at least in the consciousness of the West—into two antagonistic camps.

Religion for the Jews of pre-Enlightenment Christian Europe and for many of the adherents of the various forms of contemporary Islam, which has its immediate roots

xviii   Introduction

in majority Islamic states, became for many a "heritage" rather than a living experience in the Western, secular diaspora. What had been lived experience in *milieux de
memoire*—environments of memory—to use Pierre Nora's often-cited phrase from
1994 become *lieux de memoire*— places of memory—that refigure meaning constantly within the Diaspora (Nora 1993). What is it that such memory of ritual and
practice can or must abandon? What must it preserve to maintain its coherence for
the group? The answer depends on time and place, and yet the experience of Jews in
the Western European Diaspora seems to offer a model case clearly because of the
"narcissism of minor differences" among the three Abrahamic religions. The Jews
maintain, in different modalities, their religious identity, even if the nature of their
options created ruptures that produced new problems and over time partial resolutions and yet further conflicts and resolutions.

The essays in this volume on *Judaism, Christianity, and Islam: Collaboration and
Conflict in the Age of Diaspora* illustrate the problems of conflict and collaboration
among the various versions of the Abrahamic religions. They are case studies for
the complexity of these problems and potentials. The idea of core meanings attributed to the interrelationships between the Abrahamic religions in specific historical contexts is framed by two Israeli sociolinguists, Benjamin Hary, teaching in the
United States, and Martin Wein, in Israel, looking at what they call "religiolinguistics" across the Abrahamic religions. This idea of difference and conflict is explored
by the Muslim-American scholar Mehnaz Afridi, in her work on the image of the
Shoah as a space for interreligious reflection between Jews and Muslims. My essay
on the politics of circumcision in the contemporary Western Diaspora of Jews and
Muslims frames the debates about religious practice and ideas of health and illness
and reflects historical conflicts about religious practices in the Abrahamic religions.
The world of interreligious relationships is also the theme of the Australian political theorist Wayne Cristaudo's examination of the Christian thinker (and convert
from Judaism) Eugen Rosenstock-Huessy and his intimate correspondent the Jewish
theologian Franz Rosenzweig with the author's focus on their relationship to Islam.
That the fragmentation of the Abrahamic religions can be explored through the contrasts between them but also by examining the relationships within them is shown
by the British historian Zhou Xun looking at the meanings of "Jewishness" in secular
and multicultural Hong Kong under and after British rule. Katja Garloff's literary
approach provides yet another case study for the meanings associated with collaboration, here understood in terms of intimacy between Jews and non-Jews in contemporary German film and literature. Yulia Egorova looks at South Asia, a very different
space than Post-Shoah Germany and the potentials for Jewish-Muslim relations in
that world. David Feldman's reading of the "blood libel" attacks on European Jewry
provides a new and startling manner of seeing the relationship between Jews and
Christians in Victorian England. Jane Garnett and Michael Keith explore the East

End of London as a place for the conflict and collaboration among the Abrahamic faiths from the nineteenth century into the present. My short conclusion, on the fluid relationship between symbol and identity in the Abrahamic religions, reflects on a recurrent theme in this book: the complexity of religious meanings in our age of diasporic pluralism and the anxieties that such fluidity creates.

It is this flux in the conflicts between and the collaborations among the Abrahamic religions on the new global stage that is the core of this volume. It grew out of a most successful conference on this topic held at the University of Hong Kong under the aegis of the School of Modern Languages and Cultures and its head Professor Kendall Johnson during my tenure as Research Professor from 2010 to 2013. I am grateful to Daniel Chua (Professor of Music and Head of the School of Humanities) for his support for this undertaking and the School of Modern Languages and Cultures for its support of this publication.

References

Adorno, Theodor. *Minima Moralia: Reflections from Damaged Life*. London: New Left Books, 1951.

Appiah, Kwame Anthony. *Cosmopolitanism: Ethics in a World of Strangers* (Issues of Our Time). New York: W. W. Norton & Company, 2007.

Asad, Talal. *Formation of the Secular: Christianity, Islam, Modernity*. Stanford, CA: Stanford University Press, 2003.

Beattie, Amanda Russell. *Justice and Morality: Human Suffering, Natural Law and International Politics*. Farnham: Ashgate, 2010.

Dundes, Alan. "The Ritual Murder or Blood Libel Legend." In *The Blood Libel Legend: A Casebook in Anti-Semitic Folklore*, edited by A. Dundes, 336–345. Madison, WI: University of Wisconsin Press, 1991.

Kleingeld, Pauline. *Kant and Cosmopolitanism: The Philosophical Ideal of World Citizenship*, Cambridge University Press, 2011.

Nagourney, Adam. "Gay Marriage Stirs Rebellion at Synagogue." *The New York Times* (July 5, 2013).

Niebuhr, Gustav, "Muslim Group Seeks to Meet Billy Graham's Son." *New York Times* (November 20, 2001).

Nissan, Ephraim. "What Is in a Busby, What Is in a Top-Hat: Tall Hats, and the Politics of Jewish Identity and Social Positioning." *Australian Journal of Jewish Studies* 22 (2008): 129–190.

Nora, Pierre, ed. *Les Lieux de mémoire*, Vol. 1: *Les France: Conflits et partages*. Paris: Gallimard, 1993.

Sacks, Jonathan. *The Dignity of Difference: How to Avoid the Clash of Civilizations*. London: Continuum, 2002.

Sartre, Jean Paul. *Anti-Semite and Jew: An Exploration of the Etiology of Hate*. New York: Schocken, 1995.

Weber, Max. "Ethnic Groups (1922)." In *Theories of Ethnicity: A Classical Reader*, edited by Werner Sollors, 45–59. Washington Square, NY: New York University Press, 1996.

1
Peoples of the Book

Religion, Language, Nationalism, and the Politics of Sacred Text Translation[1]

Martin J. Wein and Benjamin Hary

The following exposition is a cultural critique of the phenomenon of sacred text translation, centering on the enormous global Bible translation project, but also including comparative references to the Qur'an, and to sacred texts of religions other than Judaism, Christianity, and Islam. This is framed by a general discussion of the triangular relationship of language, religion, and nationalism. We bring forward several propositions.

First, we make the case that Jewish studies, with its linguistic access to the original Hebrew biblical text and its specific sensitivity to this triangular interaction of language, religion, and nationalism, can provide theory and models for general disciplines, as well. Jewish studies can teach us, for example, about concepts such as the idea of a cultural bond between languages. Most importantly, the creation of a religious-linguistic-nationalist construction that is evident in the Jewish-Hebrew-Israeli case (through the continuities between biblical, Rabbinic, medieval, early modern, and modern Hebrew, intertwined with Jewish religious tradition and modern Israeli nationalism) can be traced in many other cultural contexts, too. Consequently, we question the common idea that in modernity vernaculars have replaced sacred tongues as nationalism has replaced religion; we offer an alternative view in which one merges into the other with the result being a synthesis.

In a second step we provide a brief analysis of the phenomenon and history of Bible translation with a focus on Multi-faith religious case studies. Furthermore, we investigate the notion of linguistic standardization, which is directly connected to the history of Bible translation and to the historical circles of myth surrounding it. In addition, we provide examples that demonstrate the impact of Bible translation

1. Earlier versions of this article were presented at various venues, including the annual meeting of the Association for Jewish Studies in Washington D.C. in December 2005, and twice with different focuses at Tel Aviv University, at the S. Daniel Abraham Center for International and Regional Studies in May 2011, and at the School of Education Research Forum in January 2013. We would like to thank David Blumenthal, Elizabeth Canon, Vincent Cornel, and Gordon Newby for their invaluable comments. We would also like to thank the editor K. Walsh for her profound questions and comments and Sander Gilman who agreed to include this article in the present volume. Of course we take full responsibility for the contents of the essay.

on language studies as a whole, as reflected even in academic reference tools, notably in terms of the categorization and classification of languages. For example, the global Ethnologue[2] project of Bible translation is shared by both Christian missionaries and linguists. In another example, references in the monumental *Compendium of the World's Languages* use translations of the New Testament to illustrate languages. The impact of sacred text translation has thus been unusually significant, deeply structural, and eclipses all other translation genres and projects.

In the next step, we explore the religion-language-nationalism triangle in global contexts. We find that specific Bible translations can be central to re-defining community boundaries through linguistic standardization, and sometimes even (re-)alphabetization via the invention of unique writing systems for Bible translations. This had already been a long-standing pattern in many Christian-defined communities before colonialism facilitated the global spread of this configuration. In India today, attempts are being made at overcoming historical religious-linguistic divisions stemming from colonial missionary activity, sacred text translation, and the religious transformation of languages, such as in the case of the Christian-Hindu religiolects[3] of Konkani in Goa, in order to create more multi-religious linguistic communities. In fact, communities do not actually have to use the Bible, and the religious transformation of languages can still define some of the communities' linguistic or national characteristics, such as in the case of Muslim-majority Indonesia, the largest such country in the world today. This country's official language, Indonesian, is rooted in the first printed Bible translation from the colonial era, using a Latin-based writing system.

Overall, our comprehension of the links between language, religion, and nationalism is complicated by what might be called the "theolitics"[4] of canonization, often taking the form of a "hermeneutic gleichschaltung,"[5] or forced synchronization of interpretive frameworks in a religious context. Like poetic traditions, sacred texts begin in a fluid state, transcending linguistic varieties in endless intertwined variations; this is until religious canonization sets in and further evolvement is stalled as sacred texts freeze into a fossilized testimony of historical language. Now, translations

---

2. Ethnologue: Languages of the World is a catalogue of more than 7,000 living languages used around the world. See www.ethnologue.com.

3. See Hary 2009, 12–13 and Hary and Wein 2013 for the term *religiolect*. It may be warranted to address the topic of terminology, especially since we are dealing with issues of language as we are crafting our own new language (we would like to thank K. Walsh for this observation, February 9, 2014). The terminological tools introduced here are suggestions for innovations needed for the emerging field of religiolinguistics, but they are open to selection or adaptation. We have tried to limit new or unusual terms to a minimum, i.e. to cases where no clear term for a specific phenomenon exists yet.

4. "Theolitics" is a term that has developed in recent years, describing the overlap of theology and politics. We would like to thank Sander Gilman for a consultation on this topic, email message from May 3, 2013.

5. We would like to thank Juergen Eilert for a consultation on this topic, email messages from April 26 and May 16, 2013.

become highly regulated, tightly contested, and are canonized in turn. In the modern period, the theolitics of language and religion as epitomized in sacred text translation get further entangled in collaboration and conflict with nationalism. The outcome is a thick global web of religion, language, and nationalism, similar in structure around the world, but usually experienced as unique, exceptional, and primordial from an "inside" perspective.

Jewish Studies and Beyond

In Jewish studies, the problems of definitions, boundaries, and permeability of communities have been discussed for some time now. For example, historians Pierre Birnbaum and Ira Katznelson observed: "Jewish history remains a latent and unintegrated subject, thrust to the periphery of the historical profession. Serving as their own historians, Jews have been tempted by notions of Jewish exceptionalism and have oriented most of their scholarship to specifically Jewish audiences" (1995, 13–14).

Critics of Jewish exceptionalism—for example, Amos Funkenstein—point out that many Jewish historians "obsessively try to differentiate between issues, which cannot be differentiated, between essential 'assimilation' and coincidental 'acculturation'" (Funkenstein 1996, 64). Although Funkenstein avowedly tried to break through Jewish exceptionalism, he nevertheless abstained from drawing any parallels or applying his own theory to other fields. Yet, many communities, not just Jews, in practice live in what he called the "dialectics of assimilation," since people are often part of a (diasporic) minority in one context or another, or of several minorities at the same time.

Similarly, Stuart Z. Charmé analyzes essentialist links between concepts of authenticity and authority by focusing exclusively on *inner-Jewish* religious struggles (2000).[6] Neglecting the larger historical dependence of Jewish elites on alliances with Christian and Muslim authorities, Charmé, too, misses a valuable opportunity to extend his theory of a link between claims to authenticity and claims to authority via essentialism to encompass the complete power structure of human communities, including Jews *and others* (i.e. usually Christians and Muslims).[7] Both theorists, Funkenstein and Charmé, thus unwittingly perpetuate the lack of integration of Jewish studies with other fields of inquiry, just as critiqued by Birnbaum and Katznelson.

Building on this debate and on our essay "Religiolinguistics: On Jewish-, Christian- and Muslim-Defined Languages" (Hary and Wein 2013), we wish to apply models

---

6. For example, the current Orthodox trend, notably in Israel, of delegitimizing Reform Judaism (Charmé 2000). This in some way echoes the opposite tendency in some diaspora contexts in the past.

7. For example, "The Council of Four Lands," an early modern East European autonomous Jewish administrative structure within the Christian-defined feudal system; the council was invested with power by Christian rulers and used it within the Jewish community. In the Muslim context, we may point to the venerable institution of the Jewish exilarchate based for centuries in Mesopotamia.

developed in Jewish studies to other contexts, thus creating more interdisciplinary and interreligious permeability, specifically on a theoretical level. In this contribution we argue in effect that not only Jews are the "People of the Book," but indeed many if not most modern nations are indirectly or partly based on the Bible and its various, often canonized translations—or else on the Qur'an—and are thus "*Peoples* of the Book." It should also be noted that indeed some nations could be based on *both* the Bible and the Qur'an—or on a combination of, or with, other sacred texts—and may therefore be described most accurately as "Peoples of the *Books.*"

Concerning language per se, while it is commonly assumed that Israeli Hebrew is the only living spoken language significantly based on the Hebrew Bible, a millennia-old web of historical Bible translations connects many if not most of today's standard languages back to biblical Hebrew. Thus, for example, ample Hebrew elements have been carried over into modern English via the *Septuagint* Greek, the *Vulgate* Latin, and the King James English translations of the Bible.[8] In his analysis of the stretched-out process of linguistic standardization, John Earl Joseph points out a domino effect beyond Hebrew:

> Through the framework of codification, vestigial structures of Greek and Latin survive in every [post-Classical] standardized language. The standardization tradition, passed on to each new standard language through its superposed model, insures that further characteristics become common to all of the standard languages of the world, whatever the linguistic affiliation of their dialect base. (1987, 175)

This chain of translation retains cultural as well as linguistic elements, so that the entire setup around a central book endowed with sacredness and in return endowing its own language with sacredness is replicated time and again. In other words, the King James translation or other canonized Christian translations simultaneously mark the "gold standard" of language *and* of religious faith, fulfilling much of the role that the Hebrew Bible has usually played for Jews. For instance, as Tony Crowley noted on eighteenth-century English: "The use of language in the scriptures was reckoned to have at least a dual authority as it functioned as both an exemplar of linguistic style and of religious faith . . ." (2003, 79). The message sanctifies the medium and the medium sanctifies the message. The standardization of languages is really just another form of canonization, one encompassing the entire medium.

For example, the letters used to write these very words are Roman, derived from the *Vulgate* Latin translation of the Bible. The idea of a spelling standard one has to follow is only a secularized form of the *sanctified* text and language standard in religious canons, where strict principles are imposed in the name of religious *purity*. In the case of English, the spelling used here was significantly coined by the Protestant

---

8. For a list of such elements, see Hary and Wein 2013, 101–102.

Christian King James Bible translation of 1611. Many of the words and expressions in the present text that have *taken root* in English were also introduced by this translation (e.g. "take root" from the King James translation of 2 Kings 19:30, etc.). Semantic fields as in "purity" have been amended in the light of concrete Christian or Jewish religious doctrine and abstract concepts of purity, for instance regarding notions of immaculate conception, or in the context of kosher food. The term "sanctified" offers an interesting example of a Latin-derived root (sanctus, facere—holy, make), with a Germanic suffix, an example of the *symbiotic* merger of sacred tongues and vernaculars in the formation of modern standard languages. Any text written in English, or for that matter in nearly any modern standard language, can be analyzed like this, and echoes to some degree sacred texts, usually Bible translations. Even the physical medium of a *book* is itself inspired by sacred texts such as the Bible or the Qur'an, prototypes of bound tomes with verses and chapters set on pages.

What seems like a unique exception, the Jewish focus on the Hebrew Bible (with its extension to modern Israeli Hebrew), in fact represents a much wider linguistic-religious pattern, which has been called *Kulturbund* in the study of Jewish-defined languages.[9] This biblical Kulturbund, or cultural bond, extends far beyond Jewish contexts, and encompasses most major standardized languages of the world today. In addition to a number of standard classifications of languages by families (genetic), linguistic features (typological), geographical linguistic areas, lexicosemantic typology, and holistic typology (Hary 2014), we suggest promoting a sociolinguistic way of classification of languages through a common cultural heritage (cultural bond), such as a shared sacred text tradition. Although this is a classification that was originally developed specifically only for Jewish languages, mostly by twentieth-century Jewish scholars, we believe that it is possible to take this model and expand it into a (nearly) universal classification system.

Furthermore, in contrast to a widespread view that vernaculars eventually *replaced* sacred languages, we trace how vernacular languages were actually standardized *via the filter* of sacred languages. The result was a *synthesis* or *fusion* of spoken dialects with elements from Bible-imbibed religious *linguae francae* such as Greek, Latin, or Old Church Slavonic, for example. It should be noted that Bible translations functioned in many cases as the initial core of modern literary canons, educational textbooks, dictionaries, and grammars. Thus, canonized Bible translations are the embodiment of the sacred-vernacular synthesis, or religious-linguistic fusion: a symbiotic corner stone of modern standard languages.

Since the rise of nationalism is in most contexts intrinsically linked to the creation of relatively homogenous linguistic communities on the basis of (often

---

9. The German or Yiddish term *Kulturbund* was probably introduced by Paper (1978, vii); see also Hary 2009, 9n13. On the terms Jewish-defined languages (or Christian-and Muslim-defined languages), see Hary 2009, 18–19 and Hary and Wein 2013.

authority-imposed) standard languages, the religious impact on these standard languages has frequently also been carried over onto nationalism. In spite of its ostensible secularism or declared a-religiousness in some cases, nationalism regularly styled its constituency into an exceptional and heroic "Chosen People," speaking an ancient and beautiful "Holy Tongue," and living in a divinely bestowed "Promised Land," usually adopting these concepts from the earlier religious contexts. Such religious references in nationalism can be found in places as remote from each other as Ethiopia, Ireland, Poland, South Africa, Southern Tyrol, the United States, and many more (Fishman 1997; Smith 2003).

Ireland, for example, has long been considered a "sacred island," and already Donatus of Fiesole, an early medieval Irish Catholic bishop in Italy, wrote: "With honey and with milk flow Ireland's lovely plains" (quoted in Smith 2003, 151). Clearly, this quote refers to the biblical imagery of the Holy Land as in Hebrew /eretz zavat ḥalav u-dvaš/ (for example Exodus 3:8): "a land flowing with milk and honey" (note, however, the reversed order of milk and honey in the bishop's quote). Irish historian Donnchadh Ó Corráin acknowledges that in modernity, "Irish nationalists drew on the achievements of the early medieval Irish church, the golden age, the idea that Ireland was a holy island, the early origin myths, and the history of its medieval kings" (Ó Corráin, 2011). A recent popular example of an extension to human genetic identity but simultaneously also to a hazy New Age-style spiritual realm appears on the website sacredireland.org: "Welcome Home: If you have any trace or thread of Celtic or pre-Celtic Spirit within your DNA, this site belongs to you" (Bard Na Mara, 2011).

Thus, the relationship of nationalism to religion has often been self-contradictory. On the surface, nationalism in many contexts disclaimed traditional religion by replacing it with modern *civil religion*[10] or forms of secular sacredness, the perfect example being post-Revolutionary France (e.g. Agulhon 1979; Weber 1976). Furthermore, nationalism typically aimed at exchanging traditional religious holy tongues for a seemingly secular or religiously neutral national language. However, nationalism also reemployed elements from traditional religion for the construction of modern civil religion and widely used Bible translations in the standardization of national languages. Limited participation in this process often guaranteed the acceptance to the core of the emerging nations only of select religious groups and specific language communities. Finally, it should be noted that the impact of Bible translation is also self-contradictory in its own right: on the one hand, Bible translations created

---

10. *Civil religion* (in certain contexts also *civic religion*) may be described as a concept arguing that traditional religion did not really *decline* in the modern era, but was rather *transformed* under the aegis of emerging nationalist ideologies. Nationalism typically built a "quasi-religious" set of national symbols, festivals, myths and rituals that are often based on religious heritage, but can sometimes be made to look secular and are ostensibly open or equally accessible to all members of the nation. See, for example, Cristi 2001; Hughey 1983.

new communities and opened up sacred texts to a wider public. On the other hand, these translations drew new community boundaries.

The Theolitics of Bible Translation

"There is no 'Urtext' ['original text'] of the Hebrew Bible that can be literally reconstructed; the history of its formation and its textual history overlap," notes Michael Tilly (2005, 57, our translation). Indeed, the Pentateuch and some of the other Hebrew (and less frequently Aramaic) texts that formed the sacred scriptures of Second Temple Judaism existed in at least four versions even before translation began: one developed in Egypt (Alexandrian), one in Mesopotamia (Babylonian), and two in the Holy Land (Palestinian and Samaritan). The text version that eventually became the basis for canonization was the Palestinian one. Full Jewish canonization of the Hebrew (and Aramaic) text, however, was only achieved through the Masoretic version around the eighth century CE. But Bible translation had already been started in the last centuries before the common era, with the Aramaic *Targumim*, apparently connected to a tradition of oral translation or interpretation, and, with the Greek *Septuagint* tradition, had emerged in Alexandria, Egypt. Bible translation thus began about a millennium before canonization had been completed.

Specifically, the translation of the Hebrew Holy Scriptures into the ancient *Koïne* Greek, a fairly homogenized written (and perhaps to some degree also spoken) version of Athens' *Attic* dialect, used in many Greek communities around the Mediterranean and the Black Sea, too, was unprecedented on a number of levels. The translation of "barbaric" literature into Greek was quite unusual. Conversely, also from a Hebrew point of view, the *Septuagint* tradition was extraordinary. In contrast to translations into the closely related Aramaic, which would today be classified as a Semitic language alongside Hebrew and Arabic, Indo-European Greek vocabulary and grammar significantly differed from Hebrew (Tilly 2005, 68–69). New sets of translation techniques had to be developed in order to meet these linguistic challenges.

Another problem was cultural or referential. In order to be accepted by Greek-speakers, the *Septuagint* translations of the Hebrew Holy Scriptures needed to operate within a Hellenistic framework of thought, but without losing the references and the status of the original cultural context. Giuseppe Veltri points out: "the question that needed to be answered was *if* in accordance with Jewish-Hellenist and Rabbinic understanding, the Torah could be translated in the first place . . . and how a *written translation* of the Torah should be ranked vis-à-vis the Hebrew text" (Veltri 1994, 123; his emphases, our translation). The outcome of this balancing act was a complex and multifaceted textual tradition that redefined aspects of both *Koïne* Greek and Second Temple Judaism. The long-term, indirect impact was enormous, since the language varieties of the *Septuagint* subsequently also influenced the Latin *Vulgate* and many other Bible translations. Additionally, the Hellenistic refashioning of Second Temple Judaism left a mark on Rabbinical Judaism and on various forms of Christianity (ibid., 47–48, 66–80). In Tilly's words,

> The Septuagint contains the first coherent written translation of the Hebrew Bible into another language, the most important in terms of the history of its impact [*wirkungsgeschichtlich*]. [The *Septuagint*] served the transmission of [the Hebrew Bible's] religious message into a completely different world of language, thought, and life. This enormous cultural transfer achievement enabled the deep penetration of Hebrew terminology and the Middle Eastern [*orientalischer*] world of ideas and images into European languages and cultures. (ibid, 9, our translation)

The language of the *Septuagint* tradition was not monolithic, however, and changed significantly according to the exact time and place of the translators, their theological outlook, and their degree of knowledge of Hebrew-Aramaic and *Koïne* Greek. Characteristic features of *Septuagint* Greek were Hebraisms, i.e., recognizable impact of Hebrew on all areas of the language (phonology, morphology, syntax, semantics, and more), as well as a terminological core of key biblical concepts. Lexical influence could take the form of neologisms—the creation of new words, or a narrowing or broadening of semantic fields, or even "translating" a Hebrew word into a Greek lexeme that merely sounded similar. Syntactic influence included *calque translations*, e.g. Hebrew /nishba' bə-/ literally "swear in" was rendered in the *Septuagint* into the Greek verb ὄμνυμι "swear" followed by the particle ἐν "in," thus slavishly translating the Hebrew /bə-/ "in," although *Koïne* Greek required this verb to be followed by an accusative case or by the preposition πρός "with, towards" (ibid., 69).[11]

Such methods of literal translations were often complemented by rather creative interpretive measures, sometimes for reasons of clarity in the target language of translation, and at other times for theological reasons. For example, translators and copyists did not shy away from altering the sacred text in line with their religious outlook, changing "on the seventh day God finished his work" of creating the world (Genesis 2:2) to "on the sixth day," in order to demonstrate that God indeed kept the Jewish Sabbath and did not do "work" on the seventh day (Tilly 2005, 75).

The main theolitical change introduced by the *Septuagint* tradition, however, was the consistent monotheification of the Hebrew Bible, for instance, by translating /'elohim/ into "angels," although the former is a biblical Hebrew term that is used as a singular name for God, but is grammatically plural and could be read literally as "gods." Two other biblical Hebrew divine names, /'adonay/ and the Tetragram *YHVH*, the pronunciation of which is a taboo in the Jewish tradition, were merged into one single term κύριος "(the) Lord" (ibid., 79–80).

---

11. Note that the academic acceptability of the use of Greek letters in the present text itself attests to the continuing cultural bond between classical Greek and Latin, cemented through the Bible translation of the *Vulgate* in part via the *Septuagint*.

Many of the idiosyncratic features of *Septuagint* Greek may not reflect a slip, but rather a conscious and intentional attempt to closely follow the Hebrew text, which was viewed as sacred even on a structural basis (down to word counts). The adaptation of *Koïne* Greek had the effect of increasing the exotic, transcendental, or even magic clout of the text. In fact, we can trace here the universal dilemma of translation: shall the translated text follow closely the original language or fit in more closely with the target language? As Tilly wrote, the translation "could thus either target an approximation of the reader to the original or of the original to the reader" (ibid., 67, our translation).

This linguistic tension in the translation of the *Septuagint* is in fact a hallmark of Bible and other sacred text translation. The *šarḥ* tradition, a literal translation of sacred texts from Hebrew into Judeo-Arabic, which began to flourish in the Middle East and North Africa in the fifteenth century, further exemplifies this dilemma. For the most part, each Hebrew word was rendered by a single word in the target language in the same word order, to a point of inventing terms for the sole purpose of more faithfully reflecting the original text. However, at other times the translation followed a more interpretive mode. Hary calls this the "literal-interpretive linguistic tension" (2009, 57–60).

Incidentally, the same techniques and solutions as in the *Septuagint* tradition were employed when source and target languages of the translation both belonged to the Semitic language family, as is the case in the *šarḥ*. Although the Judeo-Arabic translators/interpreters/commentators, or *šarḥanim*, had very likely no direct access to the *Septuagint*, they were still part of the same tradition of sacred text translation. They were, after all, at least partly familiar with the works of other early translators such as Onkelos (Aramaic) or Saadia Gaon (Judeo-Arabic). Moreover, some of these techniques of sacred text translation may be inherent to the human mind, to translation, language, religion, or to a combination thereof.

Thus the *šarḥanim*, too, changed the use of prepositions in Judeo-Arabic: in Later Egyptian Judeo-Arabic they consistently used the preposition /'ilā/ (or [ila])[12] "to" for marking the direct definite article, mimicking the preposition /'et/ in the Hebrew original.[13] For example, biblical Hebrew "and he sold his birthright to Jacob" (Genesis 25:33) is rendered into Egyptian Judeo-Arabic /wa-bāʿ ila bikriyyato li-yaqūb/.[14] This was a deviation from Qurʾanic Arabic, where the accusative case marker following the verb /bāʿ/ "sold" is used without *any* preposition. Furthermore, biblical Hebrew /wa-yabrēk/ "caused to kneel down" (Genesis 24:11) was denoted as Judeo-Arabic

---

12. The transcription of /'ilā/ follows standard Arabic whereas [ila] follows the colloquial realization.
13. For the treatment of this subject see Hary 1991 and 2009, 257–264.
14. This example is taken from ms. HB 15 (=CAJS Rare ms. 2555), folio 6a (=7r),1–2, located at the Center for Advanced Judaic Studies at the University of Pennsylvania in Philadelphia, which is a partial *šarḥ* of the book of Genesis, analyzed in both Hary 2009 and forthcoming.

/wa-barrak/ meaning literally in standard Arabic "to make someone kneel down."[15] The Judeo-Arabic *šarḥan* could have easily used /'anāx/ "caused to kneel down" (as did Saadia Gaon of the tenth century and later the Protestant Bible translation into Arabic in the nineteenth century), but preferred /wa-barrak/, probably for the proximity of the sound to the Hebrew original.

Also instances of interpretive modes of translation appear throughout the *šarḥ* corpus: in the Egyptian Judeo-Arabic translation of the Torah, for example, /'elohim/ is consistently translated as Judeo-Arabic /ar-rabb/,[16] with the meaning of master, owner, or proprietor (and also related to Hebrew /rav/, meaning, for example, "master, officer, lord," as well as "teacher, rabbi"[17]). This translation may reflect a theological wish to avoid the plurality of /'elohim/ (see above) and perhaps enhance the community status of rabbis. Note that the Hebrew variation /'elohey/ (as a first term of the Hebrew construct state) is translated into Judeo-Arabic /'ilāh/ with the meaning of "God" or "deity." Interestingly enough, Hebrew *YHVH* and /'adonay/ are both united into one term, just as in the *Septuagint*, and rendered as Judeo-Arabic /allah/. While the term *Allah* to a Jew using the *šarḥ* Bible may not necessarily mean the same as it does to a Muslim employing the Qur'an, this translation nevertheless demonstrates the possible blurring of religious categories and in a way even the permeability of religious boundaries.[18] It may also represent a possibly conscious theolitic (perhaps apologetic) tendency of identifying the Jewish and Muslim deities as the same.

The Global Phenomenon of Bible Translation

Overall, there have been three waves of Bible translation.[19] The tradition of Bible translation first spread through languages of the Mediterranean, East Africa, the Middle East, and the Caucasus region. This tradition included, in addition to the *Targumim*, the *Septuagint* and multilingual versions such as Origen's *Hexapla*,[20] for example, also the Syriac *Peshitta*, the Latin *Vulgate*, the Armenian and the Georgian Bibles (all likely completed only by the fifth century CE), as well as the Ethiopian Geʿez translations (Garima Gospels, sixth or seventh century). In the Armenian and Georgian cases, new writing systems were developed to facilitate Bible translation

---

15. From ms. HB 15 2b, 8. See Hary 2009, 208, 3–2.8.
16. In ms. HB 15 (=CAJS Rare ms. 2555); see Hary 2009 and forthcoming.
17. The meaning "Rabbi" referring to a teacher in the community or a person in charge of the religious life of the community originates in medieval time.
18. For crossing religious boundaries see Hary 2009, 16–19 and Hary and Wein 2013, 93–96, and for the discussion of the translation of the term "God" in the Judeo-Arabic versions of the Book of Genesis see Hary forthcoming.
19. For a useful overview, see, for example, Noss 2007.
20. From the third century, with Hebrew and Greek in several versions, including a transliteration of Hebrew into Greek characters.

and the spread of Christianity, notably Mesrop Mashtots's Armenian letters, which may have influenced Georgian writing systems, as well.

A second, somewhat feeble, medieval wave further expanded the phenomenon of Christian and Jewish Bible translation, mainly deeper into Europe and to the Atlantic rim. The earliest major translations in this period were the Old Church Slavonic translation (ninth century), but also Saadia Gaon's classic translation into Judeo-Arabic (tenth century). First Judeo-Spanish and Christian French translations, for example, were completed in the thirteenth century, while the first full Czech version and John Wycliffe's full English translation were completed in the fourteenth century.

The third wave of Bible translation, which continues today, began in early modernity and concentrated on local varieties in European colonies, or, more recently, on the so-called Third World. Malay was the first "indigenous" language to receive a printed Bible translation from 1629 onwards (in today's Indonesia, see also below), while the first translation into a Native American language was that into Massachusetts in 1663. This third, early modern, modern, and contemporary wave of Bible translation is much larger in scope and geographical reach, going far beyond the two premodern waves. Especially over the last two centuries, Bible translation has seen a veritable explosion, a boom unprecedented throughout the history of the Bible or the history of translation, with a particularly sharp increase in New Testament or partial Bible translations.

The motive behind the flourishing of Bible translation in the modern period has been for the most part Christian religious mission, as Nahum A. Sarna observes:

> Translations of parts of the Bible are known to have existed in only seven Asian and four African languages before the 15th century . . . By 1800 the number of non-European versions did not exceed 13 Asian, four African, three American, and one Oceanian. With the founding of missionary societies after 1800, however, new translations were viewed as essential to the evangelical effort . . . By 1970 some part, if not the entire Bible, had been translated into more than 100 languages or dialects spoken in India and over 300 in Africa. (2003)

Today, *Jewish* Bible translations exist in over twenty Jewish-defined languages (e.g. Judeo-Arabic, Judeo-Spanish, Yiddish), mostly in Hebrew characters. There are many more translations into Christian-defined languages but specifically intended for Jewish readerships (e.g. in Spanish, German, English). Full *Christian* Old and New Testament translations have been produced in hundreds of languages, and partial or digest translations in over 2,400 language varieties.[21] Many languages possess more than one version of the translated Bible, so the total number of (partial) Bible translations may be estimated to number many thousands. In the words of Sijbolt Noorda, "Bible translation is special in the sense that it is somehow a never-ending story. The book is as a matter of fact constantly retranslated, in very many ways and for a variety

---

21. For various estimates see Kubo and Specht 1975; MacGregor 1959; Metzger 2001; Sarna 2003.

of purposes" (2002, 8). Over recent centuries, the Hebrew Bible and especially the New Testament have thus become humanity's most widely translated and most extensively spread and printed texts.

One of the biggest Bible translators today is S.I.L. International (initially known as the Summer Institute for Linguistics). Founded in 1935, S.I.L. is an American-based Protestant missionary language research organization, specializing in Bible translations. The organization has already made hundreds of New Testament translations and is known especially for its Ethnologue project. On its website, this project identifies almost 7,000 languages in the world and often indirectly defines linguistic boundaries between groups of dialects. It lists the countries in which the languages are spoken and also provides estimates of the numbers of speakers. Ethnologue has a very wide exposure among linguists, anthropologists, and missionaries, as well as the general public.[22]

However, S.I.L. is only one part of a yet much larger global enterprise. For example, over the last years, the Institute for Bible Translation, which partly cooperates with S.I.L. and is based in a Russian-Orthodox Monastery in Moscow, has produced several dozen (partial) interdenominational Christian translations for "the non-Slavic peoples living in Russia and the other countries of the Commonwealth of Independent States" (mostly part of the former Soviet Union).[23] As *The Economist* writes, "An interlinked global network of 140 national and regional Bible Societies pools resources to reach its collective goal of putting a Bible in the hands of every man, woman and child on the planet." This ambitious initiative also has a Muslim equivalent: "Saudi oil wealth is supercharging the distribution of the Koran. The kingdom gives away some 30m Korans a year . . . Several television channels and radio stations [worldwide] do nothing [[24]] but broadcast the Koran."[25]

Nevertheless, unlike the translation approach in Christianity (and to some degree in Judaism), the Qur'an is preferably read in the original Arabic, and consequently Qur'an translations are still less widespread than Bible translations (e.g., Abdul-Raof 2005). Consider the following quotes from the website *Discovering Islam*:

> . . . the Arabic Quran (Koran) is a unique miracle. The only book in the world authored by God himself, word by word, and that is still available today in its original form . . . Each word used in the Arabic Quran was uniquely chosen by God for a purpose. You can not [sic] add or subtract a word to/from the Quran, without the corruption becoming noticeable. Scholars have discovered some

---

22. See www.sil.org and www.ethnologue.com; Erard 2005; also see Nida 1964, 21–22.
23. "Institute for Bible Translation, Russia/CIS," 1999–2012. Accessed June 6, 2013. http://ibt.org.ru/english/about_en.htm. We would like to thank Vladimir Gurevich for pointing us to this example.
24. Note that writing "nothing" in the context of the Qur'an may be considered an affront by some religious Muslims.
25. "The Battle of the Books." *The Economist*, December 19, 2007. Accessed December 19, 2007. http://www.economist.com/node/10311317.

hidden logic structures (codes) in the Quran that prove its authenticity and help in protecting its integrity from corruption. . . . There are many translations of the Quran currently available. Most of the translators of the Quran are non-Arabs and their knowledge of Arabic is limited. However, even if they were Arabs, you should not expect the translation to be perfect.[26]

This example shows the following: first, as seen in Christianity and Judaism, the translation of the Qu'ran has influenced the way that some Muslim communities think about language in general, i.e. in positivist terms of language perfection versus corruption. Second, over the last century or so translations of the Qur'an in the Muslim world (and related concepts such as the search for authenticating codes) have begun mimicking the Christian and Jewish Bible translation projects. And finally, the extension of thought about Bible translation to include Qur'an translation helps to broaden our view of the inter-religious genre of sacred text translation—of which Bible translation is a central part—beyond Christianity and Judaism.

Since in many cultural contexts writing and reading in and by themselves present quasi-sacred activities, the translator's personal degree of piety has often played a role in authenticating translations. For instance, John Rogerson points out "the dubious principle in the production of an authorized translation . . . , namely a test of religious orthodoxy as a necessary qualification for a person to be a translator."[27] As recently as 2009, a translation of the Gospel of John from the New Testament into Konkani in Goa, India, did not receive a Catholic stamp of religious approval (imprimatur), apparently because the translator was a Hindu "non-believer."[28]

In fact, the exact religious affiliation of the translator can be part of what theologically marks a Bible translation as "belonging" to one community or another. Martin Luther, for example, could at times prefer what he thought was a literal translation from the Hebrew to the German, in order to meet his theological interest and need (Kooiman 1961, 165, 172–173). Similarly, Theodore Beza worked Protestant interpretations into his revision of the *Vulgate* New Testament of 1556 (Nida 1964, 28). Felicity Heal points out how small linguistic differences could have great theolitical significance, for example, translating the *Vulgate*'s Latin *ecclesia* (adopted from the *Septuagint* Greek) as either "congregation" for Protestants or "church" for Catholics (2005, 272–274). Often competing Bible translations between Protestants and Catholics emerged, for example, in the British, Czech, German, Irish, and Spanish cases; in other cases there were competing revisions of the *Vulgate*.[29]

More recently, a controversy has erupted over the Christian Community Bible, also called the Bible for Christian Communities or the Latin American Bible, a translation

26. "The Quran." 2008–2013. Last modified April 11, 2013. Accessed April 24, 2013. http://www.discoveringislam.org/the_quran.htm [emphasis in original, compare to "Bible codes"].

27. Rogerson 2002, 24–25, 28. See also Nida 1964, 16.

28. We would like to thank Sudha Amonkar, telephone communication, January 15, 2013.

29. Heal 2005, *in passim*; Hotchkiss and Price 1996, 13–14, 41–42, 52–55, 62; Strand 1982; Wein 2009.

project started in Chile by the French Catholic Claretian priest and scholar Bernardo Hurault in 1970, allegedly in order to counter Evangelical Protestant mission in the region. The publisher of this relatively innovative edition of the biblical text (including a rearrangement of some of the order of the books in the Hebrew Bible) was closed down, apparently due to accusations of Marxism and anti-patriotism under the Argentinian regime in 1976 (Dolzani 2009/2013). The project has also been widely viewed as theologically biased, as Sander Gilman points out, "[i]n the mid-1990s, there was a general acknowledgement in the Catholic Church that the Bible for Christian Communities . . . was blatantly anti-Jewish" (2006, 4).

Furthermore, even the physical distinction between a bound Bible (Christian), i.e., a book, and a Bible scroll (Jewish) could mark a text as part of one religious group or another. The reason for this was perhaps an attempt of making a more visible distinction, given the sharing of core parts of the canon between the religions, specifically between Judaism and Christianity, but also between both of these religions and Islam.[30] Missionary and linguist Harriet S. Hill describes how members of her Christian community in Côte d'Ivoire (Ivory Coast, West Africa) complained about the paper format used for printing hymnbooks:[31] "The horizontal A5 sheet is Catholic. We are Methodist" (2006, 178).

An especially interesting twist on Bible translation is the phenomenon of interreligious translation. For example, Rabbi Moses Arragel's Castilian translation of 1422 was produced for a Catholic patron. The Judeo-Spanish Ferrara Bible (1553) was based on this 1422 translation but aimed at both Christian and Jewish readers. Two different versions were printed, where key words were exchanged, for instance, Isaiah 7:14 /'alma/ was rendered as "young woman" in the Jewish version but as "virgin" in the Catholic version, because in the Catholic reading this was a prophecy regarding Mary and connected to the virgin birth of Jesus (MacGregor 1959, 279). Contemporary interreligious translations include, for example, a number of Catholic-Protestant Bibles published in African languages, notably Chichewa, Gbaya, Ngbaka, and Swahili (Noss 2004, 21).

Finally, it should be noted that issues of female Bible translators and religious authority in the premodern period have not been adequately investigated yet; however, it is widely claimed that the first woman who translated the entire Bible (to English) was Julia Evelina Smith (1792–1886), and that this was not until 1876. In recent years, there have also been first known cases of female translators of the Qur'an, as well as of Buddhist and Sikh sacred texts. More research is needed to document women's usage of and contributions to sacred text translation throughout history and

---

30. Islam includes versions of some Biblical stories in the Qur'an, and designates figures such as Abraham (Ibrāhīm) and Jesus ('Īsā) as prophets.

31. See the idea that "the medium is the message" (McLuhan 1964), claiming that the form of communication can be as important or even more important than the content.

the role of gender identities in this framework. This is especially important in the present context, because in some cultural settings Bible translations may have been produced specifically for women, who were often less likely to be educated in the holy tongues.

Linguistic Standardization as Myth

The actual historical impact of Bible translation on modern standard languages was paralleled by circles of myths surrounding the translation process and the ideal of a stable linguistic standard. These myths were partly developed and utilized by nationalist movements later on. Nationalism often simplified the multifarious links between Bible translation and language standardization, and embellished them according to its needs, reading its own ideology into the past. Thus, Bible translation had a *real* major influence on linguistic standardization, but in addition, this impact was *amplified* by myth making.

It is important to note that linguistic and religious "founding myths"[32] already began with the *Septuagint* tradition, where the sacredness of the Hebrew Bible (in its still dynamic forms) was supposed to be transferred onto the process of translation, and onto the end product, namely the Greek text itself (Veltri 1994, 140, 150). This inter-language transition of sacredness proved a strong theological precedence, a tool of authentication and sanctification that would be imitated in many other Bible translation myths in the future. Historically, little is known about the exact circumstances of the emergence of the *Septuagint*.

A key element of the *Septuagint*'s circle of founding myths, as reflected in various partly pseudo-epigraphic documents, was its "commissioning" at the hands of a Hellenistic Egyptian king or Pharaoh, usually identified as Ptolemy II, sometimes via the chief librarian of the Library of Alexandria, and often in conjunction with the High Priest of Jerusalem's Temple and the Hellenist-Jewish community of Alexandria. Another important element of the founding myths was an alleged exchange of the Jewish scriptural "wisdom" for the liberation of variously 100,000 or 120,000 Jewish prisoners of war captured in Egypt. These elements seem an attempt at associating the founding myths of the *Septuagint* with the biblical founding myths of the Israelites and the granting of the Ten Commandments to Moses at Mt. Sinai as described in the Book of Exodus in the Hebrew Bible.[33]

The *Septuagint*'s founding myths were further embellished by various "miracles of correspondence"; for example, it took allegedly seventy-two wise men exactly

---

32. "Founding myths" purport to explain the origin of a group or a phenomenon, and are related to "origin myths." These are common types of myths.

33. A good summary of the diverse myths surrounding the emergence of the *Septuagint* can be found in Tilly 2005, 27–36.

seventy-two days to complete their work. In another version, the wise men worked separately, but the outcome of their translations was exactly the same to the dot. Such miracles allowed the commissioners to secure the text with bans on any further changes, i.e., to canonize it. The emergence of yearly pilgrimages in antiquity to the alleged site of the translation on an island off Alexandria may have helped to consolidate the founding myths via popular "re-enactment" (Tilly 2005, 27–36).

Joseph analyzed similar linguistic founding myths in later contexts, for example, surrounding the establishment of Slavic languages by Saints Cyril and Methodius, or the development of Italian by Alighieri Dante, concluding:

> The conceptual distance between absolute abstracts of any sort and religious belief is small . . . the cult of standard languages, and the Golden Age myth which underlies it, are not incidental features of Western civilization but its very cornerstone . . . The purposeful reoccurrence of such words as *deviant, deviation, moral degeneracy, perversely* and *perversity* captures the large element of religious righteousness that is intertwined within these attitudes (1987, 163–165, original emphasis).

Similarly, Jim Milroy points out that the result of the standardization of the English language was the emergence of a stringent written and spoken standard under nationalist influence in the nineteenth century, where seeming mistakes in pronunciation were viewed as "'abuses'—and this means that they are *morally* reprehensible" (2000, 16, original emphasis). Eric Hobsbawm criticizes the very concept of standard languages, claiming that it was "a sort of platonic idea of the language, existing behind and above all its variants and imperfect versions" (1990, 57).

Indeed, some of the transcendental characteristics of modern standard languages only make sense if we consider their roots in sacred tongues.[34] One such characteristic is the conservative nature of spelling in language development, as well as the aversion to spelling *misteyks*,[35] and the exaggerated punishments or social sanctions for such transgressions. While changes in other areas of the language, such as phonetics and phonology, morphology, or syntax have been quite rapid, and changes in the lexicon even very rapid (and often accepted, especially with the passing of time), changes in spelling tradition have been slow to occur. For example, today's English spelling reflects earlier stages of the language; for instance, *light* and *tonight*, where the vowel quality has changed (/i/ > /aj/) and the pronunciation of the velar fricative /x/ has disappeared. However, recently, even the traditional orthography has been questioned in popular culture, especially in the United States, where an alternative spelling of

---

34. On various language standardizations or myths surrounding them, see for instance, Armstrong 1982; Joseph 1987, 160–177; McColl Millar 2005, 77, also *in passim*; Powers 1990; Smith 1986; Smith 2003.
35. The spelling *misteyks* is clearly not standard; it is deliberately invented and chosen here as it demonstrates aversion to spelling mistakes on the part of many readers.

lite and *tonite* respectively has been introduced, beginning to appear publically in advertisement and later in the social media, although not without serious objections.

The standardization of Arabic provides another good example for religious-and linguistic-inspired myth making. First, various myths are involved in notions surrounding the appearance of the Qur'an and its exact attribution. Second, other myths have arisen regarding the use of the innumerable Arabic dialects. Arabic has long been in a state of *continuglossia*,[36] where language varieties of standard and colloquial (dialectal) Arabic are used simultaneously on a continuum stretching from one to the other, but also combining mixed varieties. Many native Arabic speakers believe that colloquial Arabic dialects are a product of deterioration and corruption of standard Classical Arabic (with the language of the Qur'an as its model). Simultaneously, however, many Arabic speakers believe that their national or local dialect happens to be the "closest" to standard Arabic and thus superior, because of the religious and linguistic prestige attached to standard Arabic (Ferguson 1968).

Additional transcendental characteristics of modern standard languages are government-sponsored language purity legislation and policies, based on *a priori* assumptions about the "nature" of a specific language, sometimes disregarding actual performance of speakers. To illustrate the power of language regulation, Joseph gave the example of a dictionary:

> The abstract ideal of the standard language has the status of a qualitative abso-
> lute . . . The dictionary . . . embodies this absolute authority to such a degree that
> most people, including educated people, confronted with a discrepancy between
> the dictionary and their own intuition, learning or reasoning, will much sooner
> deny their own knowledge than question the dictionary's authority. A lexical item
> is "not a word" if it does not appear in the dictionary. (1987, 161–162)

Today around one hundred institutions for language regulation exist around the world, often motivated by language purism, with the production of prescriptive dictionaries a central goal. In France, for example, the French Language Academy rejected the use of the term *software*, apparently because of its "foreign" (English) origin. In 1972, it recommended employing instead its newly minted term *logiciel*, based as it is on a Latin root. The term caught on and is still used today. In 1983, the term *walkman* was similarly replaced by a (pre-existing) Latin-based term, *baladeur;* however, in this case there was also a practical reason: the English term was actually a registered trademark of the Japanese Sony Corporation.[37] The French term has now

---

36. Traditionally known as "diglossia" (Ferguson 1959). Hary has introduced the term *continuglossia* in 2003 and elaborated on it in 2009, 37–38n12; 40–44. See also Hary and Wein 2013, 101n26.

37. As reported on the French Language Academy website, see http://www.academie-francaise.fr/ dictionnaire/index.html. Accessed July 24, 2012. For *logiciel* also see the website of the Centre National de Ressources Textuelles et Lexicales, http://www.cnrtl.fr/definition/logiciel. Accessed February 20, 2014. For *baladeur* also see France Terme, http://www.culture.fr/franceterme. Accessed February 20, 2014.

evolved into *baladeur numérique* (a digital music player) or *baladeur MP3* to reflect the technological evolution of the product.

In Israel, speakers of Hebrew have been using the term *mangal* "barbeque" for the last several decades. The word comes from Arabic *manqal* "fireplace, brazier, fire-pan" with the common voicing shift /q/ > /g/. The Hebrew Language Academy has gone as far as trying to eliminate not only "non-Semitic" words, but sometimes even words from closely related languages, such as Aramaic, or in this case, Arabic, which is an official language in Israel. Consequently, the Academy introduced the word *matsle* (from the Hebrew root *ts-l-h* "grill") in 2004, so far without much success among the public.

In an even more striking example, an attempt to rename fish species, the Hebrew Language Academy, in cooperation with the Fisheries and Aquaculture Department of the Ministry of Agriculture of Israel, limited its linguistic purification campaign to kosher species only.[38] The superimposition of Jewish religious dietary laws onto the Hebrew language via Israeli state agencies is not just an example of language purity policies, but also a prime case for a veritable conflation of language, religion, and nationalist policies. Although most of the popular terms for the fish species in question originated from Arabic, the Academy chose to Hebraize the majority of them, eliminating what was perceived as foreign influence.[39] In some cases, however, the ostensible Hebraization was actually a partial Latinization or Germanization, which did not follow through with consistent linguistic purification.[40]

Regarding the use of spoken language, often a neglected field of inquiry, the Israeli state radio *Reshet Gimel* refused to broadcast the popular singer Harel Moyal's single "We Don't Know You" in 2007, because of the colloquial pronunciation of one vowel (vowels are usually not written in Hebrew, so such variations occur quite often).[41]

---

38. Plater has claimed that the Hebrew Language Academy issued a statement to this effect on July 23, 2007. However, some non-kosher seafood does have Hebrew names as well. For example, shrimp has been Hebraized to /ḥasilonim/ and is used interchangeably with the word /shrimps/ (used in the plural by Hebrew speakers!), although the latter is more popular. See Plater 2007, 12–13 (in Hebrew).

39. For example, the popular fish from the Sea of Galilee, St. Peter's (Latin, *Tilapia galilaea*), or as it is known in its Arabic name, *musht*, was Hebraized in 1981 by the Academy to *amnun*. *Barbut* (Latin, *Clarias lazera*) was Hebraized in 1981 to *sfamnun*. *Buri* (Latin, *Mugil cephalus*) was Hebraized also in 1981 to *kippon*. In 1977 the popular fish *lokus* (English, Jaffa cod) and anchovy were both Hebraized by the Academy to *dakkar* and *'afyan* respectively. In actual use it seems that the non-Hebraized terms remain more popular in spoken and sometimes even written Hebrew.

40. For example, *forel* (possibly from German *Forelle*, or via Yiddish *forel*, "rainbow trout," whereby *trout* is derived from the Latin *tructa*; the scientific name is either *Salmo gairdneri* or *Oncorhynchus mykiss*); *lavrak* (maybe from Greek λαβράκι, "European sea bass"; bass has a Germanic etymology; the scientific name is *Dicentrachus labrax*); and *denis* (possibly borrowed from Arabic *denis*, "gilt-head bream"; etymology unclear; the scientific name is *Sparus aurata*) were all "Hebraized," still keeping parts of their "foreign" roots. Consequently, the Hebrew Language Academy termed them *trutat 'ein ha-keshet*, *bas ha-sela* and *sparus zahov* respectively. It appears that none of these new terms caught on in popular use.

41. In standard Hebrew /lo makirim otkha/. Moyal pronounced /mekirim/ rather than /makirim/, reflecting a typical colloquial use. See Sukenik 2007 (in Hebrew). See also readers' reactions.

Moyal, the 2004 winner of the very popular *Kokhav Nolad* television reality show, the Israeli equivalent of *American Idol*, had to re-record his song so that it would be cleared for broadcasting, only because he did not use the standard form based upon biblical Hebrew. Standard Israeli Hebrew is of course significantly derived from the original biblical Hebrew text, among others, rather than from canonized Bible translations as is common in other languages.

The Linguistic Impact of Bible Translation

Bible translation ingeniously amalgamates much of the grammar, the lexicon, and the non-elitist nature of the spoken "vernacular" varieties, with the sacredness of the languages of religious establishments, using, for example, their scripts, their traditions of orthography, and specific idioms or religious terminology. Through the process of Bible translation, these vernaculars are thus, to some degree, endowed with the religious characteristics of the holy tongues. Consider three examples of holy tongue impact on standardized vernaculars on several linguistics levels: Castilian Spanish, Russian, and (Eastern) Yiddish. These three languages each reflect the impact of their respective religious holy tongue in their orthography, vocabulary, and grammar. Thus, Castilian reflects Latin (Catholic), Russian reflects Old Church Slavonic (Orthodox Christian), and Yiddish reflects Hebrew-Aramaic (Jewish). We choose these three languages in order to provide a systematic comparison between three clearly different religious-linguistic traditions.

- Castilian Spanish is written in the Latin characters of the *Vulgate* and uses in its lexicon New Testament terminology such as *la inmaculada concepción* "immaculate conception." In the grammar, the use of the "absolute ablative" (or, *participio absoluto*) is a conscious imitation of Latin as a model for modern Spanish, particularly in writing. For example, *Dicho esto, él cerdito se fue a casa*, "Having said this, the little pig went home."[42]
- Russian employs Cyrillic characters, used in the holy tongue of Old Church Slavonic, adapted in some fashion from the Greek alphabet employed in the *Septuagint*.[43] The Russian lexicon includes a number of word pairs that come from the same "Slavic" origin: one from "native" Russian (i.e. the East Slavic branch) and the other from Old Church Slavonic (based on a South Slavic dialect). Usually the Russian-based term carries a more concrete meaning than the Church Slavonic form, which tends to be somewhat abstract or more formal. For example, *golova* "head" is Russian-based, but *glava* "head of an organization" (also "book chapter") is of Church Slavonic origin; *zdorovyj* "healthy" is

---

42. We would like to thank Donald Tuten for these examples.
43. In fact, Old Church Slavonic first employed the Glagolitic alphabet, which was itself partly based on Greek, and possibly additional alphabets. Glagolitic was eventually replaced by the Cyrillic script.

of Russian origin, but *zdravyj* "sensible, sound" of Church Slavonic origin. In Russian grammar, the suffixes used to form present active participles are of Church Slavonic origin:-*ushch*-and-*iashch*-, for example: *mogushchij* "which is able" and *gorjashchij* "which is burning." The parallel form of Russian origin is often a simple adjective. These are affixed by-*uch*-or-*jach*-, for instance, *moguchij* "powerful" and *gorjachij* "hot."[44]

- Yiddish uses a slightly adapted version of the alphabet of the Hebrew (and Aramaic) Bible, also spread through *Tsena urena* (lit. "Go out and see" [fem. pl.]), a highly popular Bible digest, the Yiddish "People's Bible." Yiddish employs in its lexicon idioms like *yeshive bokher* (lit. "yeshiva boy") "a student of a religious academy." This example represents a Yiddish phrase with two borrowed Hebrew lexical items, but with a typical Germanic word order (Genitive + Noun pattern), rather than Hebrew word order (Noun + Genitive pattern). In the grammar, Yiddish sometimes uses Hebrew grammatical elements such as the plural suffix-*im* in *doktoyrim* "doctors" attached to a Latin lexeme. (Baumgarten 1999, 236)

The relatively wide availability of amalgamated Bible translations, and their clout of holiness furthered their role in creating early standard written varieties spread by printing shops, beginning in the fifteenth century, initially in Europe. The first major book printed in Europe was Johannes Gutenberg's Christian Bible from the mid-fifteenth century, an edition of the Latin *Vulgate*. According to Benedict Anderson, a collation of "print capitalism," Protestantism, vernacular language standardization, and increasingly literate, non-elite populations drove the spread of print vernaculars, which created alternative, local language communities alongside the educational elite's Church Latin language community across Christian Western Europe (1991, 37–45).

Indeed, Bible translations could fulfill many functions in the lives of ordinary literate or semi-literate Christians or Jews, functioning as textbooks, dictionaries, grammars, or sections of prayer books. Preachers used Bible translations as a source for scriptural quotations or as models for their own speeches. Melvyn Bragg comments in his "biography" of English:

> For centuries [the translated Bible] was heard week in week out, sometimes day in day out, by almost all English-speaking Christians wherever they were [,] and its precepts, its images, its proverbs, its names, its parables, its heroes, its promises, its words and rhythms sank deep shafts into the minds of the men and women who heard it. It went to the heart of the way we spoke, the way we described the world and ourselves. [The translated Bible's] English bound the English [language varieties] together. (2003, 113)

---

44. We would like to thank Alan Cienki for these examples.

Religious concepts, sometimes theologically loaded, have thus entered the vernacular languages, profoundly transforming them on the way, creating specific forms of "biblical literacy" within a language community. To illustrate this, the Encyclopedia of North American Indians points out that:

> Many of the metaphors and narrative forms found in the Bible are so culturebound that, even where feasible, a literal translation would render them misleading or nonsensical to non-Western peoples. What possible meaning could a verbatim translation of the expression "Lamb of God" [a metaphor for Jesus] hold for a society without a pastoral tradition and unfamiliar with the cultural, theological, and emotional significance attached to the term lamb in Western Christology? (Markowitz 1996, 68)

In the English language, even with today's multi-religious and secular array of speakers, media often still assume a significant degree of implied Christian religious and textual knowledge. For example in 2007, the BBC website wrote in an article on the extinction of fish species: "When extinct species are rediscovered they are, aptly, called Lazarus species. They include the New Zealand storm petrel and a freshwater fish from Madagascar" (BBC News 2007). This passage assumes a Christian literacy among readers of an English text concerning the "return from the dead" of Lazarus, a New Testament figure (John 11: 41–44). Note the use of the term "aptly" and the lack of any explanation of the Lazarus story.

Furthermore, after Republican presidential candidate John McCain described the United States as a "Christian nation" in 2007, an English-language columnist of the Israeli newspaper *Ha'aretz*, Bradley Burston, responded:

> Every Jewish kid in America who has ever worn a kippah, every Muslim who has worn external evidence of his or her devotion to Islam, knows very well that Senator McCain was right. Every public schoolchild who was raised in a home where Jesus was not believed to be God, and who was made to sing "Joy to the world, the Lord has come!" with devotion and feeling, knows just how right McCain was. (Burston 2007)

Note here once again the multiple religious references like *kippah* (skullcap), Jesus, or Lord, which are assumed to be understood by a readership literate not only in English, but also in the "Judeo-Christian" discourse. Although Islam and Muslims are mentioned, no attempt is made to actually include a specifically Muslim readership. It appears that the target audience of English language journalism is still partly delineated by religious divides. In the age of the Internet this is particularly surprising, since the readership could potentially be global and not just British (in the case of BBC), or Israeli (in the case of *Ha'aretz*), although even these two locations are much more religiously diverse than commonly acknowledged.

Notably, Bible translations have provided not just for many features of the actual standardization of languages, but they have also imprinted linguistic reference books.

For instance, G. A. Grierson's classic reference work *Linguistic Survey of India* from 1927 lists languages and illustrates them through the Christian "Lord's Prayer," as well as the New Testament's "Parable of the Prodigal Son" (Luke 15: 11–32). At the same time, local "non-Christian" texts were sometimes added to these illustrations, making the list not as exclusively Christian as in the following example.

In the monumental reference work entitled *Compendium of the World's Languages* by George L. Campbell, linguistic classification itself was a quasi-Christian project with each language typically exemplified by the first eight verses of Chapter 1 of "St John's Gospel" (1991, 1: ix), and the consistent use of a Christian sacred text as the example for language communities, even where Christian speakers are (small) minorities (e.g., Arabic, Japanese). The religious impact on this Compendium was perhaps most obvious in Campbell's treatment of Jewish-defined languages.

First, a questionable distinction was made between Hebrew and *Ivrit* (meaning "Hebrew" in Hebrew), i.e. ancient versus modern Hebrew. Although modern Hebrew is strongly influenced by European languages, by other Jewish-defined languages, by Arabic and so on (as is the case with many languages), it is still very much based in its earlier phases—biblical, Rabbinic, medieval, as well as early modern Hebrew—and could thus be viewed as one language, not two.[45] Second, Campbell illustrates both Hebrew and what he calls *Ivrit* through the Gospel of John, rather than through a Jewish canonical text like the Book of Genesis, the first book of the Hebrew Bible. Mysteriously, a verbatim translation of the Gospel of John was used to exemplify Hebrew, while a freer, messianic, or even Christian missionary translation of the Gospel of John was offered for *Ivrit* (ibid., 565–570, 653–657).

Campbell's treatment of Yiddish revealed another interesting strategy. The author altogether abstained from providing any text illustration, although a basic set of sacred text translations into Yiddish has been available for quite some time (Hebrew Bible from 1678–1679; New Testament from 1821; Qur'an from 1987). Yiddish also happens to be one of the largest languages ever to have been pushed to the edge of extinction not via re-lingualization of its speakers, as is common, but rather through genocide. Although genocide was one of the main reasons, if not *the* main reason, for the sudden collapse of Yiddish in the mid-twentieth century, Campbell curiously fails to mention this among the many reasons he lists for the decline of this particular language (ibid., 2: 1468–1473).

The Triangle of Religion, Language, and Nationalism

In the modern period, the ancient connection between religion and language, as embodied in sacred text translation, has often helped to shape nationalism, and in

---

45. Here we differ from also Ghil'ad Zuckermann's recent claim that "Israeli" (i.e., modern Hebrew) is indeed a language separate from the earlier stages of Hebrew (2003).

return nationalist ideology tended to reshape religion and language in its search for primordiality.[46] Especially interesting in this framework is Joshua A. Fishman's proposition of the existence of a quasi-primordial "positive ethnolinguistic consciousness" (1997). To prove his point, Fishman publishes an extensive database of text samples by speakers describing their own languages, often in Romantic and nationalist or religious terms. However, rather than finding what he termed a positive ethnolinguistic consciousness, Fishman seems to have recorded standard nationalist rhetoric.[47] Instead of exhibiting some sort of anthropological universalism, it must be assumed that the vast majority of the global samples in Fishman's database had already been "contaminated" by exposure to nationalism, with specific terminology and axiomatic concepts that can be traced back to Western Europe.

Reordering Fishman's data chronologically, rather than alphabetically by language name as it was printed, it turns out that only six out of seventy-six languages which received entries (or nine of 141 sample quotations, usually one to three per language) provide examples predating the late modern period. In other words, Fishman supplies seventy languages (more than 90 percent) with examples dated only after 1800, i.e., already after the onset of nationalism, which hardly indicates a universal proto-nationalist phenomenon. Furthermore, four of those six languages with examples from before the late modern period (with five sample quotations) are Western European: Castilian (one paraphrased source from the late fifteenth/ early sixteenth centuries), English (1582, 1789), Flemish (1788), and French (1549). Since, according to most theorists, nationalism first developed in this exact region during the transition of the early modern period into modernity, before spreading around the world, none of these examples can prove Fishman's concept of a universal, inherent or primordial proto-nationalism.

The only two languages not from Western Europe, for which Fishman provides older samples, are Russian (two sources from the eighteenth century) and Telugu (from India, one mid-fourteenth century and one sixteenth century source, the latter possible paraphrasing the earlier source). For Russian, Fishman quotes Mikail Lomonosov (1711–1765), a western-European trained scientist and Alexander P. Sumarokov (1718–1777), a poet and playwright with French connections.[48] This reflects the exceptionally close links of members of the Czarist elite (beginning with the rule of Peter the Great) with Western Europe and might explain the nationalist overtones in the two samples at such an early date; however, this may not be representative for Russian as a whole.

---

46. For a good introduction to this topic, see Olender 1992.
47. It would probably be safer to claim the existence of "positive linguistic (rather than ethnolinguistic) consciousness" as people tend to have an affirmative relationship and emotional attachment to their own languages. Including ethnic issues in it may be a conceptual overextension of the phenomenon.
48. A third person quoted for Russian is M. I. Isayev (his quote is only from 1977, thus is irrelevant for our argument). See Fishman 1997, 324n170.

For Telugu, Fishman provides two sources, which might indeed be constructed in favor of his theory claiming the existence of a positive ethnolinguistic consciousness, somehow embedded in the human mind and preceding modern Western-style nationalism. Overall, Telugu is only one possible case, however, and the record is thus not substantial enough, in quantity or in quality, to corroborate Fishman's theory. Rather, it seems that the specific link between language and nationalism that he traced in his database originated in Western Europe in the early modern period, gradually spreading throughout the region, and eventually across the world, via colonialism and postcolonial independence. Indeed, Fishman himself acknowledges at the end of his book:

> The youngest citations, on average, are those from Africa, suggesting that much of ethnolinguistic consciousness there may not grow out of indigenous histori- cal traditions . . . but, rather, may have been stimulated by exposure to Western thought, either via study or, more generally, via the contrastiveness inherent in the colonial/anti-colonial experience per se. In essence, our Western European citations are largely from around the end of the 19th and the beginning of the 20th centuries, the non-Western European citations come mostly from just before and after the conclusion of the First World War, the Asian/Pacific citations are generally from the inter-war period and the American and African citations are generally post-Second World War in nature. (Fishman 1997, 301)

Fishman's meticulously documented and truly global database is nevertheless of great value for our analysis, specifically due to its ample religious references. These references were perhaps recorded somewhat accidentally, but they neatly illustrate the triangular relationship of religious, linguistic, and nationalist aspects of various communities in modernity. At times, the database shows that a particular religion is interconnected with a specific language and nationalism. A typical theme is thereby the description of a national language as a divine gift bestowed upon the believers. As Fishman writes, "[i]t is through the association of one's own vernacular with holi- ness that ethnolinguistic consciousness draws upon the power of supreme, widely unquestioned and fully canonized traditional verities and transfers some of the aura of this association to ethnolinguistic movements" (ibid., 12).

Religious references can be found in twenty-five of Fishman's seventy-six sampled languages (and in seventy-six out of the 141 quotations), most of which are unspeci- fied Christian. Some examples are explicitly or implicitly marked as Catholic, Muslim, or Jewish, as well as animist, polytheist and, in only one single case, multi-religious (Konkani, see below). Here a few examples:

- [A]bandoning our language would be true national apostasy . . . But in order that the French-Canadian nation fulfills this glorious mission, it must remain what Providence ordained it to be—Catholic and French. It must keep its faith and its language in all their purity . . . God has given us the French language;

through it He accomplished great things in our midst. It was in this language that our missionaries, our bishops, our martyrs prayed . . . For us French-Canadians, our language is intimately linked to our faith, to the religion of our great men . . . to all that is sacred to us (Jules-Paul Tardival, journalist and publisher, 1881; ibid., 219–221).

- The campaign launched [by colonial interests] against the Arabic language is an attack against our existence and against all our traditions—social, religious, linguistic . . . The death of Arabic will mean the disappearance of values and traditions . . . Arabs will simply vanish in the midst of other nations, and so will their eloquence, faith, culture and knowledge (Mohamed Jaber Al-Fayad, Iraqi nationalist, published 1984; ibid., 187).

- Even the Yiddishists [General Jewish Labor Union, a secular political group] who (may God protect us) denied the sanctity of the holy Torah, nevertheless conducted themselves as Jews . . . One need hardly add that the truly righteous and the veritable saints of every generation . . . would mix Yiddish exclamations into their very [Hebrew-Aramaic] prayers. The Torah giants would . . . always formulate their innovative interpretations and expressions only in Yiddish and Loshn-koydesh [lit. "holy tongue," i.e., a mixture of Hebrew and Aramaic] together . . . Has any other language absorbed so much sanctity of the Torah and of the process of learning the Talmud? (Shifre Rubin, rebetsin [rabbi's wife], 1992; ibid., 296–297).

In Protestantism, too, similar links have long been established. For example, in the German imagination and collective memory, the German Bible translator Luther was regularly styled into the image of a founding father not only of Protestantism, but also of standard German and, in fact, of the German nation, bundling very specific religious, linguistic, and nationalist aspects. Germany's strong Catholic minority was thus somewhat sidelined, if not quite as much as Germany's Jews. In Julie M. Winter's words:

> Luther's anti-Roman [Catholic] stance was interpreted in the Protestant tradition in Germany as a form of proto-nationalism; that is, Luther was seen historically as the liberator of the German spirit from Roman [Catholic] Christianity, and even as the creator of the Germanic form of Christianity. This association in Lutheranism of Protestantism and Germanness began largely in the nineteenth century. (1998, 15)

If a relatively small variety of religions and languages could often not be fit into the emerging national communities in Europe, in India, where a staggering variety of languages meets an equally stunning array of religious practices, nation-building must seem near-impossible. Creating an Indian nation or even just larger regional identifications with Indian states, remains quite a challenge. Thus, Mahatma Gandhi tried to develop what linguist Rocky Miranda[49] calls a "middle language," accessible to Hindus and Muslims alike, e.g. by avoiding Sanskrit elements in his Hindi, while some Muslim intellectuals correspondingly reduced Arabic elements in their Urdu in order to bridge between the two closely related religiolects of Hindi and Urdu.[50] According to Miranda, the intentional reduction of sacred-texts-derived elements in both Hindi and Urdu is regularly done until today in Bollywood movies, for example, specifically for commercial reasons, so they can be screened in both India and Pakistan.

In Goa, poet Manohar Rai Sardesai tried to do the same for the local variety Konkani, bridging mainly between Hindu and Christian religiolects (there are only few Muslim speakers, but recently also a number of Buddhist speakers). Sardesai even had some of his work printed in two writing systems in the same book (Devanagari and Roman). Altogether, Konkani can be written in five different writing systems[51] (also in Arabic, Kannada, or Malayalam). Konkani's many language varieties, some of which have been scattered across Southeast India, chiefly reflect the complex history of Portuguese colonialism, inquisition and population movements in India, with some areas ruled from Lisbon for about 450 years—among the longest continuous colonial rules in history.[52]

Printing in Goa began already in 1616 with the *Christa Purana*, a continuglossic[53] Marathi-Konkani digest of biblical stories in *purana* (Hindu myth) style and meter, heavy on the Marathi side, using a Roman writing system. A catechism titled *Doctrina Crista* in Konkani followed in 1622, a work that in many respects coined the Konkani language, including its Romanization and its role as the Catholic "language of religion" or holy tongue of Goa, as Madhavi Sardesai pointed out.[54] However, the translation of sacred texts into Konkani may have started already in the preceding era, under Muslim rule, and it continues until today, with Buddhist, Christian, Hindu, Muslim, and Sikh sacred texts being locally translated and printed in a variety of writing systems.[55]

The result of this religious syncretism and sacred text exchange has been a Konkani "ethnicity" or "nationality" with an unusually high degree of multi-religious

---

49. We would like to thank Rocky Miranda, personal communication to Martin Wein, January 21, 2013.
50. The term *religiolect* used to define Hindu and Urdu may be contested here; however, it is outside the scope of this study to discuss the boundaries between and definitions of language, variety, dialect, ethnolect, religiolect, and other related terms.
51. Using different writing systems or orthographies for languages is not unusual. See "Part X, Use and Adaptation of Script," in Bright and Daniels 1996, 625–762.
52. We would like to thank Rocky Miranda, personal communication, January 21, 2013; email messages to Martin Wein, January 27, 2013; and Madhavi Sardesai, personal communication, January 15, 2013.
53. See above for the term *continuglossia*. In the present case a continuum exists between Marathi and Konkani.
54. Madhavi Sardesai, "The Konkani-Marathi conflict and its impact on the standardisation of Konkani" (undated manuscript).
55. We would like to thank Madhavi Sardesai, personal communication, January 15, 2013.

syncretization. In Fishman's database we identified Konkani as the *only explicitly multi-religious language*, based on a sample quotation by Manohar Sardesai: "[Konkani] is well understood by all: Brahmins, Gowdas [Hindu/Christian casts/tribes], Bhats [Hindu priests], padris [Catholic priests], cooks [i.e., Christians], Kunbis [Hindu/Christian cast/tribe], everyone. Christ taught the fishermen [sometimes used as a synonym for Konkani-speakers] in their own language. The Buddha delivered his sermons in the language of the people."[56]

So can this example of multi-religious Konkani be a model for other linguistic communities, too? In Joseph's words:

> [A] given language is capable of sustaining more than one culture. Even the Arabic language, with its intense cultural bonds to Islam, has sustained Christian cultures for centuries, and has the potential to sustain any number of cultures. The same is true of every language, and in that sense language is culturally "neutral." (2004, 167)

However, is this so in practice? Over the twentieth century, even Arabic, lauded by Joseph for its integration of Christians (while ignoring the vast Judeo-Arabic tradition), has seen a process of contraction in religious terms, rather than an expansion, with the decline of Jews under Arab Muslim rule. Can linguistic and religious cultures thus really be separated?

In our next example, Lee Ki-nam, a South Korean activist, made it her calling to promote the use of *Hangul*, the Korean alphabet, around Asia. Beginning in 2003, she worked via Korean Christian missionaries in China, Mongolia, Nepal, and Vietnam, albeit without much success. In 2009, her project gained its first modest accomplishment in Indonesia, where the Cia-Cia ethnic group in the town of Bau-Bau on Buton Island near Sulawesi Island agreed to teach a group of third graders the system of *Hangul* to write their own local language variety (Choe 2009).

In response to Lee Ki-nam's claim of merely advocating alphabetization for languages without writing systems, linguist Uri Tadmor notes that Cia-Cia speakers today typically know how to write standard Indonesian in Roman alphabet, and therefore, rather than using the Roman alphabet also for their local language, "why force them to learn another script?" (Wright and Feirlough 2009).[57] According to journalist Choe Sang-Hun, some Muslim-majority countries have viewed Korean projects such as Lee Ki-nam's ostensible alphabetization drive via *Hangul* with suspicion,

---

56. Fishman 1997, 242, quoting Sardesai, "*Amci bhas amka dzay* [We want our language], Presidential address to the Eight All-India Konkani Congress, Panaji, Goa," Margao, Goa: Konkani Bhasha Mandal, 1962. Note that the reference to Buddha may also be understood within a Hindu context and that a reference to Muslim Konkani-speakers is missing (they make up for only a few percent of the language community). We would like to thank Rocky Miranda and Madhavi Sardesai for explaining the terms of the quotation to us which are added in square brackets in the quote itself.

57. We would like to thank Uri Tadmor, personal communication to Martin Wein, April 22, 2013; and René van den Berg, email message to authors, May 16, 2013.

28 Christianity, and Islam_

fearing the spread of Christianity, in this case through linguistically encoded mission (Choe 2009).[58]

This example, however minor, illustrates the highly complex situation in Southeast Asia where a number of Asian alphabets (Arabic, Chinese, various Indian scripts) have long competed with Latin characters. Specific linguistic cultures have thereby been linked to specific religious cultures. Nevertheless, the Indonesian government's national language policy centers on the establishment of a shared standard language, Indonesian, based on Malay and written in Roman letters. Ironically, this policy itself reflects the global success of Christian mission, through Bible translations in Latin characters. Indeed, the very first "colonial" (partial) Bible translation worldwide was produced by Albert Cornelius Ruyl, a Dutch East Indies Company trader on Indonesia's Ambon Island, not far from Sulawesi Island, with a bilingual Dutch and Malay edition of the Gospel of Matthew printed in Enkhuizen, in the Netherlands, in 1629, using a Latin-based writing system.[59] This case thus also demonstrates how a country that does not actually have a predominant or even significant Christian (or Jewish) population can still allow Bible translation to have a lasting impact on its standard language that is also a symbol of its national identity.

Epilogue

So has the Bible in fact imparted the template for nationalism? In his reply to Marxist historian and theorist Eric Hobsbawm, who popularized the term "invented tradition" in relation to nationalism (1983), the Roman Catholic priest, theologian, and historian Adrian Hastings writes: "[t]he Bible provided, for the Christian world at least, the original model of the nation. Without it and its Christian interpretation and implementation, it is arguable, that nations and nationalism, as we know them, could never have existed" (1997, 4). While Hastings's statement may seem convincing on the surface, we would like to raise several concerns.

The first problem is Hastings's apparent reliance on a rather questionable historical lexical stability and cogency of the term "nation" (see e.g., Breuilly 1994). Second, there is the danger of teleological reasoning by projecting concepts of modern

---

58. It may be added, however, that Korea has had a long and glorious tradition of scholarly influence around East Asia, including the development of the *Hangul* alphabet to eventually replace the Chinese-derived writing system *Hanja*, further the block printing and preservation of a key Buddhist sacred text canon, the *Tripitaka Koreana*, in the thirteenth century, and the pioneering of movable metal type printing technology, preceding Europe by decades.

59. In contrast to Brown (1816, 548) who claimed that the Malay part of this edition was printed in Arabic characters, the Württembergische Landesbibliothek in Stuttgart, which holds one of the few surviving copies, clearly describes it as "Text niederländ. u. malaisch, in lat. Schrift" [Text in Dutch and Malay in Latin script]. However, it is true that later editions (for example, Batavia [Jakarta] 1758; Calcutta 1822) were also printed in Arabic characters (Horne 1836, 50).

nationhood retroactively back onto earlier periods that were defined by entirely different political, social, economic, and linguistic systems (e.g., Connor 1994). Indeed, models of a nation were regularly crafted into modern nationalist *readings* of the Hebrew Bible. Third, we would like to take issue with Hastings's suggestion that premodern religion, specifically Christianity, was somehow (proto-) national. Conversely, we argue that modern nationalism is inherently (civil) religious. The fact that religion has *not* disappeared under the nationalist umbrella may not be self-evident, because of occasional nationalist pretenses of secularism and the transformation of *religious* into near-equivalent *nationalist* rhetoric and rites.

Finally, and most importantly, both Hastings and Hobsbawm insufficiently stressed the key role played by Bible translation, which provides the historical "missing link" between religion and nationalism. Nationalism typically tried to overcome differences in religious loyalties by embracing the standardization of vernacular language varieties, which subsequently often also played a significant role in civil religion. However, these standard vernacular languages were typically distilled via Bible translations, imprinting them with very specific religious elements. At times, such a religious marking of standard languages undermined nationalist secularism and caused rifts in multi-religious language communities.

By no means has Bible translation and linguistic standardization precipitated a rise of nationalism in all instances. However, where nationalism spread, it usually accelerated the standardization process of a select linguistic variety, intentionally or not endowing the newborn (or "reborn") nation simultaneously with a "national language" and a "national religion." The historical imprint of Bible translations and language standardization, further augmented by mythmaking, thus came to delineate many communities around the world, often permanently embedding hierarchies and power structures. George Schöpflin wrote:

> Language in the broad sense, including both symbolic and grammatical codes, exposes a community to a particular experience, to particular ways of constructing the world. Those who control the standardization process derive power from so doing. Those who can invoke myth and establish resonance can mobilize people, exclude others, screen out certain memories, establish solidarity or, indeed reinforce the hierarchy of status and values. (2000, 82–83)

This is even more relevant today, as the phenomenon of Bible translation has reached the Internet, with the recent launching of the app YouVersion containing upwards of 600 Bible translations in over 400 languages. The developers refer to this app as part of a new digital mission, and its popularity has now peaked at more than 100 million downloads. However, Adam Graber of Tyndale House, a publisher that also provides translations for the YouVersion, has compared this Bible app to Apple and Google in terms of its concentration of power, expressing caution and concern over a potential monopolization of Bible publishing (O'Leary 2013).

But is all this really still pertinent? After all, communities around the world have already been delineated through Bible translations, for better or worse. Yet, in regions like Sub-Saharan Africa and South or Southeast Asia, which are experiencing enormous population booms, new media communities, "ethnicities" or nationalities are still being created, not least through a constant effort of the classification of dialects and the codification of new standard languages, often in cooperation with Christian missionaries. While most of Europe's nations join into the European Union, the historical Western European program of nation building has a ripple effect and is still being replicated in ever-widening circles around the world today, often physically encapsulated in (translated) holy books.

Missionary projects predestine communities to draw future boundaries along the lines of the linguistic-religious identities being created through Bible translation, frequently by only one specific group or sub-group. Instead, why not employ translators from many different Christian groups and various other religious communities, too, as it has sometimes been done, such as in the cases of Chichewa, Gbaya, Ngbaka, and Swahili (see above)? Why not use, in addition to parts of the New Testament and the Hebrew Bible, also passages from the Qur'an, and material from other local or global spiritual heritages for language standardization projects? Finally, why not compile all that into one book, which could then become the cornerstone of a newly standardized, but religiously perhaps more inclusive language?

To conclude, in this exposition we have questioned, challenged, and critiqued an entire set of commonly-held axioms relating to religion, language, and nationalism, along with their collaboration and conflict, in the past as well as in contemporary life. Using theory from Jewish studies as a starting point, we found that the politics of Bible and other sacred text canonization and translation have historically played a central role in creating a myth as well as a (partial) reality of standard languages, which in turn became a vehicle for nationalism around the globe in modernity. Therefore, religion, language and nationalism are intrinsically connected today. Ideally, they need to be analyzed together, as it is the *combination* of these three paradigmatic cultural heritages, which continues to form the intellectual infrastructure and conceptual foundation of global communication, education, and community.

References

Abdul-Raof, Hussein. "Cultural Aspects of Qur'an Translation." In *Translation and Religion: Holy Untranslatable?*, edited by Lynne Long, 162–172. Trowbridge, Wiltshire: Cromwell Press, 2005.

Agulhon, Maurice. *Marianne au combat: L'imagerie et la symbolique républicaines de 1789 à 1880*. Paris: Flammarion, 1979.

Anderson, Benedict. *Imagined Communities: Reflections on the Origin and Spread of Nationalism*. London and New York: Verso, 1991.

Armstrong, John A. *Nations before Nationalism*. Chapel Hill: The University of North Carolina Press, 1982.

Bard Na Mara. "Sacred Ireland." Accessed August 9, 2011. www.sacredireland.org.

"The Battle of the Books." *The Economist*, December 19, 2007. Accessed December 19, 2007. http://www.economist.com/node/10311317.

Baumgarten, Jean. "La composante hébraïque en yiddish: repères historiques et outils théoriques." In *Vena Hebraica in Judaeorum Linguis: Proceedings of the 2nd International Conference on the Hebrew and Aramaic Elements in Jewish Languages*, edited by Shlomo Morag, Moshe Bar-Asher, and Maria Mayer-Modena, 221–241. Milan: Centro Studi Camito-Semitici di Milano, 1999.

BBC News. "How Are Species Classed as Extinct?" Accessed July 16, 2007. http://newsvote.bbc.co.uk/mpapps/pagetools/print/news.bbc.co.uk/2/hi/uk_news/magazine/6901056.stm.

Birnbaum, Pierre, and Ira Katznelson, eds. *Paths of Emancipation: Jews, States and Citizenship*. Princeton, New Jersey: Princeton University Press, 1995.

Bragg, Melvyn. *The Adventure of English*. London: Hodder and Stoughton, 2003.

Breuilly, John. "The Sources of Nationalist Ideology." In *Nationalism*, edited by John Hutchinson and Anthony D. Smith, 103–113. Oxford and New York: Oxford University Press, 1994.

Bright, William and Peter Daniels, eds. *The World's Writing Systems*. Oxford and New York: Oxford University Press, 1996.

Brown, William. *The History of Missions; or, of the Propagation of Christianity among the Heathen, since the Reformation*, vol. 2. Philadelphia: B. Coles, 1816.

Burston, Bradley. "Yes, Sen. McCain, America Is a Christian Nation." *Haaretz*, October 2, 2007. Accessed October 3, 2007. http://www.haaretz.com/news/yes-sen-mccain-america-is-a-christian-nation-1.230393.

Campbell, George L. *Compendium of the World's Languages*. London and New York: Routledge, 1991.

Charmé, Stuart Z. "Varieties of Authenticity in Contemporary Jewish Identity." *Jewish Social Studies* 6/2 (2000): 133–155.

Choe Sang-Hun. "South Korea's Latest Export: Its Alphabet." *New York Times*, September 11, 2009. Accessed October 4, 2009. http://www.nytimes.com/2009/09/12/world/asia/12script.html.

Connor, Walker. "When is a Nation?" In *Nationalism*, edited by John Hutchinson and Anthony D. Smith, 154–159. Oxford and New York: Oxford University Press, 1994.

Ó Corráin, Donnchadh. "Nationality, Nation, Nationalism." *Multitext Project in Irish History*. University College Cork, Ireland. Accessed August 9, 2011. http://multitext.ucc.ie/d/Nationality_Nation_Nationalism.

Cristi, Marcela. *From Civil to Political Religion: The Intersection of Culture, Religion and Politics*. Waterloo, Ontario: Wilfried Laurier University Press, 2001.

Crowley, Tony. *Standard English and the Politics of Language*. New York: Palgrave Macmillian, 2003.

Dolzani, P. Martín. "Sacerdotes que dijeron sí: Padre Bernardo Hurault." *Sociedad San Pablo*, September 5, 2009, last update 2013. Accessed July 17, 2013. http://www.paulus.net/index.php?option=com_content&task=view&id=1072&Itemid=523.

Erard, Michael. "How Linguists and Missionaries Share a Bible of 6,912 Languages." *New York Times*, July 19, 2005. Accessed July 19, 2005. http://www.nytimes.com/2005/07/19/science/19lang.html?pagewanted=all&_r=0.

Ferguson, Charles. "Diglossia." *Word* 15 (1959): 325–340.

————. "Myths about Arabic." In *Readings in the Sociology of Language*, edited by Joshua Fishman, 375–381. The Hague: Mouton, 1968.

Fishman, Joshua A. *In Praise of the Beloved Language: A Comparative View of Positive Ethnolinguistic Consciousness*. Berlin: Mouton de Gruyter, 1997.

French Language Academy website. n.d. Accessed July 24, 2012. http://www.academie-francaise.fr/dictionnaire/index.html.

Funkenstein, Amos. "The Dialectics of Assimilation." *Zmanim* 55 (1996): 64–71 [in Hebrew].

Gilman, Sander. *Multiculturalism and the Jews*. New York: Routledge, 2006.

Grierson, George Abraham. *Linguistic Survey of India*. Delhi, Varanasi, and Patne: Motilal Banarsidass, 1927.

Hary, Benjamin. "On the Use of *'ilā* and *li* in Judeo-Arabic Texts." In *Semitic Studies in Honor of Wolf Leslau on the Occasion of His Eighty-Fifth Birthday, November 14th, 1991*, edited by Alan Kaye, vol. 1, 595–608. Wiesbaden: Otto Harrassowitz, 1991.

————. *Translating Religion: Linguistic Analysis of Judeo-Arabic Sacred Texts from Egypt*. Leiden and Boston: Brill, 2009.

————. "Is Judeo-Arabic A Semitic Language?" Paper delivered at the forty-second North American Conference on Afro-Asiatic Linguistics, Leiden, 2014.

————. *Sacred Texts in Judeo-Arabic: The Tradition of Šarḥ in Egyptian Judeo-Arabic, With Critical Editions and Translations of the Book of Genesis, the Book of Esther and the Passover Haggadah*. Leiden and Boston: Brill, forthcoming.

Hary, Benjamin, and Martin J. Wein. "Religiolinguistics: On Jewish-, Christian-and Muslim-Defined Languages." *International Journal of the Sociology of Language* 220 (2013): 85–108.

Hastings, Adrian. *The Construction of Nationhood: Ethnicity, Religion and Nationalism*. Cambridge: Cambridge University Press, 1997.

Heal, Felicity. "Mediating the Word: Language and Dialects in the British and Irish Reformations." *Journal of Ecclesiastical History* 56 (2005): 261–286.

Hill, Harriet S. *The Bible at Cultural Crossroads: From Translation to Communication*. Manchester and Kinderhook, New York: St. Jerome Publishing, 2006.

Hobsbawm, Eric. *Nations and Nationalism since 1780*. Cambridge: Cambridge University Press, 1990.

Hobsbawm, Eric, and Terence Ranger, eds. *The Invention of Tradition*. Cambridge: Cambridge University Press, 1983.

Horne, Thomas H. *An Introduction to the Critical Study and Knowledge of the Holy Scriptures*, vol. 2. Philadelphia: Desilver, Thomas and Co., 1836.

Hotchkiss, Valerie R., and David Price. *The Bible of the Reformation*. New Haven and London: Yale University Press, 1996.

Hughey, Michael W. *Civil Religion and Moral Order*. Westport: Greenwood Press, 1983.

Joseph, John E. *Eloquence and Power: The Rise of Language Standards and Standard Languages*. London: Frances Pinter Publishers, 1987.

————. *Language and Identity: National, Ethnic, Religious*. New York: Palgrave Macmillan, 2004.

Kooiman, Willem Jan. *Luther and the Bible*. Philadelphia: Muhlenberg Press, 1961.

Kubo, Sakae, and Walter Specht. *So Many Versions? Twentieth Century English Versions of the Bible*. Grand Rapids, Michigan: Zondervan, 1975.

MacGregor, Geddes. *The Bible in the Making*. Philadelphia and New York: J. B. Lippincott Company, 1959.

Markowitz, Harvey. "Bible Translations." In *Encyclopedia of North American Indians*, edited by Frederick E. Hoxie, 67–69. Boston: Houghton Mifflin Company, 1996.

McColl Millar, Robert. *Language, Nation and Power: An Introduction*. New York: Palgrave Macmillan, 2005.

McLuhan, Marshall. *Understanding Media: The Extensions of Man*. New York: McGraw-Hill, 1964.

Metzger, Bruce M. *The Bible in Translation: Ancient and English Versions*. Grand Rapids, Michigan: Baker Academic, 2001.

Milroy, Jim. "Historical Description and the Ideology of the Standard Language." In *The Development of Standard English 1300–1800: Theories, Descriptions, Conflicts*, edited by Laura Wright, 11–28. Cambridge: Cambridge University Press, 2000.

Nida, Eugene A. *Toward a Science of Translating, with Special Reference to Principles and Procedures Involved in Bible Translating*. Leiden: E. J. Brill, 1964.

Noorda, Sijbolt. "New and Familiar: The Dynamics of Bible Translation." In *Bible Translation on the Threshold of the Twenty-First Century: Authority, Reception, Culture and Religion*, edited by Athalya Brenner and Jan Willem van Henten, 8–16. New York: Sheffield Academic Press, 2002.

Noss, Philip A. "Traditions of Scripture Translation: A Pan-African Overview." In *Bible Translation and African Languages*, edited by Gonsell L. O. R. Yorke and Peter M. Renju, 7–24. Nairobi: Acton Publishers, 2004.

———, ed. *A History of Bible Translation*. Rome: Edizioni di storia e letteratura, 2007.

O'Leary, Amy. "In the Beginning Was the Word; Now, the Word is on the App." *New York Times*, July 26, 2013. Accessed July 29, 2013. http://www.nytimes.com/2013/07/27/technology/the-faithful-embrace-youversion-a-bible-app.html?hpw&_r=1&.

Olender, Maurice. *Languages of Paradise: Race, Religion and Philology in the Nineteenth Century*. Cambridge, MA and London: Harvard University Press, 1992.

Paper, Herbert, ed. *Jewish Languages: Theme and Variations*. Cambridge, Massachusetts: Association for Jewish Studies, 1978.

Plater, Nurit. "How Do You Want Your Trout?" *Yediot Aharonot* (July 24, 2007): 12–13.

Powers, William K. "Comment of the Politics of Orthography." *American Anthropologist* 92/2 (1990): 496–498.

Rogerson, John W. "Can a Translation of the Bible be Authoritative?" In *Bible Translation on the Threshold of the Twenty-First Century: Authority, Reception, Culture and Religion*, edited by Athalya Brenner and Jan Willem van Henten, 17–30. New York: Sheffield Academic Press, 2002.

Sarna, Nahum M. "Old Testament, Canon, Texts and Versions." In *Encyclopaedia Britannica Deluxe*, CD-ROM Edition, 2003.

Schöpflin, George. *Nations, Identity, Power*. London: Hurst, 2000.

Smith, Anthony D. *The Ethnic Origin of Nations*. Oxford: Blackwell, 1986.

———. *Chosen Peoples: Sacred Sources of National Identity*. Oxford: Oxford University Press, 2003.

Strand, Kenneth A. *Catholic German Bibles of the Reformation Era: The Versions of Emser, Dietenberger, Eck, and Others*. Naples, Florida: Ann Arbor Publishers, 1982.

Sukenik, Tamar. "Harel Moyal Will Re-Record A Song Rejected for Broadcasting by Reshet Gimel Because of A Mistake in Hebrew." *Haaretz*, June 12, 2007. Accessed June 24, 2007. http://www.haaretz.co.il/hasite/spages/869705.html.

Tilly, Michael. *Einführung in die Septuaginta*. Darmstadt: Wissenschaftliche Buchgesellschaft, 2005.

Veltri, Giuseppe. *Eine Tora für den König Talmai*. Tübingen: J. C. B. Mohr, 1994.

Weber, Eugen. *Peasants into Frenchmen: The Modernization of Rural France, 1870–1914*. Stanford: Stanford University Press, 1976.

Wein, Martin J. "Chosen Peoples—Holy Tongues: Religion, Language, Nationalism and Politics in Bohemia and Moravia in the Seventeenth to Twentieth Centuries." *Past and Present* 202 (2009): 37–81.

Winter, Julie M. *Luther Bible Research in the Context of Volkish Nationalism in the Twentieth Century*. New York: Peter Lang, 1998.

Wright, Tom, and Gordon Feirlough. "To Save Its Dying Tongue, Indonesian Isle Orders Out for Korean." *The Wall Street Journal*, September 12, 2009. Accessed June 24, 2013. http://online.wsj.com/article/SB125261759118600981.html.

Zuckermann, Ghil'ad. *Language Contact and Lexical Enrichment in Israeli Hebrew*. New York: Palgrave Macmillan, 2003.

2
Jews and Muslims

Collaboration through Acknowledging the Shoah

Mehnaz M. Afridi

This chapter discusses tensions between Jews and Muslims concerning issues such as genocide and politics. My own personal and academic experiences have led me to explore opportunities of collaboration for these two groups, who have typically seen each other through the lens of conflict. This account of contemporary research and my own experiences—academic and personal—will conclude that collaboration can occur if one can create case studies of suffering of one group even when the other group denies this pain in contemporary life, whether through political or social means. This case study hopes to offset the imbalance of these two groups by providing an account of the denial of one group's suffering. Jews and Muslims have been in conflict since the creation of the state of Israel in 1948, and this has led to an overarching Holocaust denial and Zionist phobia among Muslims over the past sixty years. Much of this is based on a lack of historical and social context, and dwells rather in a mythological understanding of Jewish conspiracies in areas of the Holocaust, political power, and rejection of Muslims. On the other hand, Islam phobia (a term coined by Runnymede Trust Report in 1991) is a deep and recent problem in the language of the media in Europe and the United States. Research demonstrates that Jewish communities fear Muslims and see Islam as a threat to their governments and societies. I discuss these conflicts and attempt to build a case study to understand how we might understand the underlying fear of one another and collaborate through initiatives of contact, literature, and the acceptance of the other's suffering, as in the case of genocide and specifically the *Shoah*.

Conceptions of genocide influence the ways in which we view history. Who was the oppressed and who was the victim? Which community destroyed and which abstained? Throughout the ages, reports of genocide ignite interest in the headlines, which then fades because of feelings of shock, awe, helplessness, and ignorance. We have watched genocides take place through moving images, pictorial graphics, radio waves, and written journalism, and yet we distance ourselves from these reports and prefer to focus on the ordinary events of the world. Genocide that continues to be sustained in the world today has become a banal and ignored issue. The example of *Shoah* as a point of conflict within Jewish and Muslim communities has lost its colossal impact and has been politicized. Memories of horrific events are buried under the more political issues that surround Jews and Muslims, Turks, and Armenians. The memory of evil remains to be simplified and as Agamben notes:

> The unprecedented discovery made by Levi at Auschwitz concerns an area that is independent of every establishment of responsibility, an area in which Levi succeeded in isolating something like a new ethical element. Levi calls it the "gray zone." It is the zone in which the "long chain of conjunction between victim and executioner" comes loose, where the oppressed becomes oppressor and the executioner in turn appears as victim. A gray, incessant alchemy in which good and evil and, along with them, all the metals of traditional ethics reach their point of fusion. (Agamben 1999, 21)

The fusion of this sort is difficult to discuss for most people but it is a significant factor in exposing how communities create conflict rather than collaboration by living within the perceived boundaries of either the "oppressed" or the "oppressor" zones.

Most audiences do not wish to view televised genocide. This was the case with the Holocaust in Nazi Germany, and it is true as well of the current affairs in Darfur, Sudan. Acceptance and acknowledgment of the "other's" genocide, suffering, and history can lead to collaboration. I argue that grappling with the pain and fears of the past can cause a new way of looking at religious identity, which can then lead to collaboration. This chapter focuses on the two religious groups, Jews and Muslims, and the case of the Holocaust. I will use the term *Shoah,* so that the reader is not confused by other significant holocausts or genocides. Although as I argue Holocaust denial within Muslim countries is common, I also want to make clear that perpetrator and victimhood are not always consistent, as:

> . . . consider how little we know about the Kurds who were encouraged by the Special Organization to take advantage of the helpless Armenians and who were later subjected to mass deportation, or the Twa, a tiny minority in Rwanda who were suppressed by the Hutu and the Tutsi throughout history and who in 1994 were incited to take part in genocide. (Stone 2008, 44)

Therefore the assumption that Muslims can fully understand the *Shoah* and the memory of such an event is naïve, as the victims can be seen as the perpetrators. Perpetrators can be seen as victims depending on the perspective, this seems sadly to be a truism in the case of Jews and Muslims recognizing one another's suffering.

My case study has its beginnings in biographical and intellectual anecdotes that led me to the path of interviewing survivors and discussing the Shoah as a Muslim. My journey began when I realized that Judaism, Jews, and the Holocaust were omitted from the educational curriculum at my school in Dubai, UAE. For me, this led to an interest in studying Judaism, and the Holocaust. I was interested in the unspoken taboos around the topic of Arab hatred toward Israel. It seemed that this silence was partially due to the stark, and at times justifiable, victimized image of the Palestinian.

It was through such a perspective that I sought to uncover the place where Muslims and Jews may be able to move toward reconciliation on a religious or political level. My liberal Muslim upbringing in Western Europe included exposure to all faiths and an acceptance of all people as equal under the principles of Islam, which were nurtured within me by my parents. My interest and education in post-genocide identity stem from the buried genocide and wars that my Muslim parents witnessed as refugees during the partition of India and Pakistan. I have yet to fully confront that history and realize that through the process of reaching toward understanding and the act of speaking up for the "other," in this case, the Jew, the path of my intellectual life may seem to provide plenty of material to a Freudian psychoanalyst.

On February 27, 2010, I looked into the sky-blue eyes of Albert Rosa, an 85-year-old survivor, for three hours as he spoke about his experience of the Shoah at Auschwitz-Birkenau camp. As I left him, he told me that he wanted someone to write his life story since he had very little formal education and would not be able to express in writing his feelings about the Shoah. He asked me, "How can I express in words how I felt when my sister was bludgeoned to death in front of me by a Nazi woman or when I saw my elder brother hanging from a rope when I had tried to defend him?" I looked into his eyes that had pierced into me all day and wondered how *I* could tell his story in words without losing the sense of the emotional and physical strength it had taken him to survive the horror of his life in the camps. He spoke of maggots crawling on his body as he was ordered to move dead bodies, the gold he stole from the teeth of the dead, the urine he saved to nurse his wounds from a German Shepherd, the roots that he dug out with his fingers for nourishment, the ashes he breathed in from the crematorium as he built the Birkenau camp. I live in a strange space and time these days, pondering on what it is about Jews and the Shoah that compels me to write this testimony? And when I reflect on this question, I hear the voices, I see the expressive eyes, I feel the strength, the pride, and the memories of men and women who have lived unimaginable lives and have taken the time to sit and tell their stories to a stranger, a Muslim woman. When I left Albert's home, I gave him a hug because my words of gratitude seemed incomplete, and he smiled as he hugged me back. He said: "This is the first time in my life that I have hugged a Muslim woman." I told him that this should not be a surprise or the last time since "Muslim women are not so cold or segregated as people might think!" Albert and I together took the first step in true dialogue by humanizing one another.

In the past few years, I have attended several events that speak about Jewish-Muslim relations or Israel and Palestine, and my own participation in these events has led me to questions about reconciliation, education, and interfaith relations. Most of these events that begin with the good intentions of peace or mutual re-education about Judaism and Islam have resulted in a deep polarization over the politics of Israel and Palestine. These events are often filled with political fervor and result in polarization that includes either the denigration of the state of Israel or disregard for the plight of the Palestinians. Balance is very difficult to achieve.

As a Muslim woman, growing up in diverse environments, my faith taught me to believe that humans regardless of race, religion, gender, or nation can speak up for one another. As a Muslim, I am obligated by my faith to speak out against all injustices, false rumors, and oppression. As the Qur'an states:

> O you who believe! Stand out firmly for justice, as witnesses to Allah, even if it be against yourselves, your parents, and your relatives, or whether it is against the rich or the poor . . . (Qur'an 4: 135)
>
> Let not the hatred of a people swerve you away from justice. Be just, for this is closest to righteousness . . . (Qur'an 5: 8)
>
> God does not forbid you from doing good and being just to those who have neither fought you over your faith nor evicted you from your homes . . . (Qur'an 60: 8)

My work on the Shoah stems from the ethical responsibility to speak out against false testimony and direct witnessing as the Qur'an states that "Let not the hatred of a people swerve you away from justice." Hatred of a group of people is considered a fundamental flaw and Islam recognizes this when it speaks about justice and human rights. Some might argue that Israelis have dispossessed thousands of Palestinians and according to the laws of Islam it is sanctioned to fight for one's justice, so why not deny rights to the Jews? The answer, of course, is that Jews like Muslims are not all alike and denying the right of any human being under Islam is unjust. It is fair to fight for justice but it is not just to terrorize and create a prejudice against a whole people: the Jews. This is about the Shoah and not the politics of Israel/Palestine, because I hope that Jews through Muslim eyes may be humanized and given their unique place in the list of genocides. Reconciliation and interfaith work requires discomfort, dislocation, and self-critique.

There is sadly so much suffering in the world and I witness this suffering in my country of birth, Pakistan, where women are mistreated, governments are corrupted, and the poor are deprived of opportunities. Why did this become my journey? Perhaps, I see that part of the antagonism that has seeped into Pakistan has a direct bearing on this project of mine. Pakistan continues to burn Israeli flags and mistrust Jews, and I have a duty to Pakistanis and others around the world to work to help seek another perspective.

In 2010, I sat with Elizabeth Mann in the Hertz Theater at the Museum of Tolerance, Los Angeles, riveted by her story as a survivor of Auschwitz. It was deeply emotional and I experienced one of the most difficult moments of my life as she sobbed and I laid my hand upon her knee. She said to me: "Mehnaz, I hope you don't take offense to this but I'd like to say something to you." I told her nothing could offend me, she continued with hesitation and said that she believed in souls that linger on for thousands of years and that she thought I might have had a Jewish soul thousands of years ago. I smiled, and said "perhaps" but as a Muslim it was not surprising that my soul might have been Jewish after all we came from the same source: Abraham. To me it did not matter; all that mattered was that she trusted me and was free to talk with me. I felt like I could have listened to her for days as we walked arm in arm outside the theater. I hope that through writing this chapter I can bear witness to the humanity of my Jewish friends (survivors) who are willing to talk with a Muslim with freedom and trust.

One of the many events that encapsulated my desire to give testimony to the Shoah was one of several experiences of the relativity of the Holocaust that require attention. In November 2006, I was invited to New York City to participate in the Wise, or Women's Islamic Initiative in Spirituality and Equity, to discuss the role of the *Shura* (or, Consultation) Council in diverse Muslim countries and whether Muslim women could create the first Muslim women's *Shura* council with power over both Islamic and civil laws. A hundred or more Muslim women from North America, Europe, Africa, Asia, Eastern Europe, and several Arab countries participated. On the last day, I was asked to initiate the interfaith panel. Moments before my introduction, as I prepared to take the podium, I was approached by a woman from McGill University who pointedly asked me: "Mehnaz, since you study contemporary Judaism and Islam, isn't it true that *only* 2 million Jews died during the Holocaust?" I was stunned and appalled by this young woman's question. She was a highly educated individual—earlier in the day I had heard her battling in favor of human rights and favorable laws for Muslim women. She is a woman who speaks four languages and is highly skilled in debating the Qur'an and its interpretation, yet she had posed this question to me. I was speechless with only a few seconds to go on stage I told her that she should talk with me immediately after my panel. Unfortunately, she did not talk with me nor did I get her contact information. This story epitomizes the casual acknowledgment of the death of 2 million Jews and the unwavering refusal to accept 6 million deaths. As if 2 million deaths were not enough to deserve attention. The debate about the numbers of Jews killed during the Holocaust requires some attention. Astonishing as it is that to some 2 million Jews' dead is an ordinary fact, not at all an unsettling one, whereas 6 million becomes too straining to accept.[1] This incident is not the first or the last one that I have encountered within Muslim communities but numerous times I have been asked how it was possible that 6 million Jews were killed especially since they had been assimilated in European culture. Weren't they aware of what was going on around them? How did they not rebel? What is so unique about

---

1. In Deborah Lipstadt's *Denying the Holocaust: The Growing Assault on Truth and Memory*, one can find a thorough discussion of the publication of *The Myth of the Six Million* published by Noontide Press in 1969, a consortium of the anti-Semitic lobby. Such books, pamphlets, and writings of Holocaust denial can be found that were written after World War II. Anti-Semitism had much earlier beginnings in Europe and America within rightwing lobbies.

the Holocaust? And why are the Palestinians taking the burden of European crimes? Where are the facts? In light of the creation of the state of Israel, many Muslims believe that the Europeans in power, mainly the British and then the Americans, gave Jews a state because of the Holocaust. Israel is seen as a state that was illegally created in what was Palestine to appease the guilt of Western powers. In this reading, the state of Israel emerged in 1948 when the state was created. Muslims feel betrayed by the Western powers and believe that Israel was given aid, warfare, and nuclear technology to assert a non-Arab/Muslim power in the Middle East. So, the question of power remains highly problematic and Muslims/Arabs believe that Jews control the United States with a strong lobby in Washington, D.C. and a long-standing presence in Europe. Recently, a Muslim woman who is very active in pursuing human rights for all Muslims and non-Muslims responded to my idea for this book with the following remarks: "Are you going to discuss how the Jews have taken on the Nazi psychology and how sad it is that the Jews once victims of genocide are inflicting the same on the Palestinians . . ." I am inundated with these questions and more. My dinner table can speak of how many Muslims, Christians, and others have accused Jews of worldwide control and of the skepticism that still surrounds the Holocaust. I wish that this table could bear witness to the ignorant belief that Jews today embody the old European stereotype of murderers, conspirators, sparing folk, and political directors of the US government. I am horrified by this for a number of reasons: first, the idea that somehow 2 million dead seems palatable to people because the number is 4 million fewer than the 6 million number; second, that this lower number is so readily accepted; and third, the way in which the Holocaust has been seen as a less tragic historical event for non-Jews. As Robert Satloff points out in his pivotal book, *Among The Righteous: Lost stories from the Holocaust Long Reach into Arab Lands*: "the blatant refusal of Arabs to have anything to do with the Holocaust or even accept the number 6 million becomes symptomatic of how Arabs see Jewish history and Western alliances with Jews" (Satloff 2006, 164). He further quotes from Mahmoud Abbas's (Yasser Arafat's successor) own doctoral work where Abbas asserts that:

> But after the war it was announced that six million Jews were among the victims, and that the war of annihilation had been aimed first of all against the Jews, and only then against the rest of the people of Europe. The truth of the matter is that no one can verify this number, or completely deny it. (Satloff 2006, 164)

Not only does Satloff point out the relativism of the Shoah amongst Muslims, but he further elaborates this point, stating:

> The purpose of Abbas's dissertation, like many others produced by Arab "scholars" of the last half-century, was to inject relativism into the discussion of the Holocaust. Yes, Jews suffered, this argument goes, but in a century that produced genocides in Cambodia, Bosnia, and Rwanda, the mass killings of Jews during World War II was hardly unique. (Satloff 2006, 164)

In addition, Satloff's book brings to light the role of Muslims in Morocco and Tangiers that saved Jewish lives but also explores the actions of those who became perpetrators and bystanders in their own lands. His research also points to more evidence of Muslims' personal and direct knowledge of the Holocaust and in this case, prisoner camps similar to concentration camps. He states that his goal in writing this book was:

> I decided that the most useful response I could offer to 9/11 was to combat Arab ignorance of the Holocaust. The question was how to do it. An adversarial approach, I soon realized, was the wrong way to engage Arabs if I truly wanted to change attitudes on a taboo topic. To do that, I needed to make the Holocaust accessible to Arabs; I needed to make the Holocaust an Arab story. (Satloff 2006, 5)

How can I then make this story not just an Arab story but a Muslim testimony to the Shoah? As I delve into mounds of research I find many stories of Muslims that were directly connected to the Shoah, those who helped, those who were in camps with Jews, and those who turned away. These Muslims have been silent, and one might ask why? There are many positive stories about the role of Muslims in the Holocaust that are historically recorded from Albania to Morocco to Ukraine. For example, Norman Gershman in his book, *Besa: Muslims Who Saved Jews in World War II*, has recorded testimonies and photographs of Albanian and Slavic Muslims who risked their lives to save Jews in their communities. The book tells short stories through photographs that illuminate the character of Muslims who saved Jews.

The reality of the Shoah for Muslims is skewed by Muslim politics and long-standing myths—one of these is the idea that while many Jews may indeed have been killed along with other casualties in World War II, the number killed was not 6 million. Hence, the "cover" of war is used to shield these numbers. Similarly, Turks today will argue that the Armenian Genocide was not genocide but the "cover" of war to defend Turks against the Armenian rebellions and their allegiance to the Russians during World War I.

There is a pervasive myth within the Muslim community that Jews used the Holocaust as an excuse to colonize Palestine. Jews were seen to be given absolute support from Europe and the United States as a direct response to the Holocaust and to the guilt associated with it. During a UN Anti-Racist conference, held in April 2009, Mahmoud Ahmadinejad asserted that Israel, the United States, and Europe were perpetrating genocide on the Palestinian people. Headlines trumpeted: "Ahmadinejad Accuses Israel of Genocide, Europeans Walk Out." For a Muslim Prime Minister like Mahmoud Ahmadinejad to call the International Conference to Review the Global Vision of the Holocaust in December 2006, with the specific intention of supporting the denial of the Holocaust is reprehensible. The attendees at the conference were all holocaust deniers and included David Duke and also Yisroel Dovid Weiss of Neturei Karta; the discussion was billed as allowing a space for free and open dialogue about the Holocaust. What went unnoticed was that Khaled Kasab Mahameed, an Israeli-Arab who has opened a Holocaust Museum in Nazareth, was not allowed to attend the conference because he holds Israeli citizenship, but he was quoted saying:

> The Holocaust did happen and that Iranian President Mahmoud Ahmadinejad's position of Holocaust denial is wrong. Everything that happened must be internalized and the facts must not be denied . . . It is the obligation of all Arabs and all Muslims to understand the significance of the Holocaust. If their goal is to understand their adversary, they must understand the Holocaust . . . The naqba [disaster] the Palestinians experienced in 1948 is small compared to the Holocaust, but the political implications of the Holocaust have made its terrors a burden on the Palestinian people alone . . . The Holocaust has all the reasons for the creation of the Arab-Israeli conflict, but also has potential to bring peace. (Stern 2006)

I think that Mahameed's thinking is crucial to understanding the ongoing anti-Semitism within Muslim communities and Islamophobia within Jewish communities. If, as he states, "the Holocaust has all the reasons for the creation of the Arab-Israeli conflict, but also has potential to bring peace," I believe that through voices like his we can hope to bridge this gap through education and facts.

An example of collaboration is the humanitarian rescue and help that Muslim Albanians provided to the Jews who were escaping the Shoah. During World War II, Albanian Muslims hid more than 2,000 Jews from Albania, Greece, Austria, Italy, and elsewhere. Not only did Albanians refuse to cooperate with the Nazi regime, there were also more Jewish people living in Albania after the war than prior to the war. Under the circumstances, it would have been very easy, when Nazi troops were there, to give people up. The notion of Muslims sheltering Jews during the war has a contemporary resonance because of the current state of Muslim-Jewish relations around the world. Albanian Muslims were among the more than 22,000 non-Jewish rescuers honored at Yad Vashem, the Holocaust memorial in Jerusalem—yet their deeds remained relatively unknown for decades (Sarner 1997).

As evidenced in growing literature that the Shoah and its connection to Jewish-Muslim relations is indelible, there has been some important scholarship relating to Muslims and the Holocaust such as Robert Satloff's *Among the Righteous: Lost Stories from the Holocaust's Long Reach into Arab Lands* (2007), Jeffrey Herf's *Nazi Propaganda for the Arab World* (2010), Fairborz Mokhtari's *In the Lion's Shadow: The Iranian Schindler and His Homeland in the Second World War* (2012), and Karen Ruelle and Deborah Desais's *The Grand Mosque of Paris: A Story of How Muslims Rescued Jews During the Holocaust* (2010). This literature and especially novels like Boualem Sansal's *The German Mujahid* (2009) reveal the generational and global connections of the Shoah and colonialism. Sansal's work is banned in his native Algeria; however, he exposes several explosive themes like the moral implication of the Shoah and contemporary Islamic fundamentalism in Algeria of the early 1990s. He further elaborates the emergence of grim Muslim ghettos in. The following conversation takes place as the protagonist and son, Malrich, meets an SS guard friend of his father's from the past:

> I would have been only too happy to wander through his brain, I'm sure I would have found something charming grottos and ravine the bastard did not know he had, there's clearly no end to cretinism, what I had seen was only the tip of the iceberg. I felt . . . like . . . nothing. You don't kill madmen, you don't exterminate the handicapped, you pray for them. But for all his madness, his sickness, he managed to hurt me with a line: "You're your father's son alright!" (Sansal 2009, 64)

Malrich attempts to somehow come to terms with what has happened to him and learn about the Holocaust—which, he admits, "he didn't know anything about . . . I'd heard bits and pieces, things the imam said about the Jews and other stuff I'd picked up here and there"—he resolves that "where my father and Rachel had failed, I had to survive" (Sansal 2009, 68). But both brothers' lives are inescapably determined by their father's actions. Rachel literally turns himself into a concentration camp victim, growing more emaciated and haunted until, head shaved and wearing striped pajamas, he gasses himself on the anniversary of his father's death, "the day Hans Schiller finally eluded the justice of men." Malrich, on the other hand, directs his shame outward to save his beloved "Sensitive Urban Area, Category 1" housing project, which has slowly but surely been taken over by Islamists who are creating "a concentration camp," with an atmosphere of "all conquering Islam." Telling his friends that "we're going to live, we're going to fight," Malrich considers it his legacy and his duty to first declare war on the "Nazi jihadist fuckers," and then to "tell the truth, all over the world" (Sansal 2009, 87). Through a thorough comparison and analysis of understanding of the suffering and truth of the Shoah, Malrich sees many issues with his own community and a suffering that may be different from the Shoah, but that is real and interminable in his mind.

This brings me to the question: Why is it that Muslims are able to deny the Holocaust and have no historical understanding of Judaism, Jews, or the history of Zionism? One of the fundamental problems in understanding the Holocaust in the majority of Muslim countries is the lack of education and the censorship of the word "Israel" in history and geography books. Even Sansal's novel is censored in his native Algeria, where perhaps it could be read widely and seen in multiple ways as a lesson in understanding another's pain or suffering. Simultaneously, it could serve as place of postcolonial discussion and an illustration of the image of the other in fiction.

When I was living in Dubai, UAE, in the 1980s, I attended Choueifat, a school that was based on the Lebanese French Baccalaureate system. There, I and my fellow students were witnesses to censorship and hatred toward Israel and Jews. Our Arab

Christian and Muslim supervisors would march into our history and geography classes with scissors or thick markers. They would approach every desk and cut or cross out the word "Israel" from our textbooks. These books were European authored textbooks that recognized Israel. As a young child, I was curious as to why they would make such a production of this event and take time from class rather than creating an alternative textbook that provided Muslim/Arab perspectives on Israel. Essentially, Muslims are not taught history in the same way that we learn history in the United States or Europe. It goes without saying that we in the United States have had to change our own views of history, as various groups in our country have raised their own experiences and pressured the mainstream to take their voices seriously. That can be seen in histories that cover native Indian Genocide, African Slavery, Vietnam, and the Civil Rights movement. However, these changes have not been integrated into most Muslim curriculums. History is interpreted differently by different people globally and since the seventeenth century, the European and American historical lens has dominated the media and educational realm as Tamim Ansary in *Destiny Disrupted: A History of the World through Islamic Eyes* notes when he writes about his perception of Islamic and Western history:

> Here are two enormous worlds side by side; what's remarkable is how little notice they have taken of each other. If the Western and Islamic worlds were two individual human beings, we might see symptoms of repression here. We might ask: "What happened between these two? Were they lovers? Is there some history of abuse?" But there is, I think, another less sensational explanation. Throughout much of history, the West and the core of what is now the Islamic world have been like two separate universes, each preoccupied with its own internal affairs, each assuming itself to be the center of human history, each living out different narrative—until the late seventeenth century when the two narratives began to intersect. At that point, one or the other had to give way because the two narratives were crosscurrents to each other. The West being more powerful, it's current prevailed and churned the other one under. (Ansary 2009, xxi)

Ansary's point is that Islam alongside the "West" has been consumed by its own internal voices and significance and the two have failed to include one another in their historical lens or, in this case, curriculum projects. For example, post-holocaust literature took a long time to surface in the United States and Europe, and it was not until the 1970s that Elie Wiesel broke the silence about the Holocaust and history books were increasingly pressured to add Holocaust history apart from just World War II, that had previously offered only a slight glimmer of information about the Jewish Genocide. The types of organized and structured institutions created by Jewish-Americans and Holocaust survivors resulted in a new awareness within the American and European educational systems. In other words, things take time but someone has to break the silence, the cycle, and offer the truth.

Elie Wiesel wrote the small but gripping book *Night* that testified to the horrors that befell him and others in the camps. He was born in a small village in Romania on September 30, 1928. He had the traditional upbringing of an Eastern European Jew in pre-World War II Europe. Wiesel's Jewish faith and his family were at the center of young Wiesel's life. This life was lost forever in 1944, when fifteen-year-old Wiesel and his family were deported by the Nazis to Auschwitz in Poland. His mother and a sister were gassed to death and his father died of starvation in detention. Wiesel was transferred to the Buchenwald concentration camp where, on April 11, 1945, he was finally liberated by American troops. For years, like many other survivors, he dealt with the trauma of this experience by maintaining a silence. After studying at the Sorbonne and working as a journalist, Wiesel broke this silence with the haunting book, *Night*. Wiesel's prose is poetic in describing the jolting experience of his brutal detention:

> Never shall I forget that night, the first night in camp, which has turned my life into one long night, seven times cursed and seven times sealed.
> Never shall I forget that smoke.
> Never shall I forget the little faces of the children, whose bodies I saw turned into wreaths of smoke beneath a silent blue sky.
> . . .
> Never shall I forget these things, even if I am condemned to live as long as God Himself.
> Never. (Wiesel 1960)

Since then, Wiesel has acted as a moral sentry guarding the memory of those years. He has used his influence on behalf of Jews persecuted in the former Soviet Union and oppressed peoples elsewhere. He has always made clear that the victims of the Holocaust will win an ultimate victory only if we the living never forget the horrors of those years; if we never forget the depravity and evil to which a modern civilized nation can fall; and if we should never forget the lessons of the Holocaust. For his work, Wiesel received the Nobel Peace Prize in 1986. The purpose of post-holocaust narrative and literature is to continue with the testimony and to not allow these experiences to be forgotten. However, if some educational curriculums omit genocidal events in our children's history books or in our communities it seems very bleak. How do we continue to tell one another's stories so we can continue to humanize rather than dehumanize?

A second issue with the majority of Muslim educational curriculum is the tight focus on Islamic studies and the deficiency of information about other world religions. The deficiencies in information about the humanities and about cultural history have created a vacuum for many young Muslims, especially those who come to the US (some of them my students) for higher education, who are immediately skeptical of attempting to think critically about Islamic history or to be open to learning about other faiths. There have been some initiatives on the part of The Organization of Islamic Cooperation to start multi-faith education in universities in Malaysia, Pakistan, and Saudi Arabia.[2] These are very new programs but they are necessary in order to bridge the gap between Muslims and other faiths as the programs allow Muslims to interpret Jewish and Christian revelations through the lens of Islam or the Qur'an.

As a student of Judaism and Protestant theology, I have been enriched by learning about these faiths and felt that I was given another perspective outside of my own lens that had come from reading the Qur'an. To read one another's sacred texts and histories can help us to avoid the damage and misunderstanding between us. Studying one another's texts offers all of us new ways of creating bridges. When I received my Bachelor's degree in English and Religious Studies from Syracuse University, my father attended my graduation and asked the chair of my department, "How can one *study* religion, is religion not all encompassing?" My chair was stunned and did not have a ready answer. My father was a banker and was supportive of my studies, but he could not grapple with the idea that his daughter was interested in the phenomena of God. How can you study God, he would ask. The idea that religion has history, culture, and a rich array of contextual nuances escaped his thinking; the world in which he grew up taught him to accept God and Islam without hesitation. My father and other members of his family were not even taught about the skeptics within Islamic history and literature; their own history and philosophy was omitted by their environment. Islamic history provides rich resources for reasoning, scientific inquiry, and skepticism. One has to only look at the historical exchanges between Avicenna and Maimonides[3] to grasp the diversity of thought and reliance on the intellect during the Islamic enlightenment. The lack of education and diversity in curriculums creates vacuums and myths help me to understand why there is anti-Semitism and holocaust denial in mainly non-Jewish communities.

My own experience in talking with many Muslims and non-Muslims is that there continues to be an uncanny insistence that the Holocaust is not a unique event and that Jews have fabricated 6 million deaths as a vehicle to obtaining Israel as their own land. As an academic who is on many group email list serves, I have seen the discussion of the Jewish holocaust take on new twists. The Shoah is posited as a genocide that has become privileged above others and then it is dismissed through academic arguments. I have witnessed some interesting discussions about this that need to be explored; this line of thinking relies on the idea that Jews have had too much

---

2. The Organization of Islamic Cooperation is funded by the United Nations to set up educational models in Muslim countries that are interfaith in cooperation. I attended a meeting at the United Nations where the organization spoke about these initiatives on September 28, 2012, at the UN Plaza 777.

3. For specifics, see *http://plato.stanford.edu/entries/maimonides-islamic/* at the Stanford Encyclopedia of Philosophy.

attention, have too much power, and that other genocides are equally as important and significant. I am not arguing here that other genocides are not equally important, but what stuns me is that Jews are somehow vilified for giving a strong and unified voice to their own calamity that *they* have named a "Holocaust" or *Shoah* in Hebrew. The following email exchanges are common:

> First person: Holocaust is the term used specifically to refer to the genocide of Jews in WWII, the enormity of the massacre deserves a specific name. Whether 6 of 6 million the pain is the same to the families who have lost the dear ones. However, the 6 million numbers is too large a number not to be identified distinctly.
> The term Genocides can be used for all other atrocities.

And then the response:

> Second person: "Holocaust is the term used specifically to refer to the genocide of Jews in WWII" is not a justification for its continued use that way. The enormity of the massacre is beyond doubt. But that does not justify a specific name for it. Indeed, I am not sure whether you are familiar or not, but in terms of scale, there have been other genocides much bigger than the Nazi Holocaust.
> I also find no justification for separating Nazi Holocaust from all other genocides. This is clearly diminishing all other genocides. There is another reason why such specialness must not be allowed. Treat any people as special and you might face the prospect that such special status would be abused to victimize others. Unfortunately, instead of being a prospect, it has become a reality.
> If I have to call upon my fellow Muslims that they should not think that their suffering in the world in the hand of others is not unique, it would be unprincipled to acknowledge that somehow others are special. In this world if we cannot accept the entire humanity on this equal footing, every group will consider themselves special and when they attain power they may abuse others, as in the case of Israel.[4]

The exchange above is quite common even amongst academics and it is this precise point that creates a deep gulf. I argue that the Holocaust is unique and that the slaughter of Jews in every country at this time, including Arab countries, is terrifyingly unique. One has to only look at the history of different cases of genocide to see the glaring difference. I am not at all stating that the genocides involving Native Indians, Cambodians, Darfurians, Rwandans, and Bosnians are to be taken lightly; in fact, they should perhaps be taken even more seriously in light of the Holocaust. The main thrust of many survivor testimonies from the Holocaust delivers one main message and that is not to forget. Such stories of atrocities must be told again and again so that they do not happen again in future generations. There are several reasons that I would argue that the Holocaust is unique: 1. Jews were sought out and killed worldwide as far as the Nazi and Vichy governments could reach; 2. Jews were seen as dangers to

---

4. I have kept this as an anonymous correspondence in an email exchange, February 8, 2009.

society both as human beings and as economic barriers; 3. Jews were massacred in the most technological and mechanical manner; 4. Jews were easy targets of hatred because of the long-standing mythical history of Jews having committed deicide against the Christians, not to mention many myths of the blood libel that are still discussed in many parts of the world both Christian and non-Christian; 5. Jews were not from a nation or country where they could fight or take arms. Jews were nation-less in terms of a place where they could have had a stronghold to fight against the WWII players; 6. Jews were living in Europe as assimilated citizens for hundreds of years, and the Holocaust was not a war between two countries but a war against a minority within a country.

I hope that my fellow Muslims will read my article and understand that my commitment to Islam was inspired by studying Judaism. My respect and understanding of Judaism was inspired by working as a teaching assistant at Syracuse University under Alan Berger in a post-Holocaust class. I was in a master's program interested in critical theory and post-colonialism, and had never studied anything Jewish except for reading texts by Jewish authors. As a Muslim, I was always caught between accepting Jews and rejecting Jews on the basis of political nuances in my family against Israel and in Pakistan, the country of my birth. Since the year 1990, my clarity about Judaism has encouraged me to feel even closer to my own Islamic faith in ways that I would have never imagined. I began to see many parallels between both faiths and a congruence of identity questions as living as a minority in non-Jewish and non-Muslim communities. As a student I was engaged in postmodern understandings of identity and culture, and I had been given the tools to think critically about the world, but I lacked historical and religious foundations. I decided to pursue Religious Studies in both Judaism and Islam. From this initial idea for my studies, I began to explore my own personal past as a Muslim child growing up in Europe, which has helped me to understand Jewish identity, but more importantly what racism, prejudice, and hatred can bring to bear toward humanity.

Samantha Powers's *A Problem from Hell: America and the Age of Genocide* (2002) focuses on America and on how genocide is ignored, silenced, and at times denied. I wanted to sharpen the focus and give attention specifically to genocide. I wanted to speak about the ebbing anger and turmoil within me as I experienced anti-Semitism in many Muslim communities. I also wanted to explain to myself and others that genocide is still happening and it is an ongoing human problem as Hannah Arendt coined the term "banality of evil." It is an understanding of this banality that moves me to write (Arendt 1963). In the many classes that I have taught on genocide, I have increasingly found myself discussing the Shoah as unique. As a Muslim, I have found the past few years difficult in light of the war on terrorism, Iraq, Afghanistan, and Pakistan. However, the denial of the Holocaust amongst Muslims and Muslim nations continues to be even more painful to me. For me, it is one thing to recognize

that there have been accounts of war and genocide all over the world since the incep-
tion of recorded history, but quite another to deny any human slaughter which is to
deny human life for all. This principle stems from my understanding of Islam and
Judaism—since the Jews planted the future birth of Islam, they are our community
from the time of Ibrahim to the time of Moses. As the Qur'an states:

> It is He Who sent down to thee (step by step), in truth, the Book, confirming what
> went before it; and He sent down the Law (of Moses) and the Gospel (of Jesus)
> before this, as a guide to mankind, and He sent down the criterion (of judgment
> between right and wrong).—3:3
>
> This day [the day of the Prophet's "Farewell Address" on which the last verse of
> the Qur'an was revealed] have I made perfect for you your religion, and have
> completed My favor towards you, and am satisfied with Islam for you as your
> religion.—5:3
>
> In truth We have sent the Qur'an to you, confirming all the previous heavenly
> books that were revealed before you and bearing witness to them.—5:48

It is essential to understand that Holocaust deniers and relativists have described the
Holocaust as simply one political incident among many in the twentieth century.
As Deborah Lipstadt asserts: "If Holocaust denial has demonstrated anything, it is
the fragility of memory, truth, reason, and history" (Lipstadt 1994, 216). Although
I know that it is both idealistic and perhaps naive, I truly believe that if my fellow
Muslims were to understand and accept the Holocaust, Israel, and Judaism fully,
we would be in a better place both spiritually and politically. If a Muslim believes
that Jews are our enemies then he or she must be listening to the extremist factions
that go so far as to blatantly and openly call for the extermination of Jews. I had the
opportunity of visiting Israel in 1995, which opened up questions for me both intel-
lectually and personally.

While I was a student at Syracuse University in the Department of Religion,
Dr. Alan Berger (in whose class I was a teaching assistant) asked me if I ever wanted
to visit Israel. I was taken aback from his question because I knew that the word
"Israel" to me, who grew up with Pakistanis and Muslims, was almost a taboo word.
I also knew that at the time (the 1980s) there were two countries that I was prohibited
from visiting by my government: Israel and South Africa. My passport clearly stated
that I was not allowed entry to these countries. I asked Dr. Berger how I would go
there and what would I do? He told me about a mini-grant at the Hebrew University
for five weeks that I could apply for, he handed me the paperwork and he left.
As I walked back to my dorm room, I felt nervous but at the same time excited at
the possibility of visiting the Dome of the Rock and Haram al-Sharif, after all these
were important Muslim places of worship, and I remembered fondly the postcards
I had received from my Swiss godmother when she visited Jerusalem. I also wanted
to see for myself what Israel was like, who Israelis were, and how the Palestinians

were treated. I became obsessed with the idea of traveling to Israel and embarked upon my journey in 1995 to the chagrin of my family and friends. People warned me of the dangers, the fears, the climate, the attitudes toward Muslims, and the risk I was about to embark upon with a tiny piece of white paper from the Israeli embassy in New York that gave me entry into Israel. I was told that I would not be helped if anything were to go wrong because I had a mere green card and a Pakistani citizenship. I was excited with the temporary prospect of being dispossessed like my fellow Palestinians and my fellow Jews. I had been reading *The Book of Questions* (1991) by Edmond Jabès who had lived in Egypt all his life but had been exiled to Paris in 1952 because he was Jewish. Jabès as a writer inspired me to understand how exile, longing, home, and identity were part of Jewish theology, politics, and psychological condition before, during, and after the Shoah, and I understood that Jews were somehow always in the condition of exile until the redemption from God. Jabès's universe is defined by homelessness, and in this particular book he tells the story of two holocaust victims, Sarah and Yukel, through poetry, prose, and a rabbinic interpretation. He states:

> "Yukel, which is the land you call Jewish, which every Jew claims as his own without ever having lived there?"
> "It is the land where I have dug my well."
> "Yukel, which is this water of our land, so good against thirst that no other water can compare?"
> "It is water fifty centuries have forgotten in the hollow of our hands." (Jabès 1991, 59)

Jabès's words came alive as I entered Jerusalem: the hollowness, the land, the ephemeral identities pitted up against each other at the Wailing Wall, and water that holds no form but pours and pours from a well in the desert. My trip to Jerusalem changed my life. I was able to be with students at Hebrew University who were from all walks of life, countries, and socio-economic backgrounds, but they were all Jews or Christians. My ability to visit the Dome of Rock with the gatekeeper's permission was granted at all times because I was a Muslim from Pakistan. I was also able to frequent places with the Hebrew University students since everyone assumed I was just another Jew from America. This duality and freedom gave me access to personal feelings and perceptions of Israelis and Palestinians, and allowed me to hear their thoughts on peace, hatred, interminable memories of war, and even a love for one another. This is a complex relationship that has been undermined by political parties on both sides and by renewing cycles of violence and dehumanization. I thought that my time in Jerusalem would prove valuable, but I did not know nor realize how much I would become invested in this struggle and in unraveling the misperceptions of both sides.

When I reflect on Jerusalem, I believe that the most important expression of literature devoted to the issues and pain on both sides can be found in the works of Yehuda Amichai and Mahmoud Darwish, the beloved poets of both sides who resonate with one another, and through their words we witness the deep similarities in both Israelis and Palestinians. Darwish has called the conflict a "struggle between two memories" (Shehadeh 2009). His poems challenge the Zionist tenet, embodied in such poetry as Haim Bialik's, of "a land without a people for a people without a land." While he admires the Hebrew poet Yehuda Amichai, "his poetry put a challenge to me, because we write about the same place. He wants to use the landscape and history for his own benefit, based on my destroyed identity. So we have a competition: who is the owner of the language of this land? Who loves it more? Who writes it better?" Amichai writes:

> Jerusalem
> On a roof in the Old City
> Laundry hanging in the late afternoon sunlight:
> The white sheet of a woman, who is my enemy,
> The towel of a man, who is my enemy,
> To wipe off the sweat of his brow.
> In the sky of the Old City
> A kite.
> At the other end of the string,
> A child
> I can't see
> Because of the wall.
> We have put up many flags,
> They have put up many flags.
> To make us think that they're happy.
> To make them think we're happy. (Amichai 1996, 32)

The sentiments of these poets imprint a vision of love and peace coupled with the longing of each poet for the other's humanity. With this thinking, I imagine that Muslims and Jews can take from these words an awareness of the absence and the presence of peace. In Jerusalem I had some deeply moving experiences that have shaped me in my approach to the conflict between Israel and Palestine.

This intellectual journey that has shaped my testimony continued in 2006 when I visited Camp Dachau just outside of Munich with my husband and then three-month-old daughter. The experience of being at Dachau transported me away from categories of Jews, Muslims, Christians, Germans, and Nazis, and toward the baby in my arm who was witnessing at the beginning of her life one of the centers of the death of humanity. *Job: The Story of a Holocaust Survivor* (2002), a memoir by Joseph Freeman, compelled me to interview survivors. I began to ask myself over and over again how and why humanity wanted to deny the voices of pain and hope.

Joseph Freeman was born in Poland in 1915, and he immigrated to the United States after surviving several different camps including Dachau. Reading his story and others became a vessel through which I began to see how intricate the Nazi agenda was and how meticulous the SS guards had been in order to persecute and use the Jews as workers. As I reflect on the Holocaust not too far away is a place called Darfur where genocide is ongoing, I feel chills down my spine when I think of what is occurring in Darfur today, Arab Muslims murdering African Muslims for land and control, and I am reminded that Muslims are sitting upon the bench as the Jews and United States provide humanitarian aid. I can imagine that an African Muslim today could resonate with Joseph Freeman sixty years ago when he wrote:

> There was no water in the camp after weeks without washing, shaving, or chang-
> ing our clothes, we smelled and looked nearly inhuman. At night insects attacked
> us, and the rain poured in from still unfinished roof. We lay in water. Our clothes
> froze against our skin. Many died from the cold. (Freeman 1996, 67)

Today genocide has to be defined, seen, argued, and has to be internationally rec-
ognized by the UN before any action can be taken. This action was made possible because of Raphael Lemkin, a Polish Jew, who lobbied to instantiate international law when he heard about the Armenian disaster. What then are the Muslims going to do about Darfur? Are we going to let millions to be displaced and killed from burning and malnourishment? Is this a Jewish problem? No, this is a human problem. As one victim expressed at the end of the documentary *Devil Came on Horseback* (2007), "Where are the Muslims? We are Muslims and no Muslim has helped us, only America, thank you America."

References

Agamben, Giorgio. *Remnants of Auschwitz: The Witness and the Archive*. Trans. Daneil Heller-
    Roazen. New York: Zone Books, 1999.
Ansary, Tamim. *Destiny Disrupted: A History of the World through Islamic Eyes*. New York:
    Public Affairs, 2009.
Arendt, Hannah. *Eichman in Jerusalm: A Report on the Banality of Evil*. New York: Penguin,
    1963.
Asad, Muhammad, trans. *The Message of the Qur'an*. Gibralter: Al-Andalus, 1980.
Bloch, Chana and Stephen Mitchell, trans. *The Selected Poetry of Yehuda Amichai*. Berkeley:
    University of California Press, 1996.
Freeman, Joseph. *Job: The story of a Holocaust Survivor*. St. Paul: Paragon House, 1996.
Jabès, Edmond. *The Book of Questions: Volume One (The Book of Questions, The Book of Yukel,
    Return to the Book)*, trans. Rosemarie Waldrop. Middleton, CT: Wesleyan University
    Press, 1991.
Lipstadt, Deborah. *Denying the Holocaust: The Growing Assault on Truth and Memory*.
    New York: Plume, 1994.

Powers, Samantha. *A Problem from Hell: America and the Age of Genocide.* New York: Harpers, 2002.

Sansal, Boualem. *The German Mujahid.* Cathedral City, CA: Brunswick Press, 2009.

Sarner, Harvey. *Rescue in Albania: One Hundred Percent of Jews in Albanian Rescued from the Holocaust.* Cathedral City, CA: Brunswick Press, 1997.

Satloff, Robert. *Among the Righteous: Lost Stories from the Holocaust's Long Reach into Arab Lands.* New York: Public Affairs, 2006.

Shehadeh, Raja. "Mahmoud Darwish—a Poet of Peace in a Time of Conflict." *The Guardian.* Accessed January 28, 2014. http://www.guardian.co.uk/books/booksblog/2009/aug/07/mahmoud-darwish-poetry-palestine.

Stern, Yoav. 2006. "Founder of Holocaust Museum in Nazareth Invited to Tehran." *Haaretz.* Accessed December 12, 2006. http://www.haaretz.com/hasen/spages/789142.html.

Stone, Dan, ed. *The Historiography of Genocide.* New York: Palgrave Macmillan, 2008.

Wiesel, Elie. *Night.* New York: Bantam Books, 1960.

3
How Health and Disease Define the Relationship among the Abrahamic Religions in the Age of Diaspora

Sander L. Gilman

Religion and Health

During the twenty-first century an issue has reappeared that can help us focus on how the relationship between the Abrahamic religions, at least in Western Europe and North America, has continued to shift. Infant male circumcision, a ritual practice strongly identified with Judaism, has come to be a litmus test for cultural adaptability for Muslims in the West. The Princeton cultural anthropologist James A. Boon has argued "foreskins are facts—cultural facts whether removed or retained. Absent versus present, prepuces have divided many religions, politics, and ritual persuasions . . . (non)circumcision involves signs separating an 'us' from a 'them' entangled in various discourses of identity and distancing" (1994, 556).[1] It is this theme—that circumcision is a cultural fact that provides meaning when there is a confrontation between traditions and peoples that advocate and disparage the practice—that I wish to pursue in this essay. I will trace multiple religious and medical approaches to circumcision to illustrate that each continually occupies and creates cultural meanings for and from this procedure.

Circumcision, as Boon has shown, can be seen as a case study, as an index of difference in societies, but it can also take on nuances that those societies give it in regard to other, highly valued arenas of the production of other forms of meaning. Foreskins are thus not only cultural facts, they are the space for the accretion of multiple cultural connotations depending on the salience of other systems of value in a given society at a given moment.[2] Certainly one of the major points of confusion in the history of circumcision is the elision (and now the assumption) that the meaning of this practice within religion is coterminous with that in medicine. These are two

---

1. See also Boon 1982, 162–168; 1990, 55–60; and Boon 1999, 43–47 where he contrasts Montaigne and the nineteenth-century American commentator P. C. Remondino's views.

2. On the history and culture of circumcision see Waszak 1978; Grossman and Posner 1981; Grossman 1982; Collins 1985; Morris 1985, 218–220; Lévi-Strauss 1988; Allan 1989; Trachtenberg and Slotkin 1989; Schwartz 1990, 141–176; Trachtenberg 1990; Chebel 1992; Gollaher 2000; Mark 2003; Cohen 2005; Silverman 2006; Judd 2007. Recently, I have provided a long comment on Fox and Fox 2012 in *Global Discourse: An Interdisciplinary Journal of Current Affairs and Applied Contemporary Thought* 3:2 (2013): 376–378.

different worlds of meaning, although they constantly borrow one from the other. Yet in this process there is always a shift in the meaning ascribed to that which is borrowed. Thus "medical testimony" before a court is superficially related to medicine as it draws on the status of medicine in its forensic claims, but is ruled by radically different meanings. This is also true in the function of circumcision within the worlds of theology and medicine, even though this is not always clearly the case.

The recent debates on circumcision in the West (specifically in Europe and the United States) have made this conflation of the medical meaning of circumcision with all possible meanings of the practice evident in an interesting and often conflicted way (Harrison 2002, 300–316). In August 2012, the American Academy of Pediatrics reversed its stand on infant male circumcision. Originally in 1971 they had stated "There are no valid medical indications for circumcision in the neonatal period" (American Academy of Pediatrics 1971). By 1999 they began to waffle: "Existing scientific evidence demonstrates potential medical benefits of newborn male circumcision; however, these data are not sufficient to recommend routine neonatal circumcision" (American Academy of Pediatrics 1999). In August 2012 there was no longer any hesitation:

> Systematic evaluation of English-language peer-reviewed literature from 1995 through 2010 indicates that preventive health benefits of elective circumcision of male newborns outweigh the risks of the procedure. . . . Although health benefits are not great enough to recommend routine circumcision for all male newborns, the benefits of circumcision are sufficient to justify access to this procedure for families choosing it and to warrant third-party payment for circumcision of male newborns. (American Academy of Pediatrics 2012)

Here we see the sweep from no health benefit to sufficient health benefit, from religious practice to medical intervention, from discouraging to encouraging in less than fifty years.

In May 2012, the equivalent German organizations (the *Dachverband der Kinder- und Jugendmedizinischen Gesellschaften* and the *Berufsverband der Kinder- und Jugendärzte*) had stated exactly the opposite. Their argument that circumcision violates the bodily integrity of the infant—as well as putting the infant's health at risk—was supported by a German court ruling later that year banning the procedure for these reasons. The case brought before the court involved the circumcision of a four-year-old Muslim boy that was performed by a doctor at the parents' request. Complications occurred with the operation that resulted in the Cologne public prosecutor charging the doctor with the grievous bodily harm of the infant. The district court, hearing the case in the first instance, acquitted the doctor on the grounds that there was parental consent and that he had performed the procedure as a ritual act based on Islamic practice (Deutsche Akademie für Kinder- und Jugendmedizin 2012). The first court's position supports a view of circumcision as a procedure to be encouraged as a prophylaxis; the later ruling sees it as a non-medical procedure that is harmful and violates an infant's human rights.

What is fascinating about this debate is that it takes place within institutions of medicine, specifically pediatrics, in cultures that place the highest premium on medicine providing objective truths, especially in their application of medical knowledge within judicial processes. That the West moves from a culture of religious belief (including concerns about circumcision) to a culture of science in the hundred years leading up to the European Enlightenment is a commonplace understanding, best articulated in terms of the warfare between "theology" and "science" (as in the title of a major book of 1896 by the former American Ambassador in Berlin, Andrew Dickson White). "Theology" is a specific religious claim or structure rather than religious belief itself; while "science" more and more in the course of the nineteenth century comes to focus on medicine as its litmus test for acceptable authority. But, as we shall see, this movement toward medicine as a litmus test actually occurs long before the nineteenth century, when a system with a cultural acceptance of circumcision within religious practice comes into conflict with a system that denigrates it but has a powerful autonomous medical tradition. This seems very different from the pattern that Boon found on Java where two religious systems, one circumcising, one not, were/are in conflict. As we shall see in asymmetrical systems, such as those where science trumps theology, the acceptance or rejection of the practice is often colored by the status of circumcision in medicine rather than theology.

Boon's characterization of the conflicted meaning of circumcision traces a long and fraught history and the practice has included female as well as male genital cutting (Gilman 1999, 53–58). In this essay, I focus on male genital cutting, even though, as I shall mention, a general negative consensus about female genital cutting colors the present debates in the West. While a multitude of societies have practiced and continue to practice male circumcision (the procedure is documented as early as the twenty-third century BC in Egypt) its place in contemporary debates is focused on its continued ritual practice in Judaism and Islam. Uha, in the twenty-third century BC, describes a mass Egyptian ritual circumcision of future priests and boasts of his ability to stoically endure the pain: "When I was circumcised, together with one hundred and twenty men . . . there was none thereof who hit out, there was none thereof who was hit, and there was none thereof who scratched and there was none thereof who was scratched" (Dann 2006, 73). This was a religious test linked to the coming of age of young men destined for the priesthood. No discussion of any medical efficacy is present, even given the wide range of Egyptian medical papyri. Circumcision is defined as a religious act even though, or perhaps because, it involves amputating a part of the body and it is an action often depicted as part of Egyptian medicine.

To those who practice it, infant male circumcision has been a powerful sign of group identity: it defined the community of the ancient Egyptians and later of the

Jews and Muslims who adopted it. (Jews must perform the ritual on the eighth day after birth while Muslims can and do circumcise up to the fourteenth year of life.) This communitarian view has had a powerful resonance in Jewish history after the destruction of the second Temple, when it became the primary sign of Jewish identity. Even slaves were circumcised, indicating the significance of male circumcision as one of the central communitarian act defining the bounds of the group. As in *Genesis* 17: 13–14:

> He that is born in thy house, and he that is bought with thy money, must needs be circumcised; and My covenant shall be in your flesh for an everlasting cov-enant . . . And the uncircumcised male who is not circumcised in the flesh of his foreskin, that soul shall be cut off from his people; he hath broken My covenant.

Temple Judaism practiced the ritual of infant male circumcision as a religious one, needing only a divine rationale for its undertaking.

As the world of the Jews became more and more Hellenized in the second century BC, the claim of a communitarian identity through infant male circumcision was contested. Indeed this was the very moment where its absolute necessity as the defin-ing action for membership in the religious community was made paramount. Thus, in the land of Israel circumcision is a problem for some Jews as we read in 1 *Maccabees* 1:15–1:15 where such Jews during the first century BC "removed the marks of cir-cumcision, and abandoned the holy covenant. They joined with the Gentiles and sold themselves to do evil."

That circumcision was condemned in Greco-Roman antiquity is clear. In the Satyricon, Petronius has Cito say, "Circumcise us, that we may appear to be Jews" (Arrowsmith 1959, 102.4). Tacitus in *Histories* observes that the Jews "have instituted circumcising the genitals in order to be distinguished by this difference." It is a custom that Tacitus finds "base and abominable, persisting due to their depravity" (Tacitus 1969, 5.5). But it is also clear that circumcised males sought out the most advanced medical techniques of the day to remove this sign of circumcision. Surgery, as we read in the work of Aulus Cornelius Celsus (25 BC–AD 50), was undertaken to restore the foreskin and therefore reconstitute a healthy body:

> But in one who has been circumcised the prepuce is to be raised from the under-lying penis mound the circumference of the glans by means of a scalpel. This is not so very painful, for once the margin has been freed, it can be stripped up by hand as far back as the pubes, nor in doing so is there any bleeding, The prepuce thus freed is again stretched forwards beyond the glans: next cold water effusions are freely used, and a plaster is applied round to repress severe inflammation. And for the following days the patient is to fast until nearly overcome by hunger lest satiety excite that part. When the inflammation has ceased, the penis should be bandaged from the pubes to the corona; over the glans the plaster is applied with the other end of the probe. This is done in order that the lower part [between

the corona and pubic area] may agglutinate, whilst the upper part [the new foreskin covering the glans] heals without adhering. (Celsus 1938, 118)

Celsus recorded these surgical procedures for elongating or replicating the male foreskin, for he saw this as one of the roles that medicine played in reconfiguring the male
body as a healthy one, able to enter into the social activities in the Gymnasium (Rubin
1980, 121–124). Thus out of parochial Jews, cosmopolitan Greco-Romans were made.

Indeed in time circumcision came to be banned among the Jews by Antiochus IV
(215–164 BC). For as Josephus writes:

> Menelaus and the sons of Tobias were distressed, and retired to Antiochus, and
> informed him that they were desirous to leave the laws of their country, and the
> Jewish way of living according to them, and to follow the king's laws, and the
> Grecian way of living. Wherefore they desired his permission to build them a
> Gymnasium at Jerusalem. And when he had given them leave, they also hid the
> circumcision of their genitals, that even when they were naked they might appear
> to be Greeks. Accordingly, they left off all the customs that belonged to their own
> country, and imitated the practices of the other nations. (Whiston 1954, 256)

In other words the religious practice of the Jews came in conflict with the attitudes of
the Greeks and Romans toward any "disfiguring" of the body with as potent a result
as Boon saw on Java. The dominant political and cultural elite saw the act as barbaric
mutilation without any redeeming features whatsoever. How could one justify the act
except by a reactive, conservative theological position such as the one taken by the
Maccabees?

The Jewish philosopher Philo of Alexandria (20 BC–AD 50) wrote in this
strongly Hellenistic culture where, according to Josephus (in his *Against Apion*), the
Alexandrian Apion derided the practice of circumcision. Philo in De specialibus
legibus advocated for the practice, noting that it was a prophylaxis against diseases of
the penis—"preventive of a painful disease, and of an affliction difficult to be cured,
which they call a carbuncle"—and also promoted the well-being of the individual and
assured fertility (Borgen 1997, 159). Circumcision may be a Jewish ritual that alters
the body, but it also presents a health advantage. The Greek historian Herodotus
(484–425 BC) (2:37) dismisses this claim when he writes about the Egyptians (and
those that learned circumcision from them) that they "practice circumcision for the
sake of purity, considering it better to be pure than comely."[3] Here we see the power
of what I am calling the "health exception," the evocation of medicine, for good or for
ill, in regard to a practice that had been considered purely religious. The health exception works in both directions: it is seen as recuperative, preventing or curing, or it is
seen as destructive and harmful because it disrupts the natural beauty of the male
body and disfigures it, a sign of illness. The health exception exists when there is no

---

3. Cited by Boon1982, 29; I have corrected the translation to reflect the comments by Cohen 2005, 230.

consensus about the practice of infant male circumcision in a society with competing values and with a strong medical tradition.

Modernity, at least in the Western Diaspora, came to regard infant male circumcision as the key marker of a Jewish religious identity. As Spinoza in his Tractatus Theologico-Politicus (1670) noted: "the sign of circumcision is, as I think so important that I could persuade myself that it alone would preserve the nation forever" (1951, 15). Yet for Christians of Spinoza's age, circumcision had been dismissed by Paul as inherently Jewish and, therefore, after the rise of Christianity, as not defining the universal claims of Christianity, but only the parochial views of the Jews. It was a Noahide law, pertaining only to the Jews. Boon comments that "at the mention of circumcision the Balinese dike of tolerance collapsed; the outpouring in Indonesian went something like this: What are they doing that here for? That's the trouble with Muslims, too fanatical" (1977, 212). Certainly the "dike of tolerance" in Europe was regularly breached when circumcision was raised in the context of Jewish practice.

The view that the Jews, again to quote Boon, were "too fanatical" about circumcision was espoused by the Church Fathers, Eusebius and Origen, and it continued through the Renaissance (Erasmus) and through the Reformation (Luther). As Immanuel Kant notes in his Religion Within the Boundaries of Mere Reason (1793):

> The subsequent discarding of the corporeal sign which served wholly to separate these people from others is itself warrant for the judgment that the new faith [Christianity], not bound to the statutes of the old, nor, indeed, to any statute at all, was to contain a religion valid for the world and not for one single people. (Kant 1996, 155–156)

This view of a Jewish particularism defined by circumcision is held even by liberals such as the Italian physician Paolo Mantegazza, clearly, if mockingly, an advocate of hygiene:

> Circumcision is a shame and an infamy; and I, who am not in the least anti-Semitic, who indeed have much esteem for the Israelites, I who demand of no living soul a profession of religious faith, insisting only upon the brotherhood of soap and water and of honesty, I shout and shall continue to shout at the Hebrews, until my last breath: Cease mutilating yourselves: cease imprinting upon your flesh an odious brand to distinguish you from other men; until you do this, you cannot pretend to be our equal. As it is, you, of your own accord, with the branding iron, from the first days of your lives, proceed to proclaim yourselves a race apart, one that cannot, and does not care to, mix with ours. (Mantegazza 1935, 99)

While circumcision is seen as creating a communitarian identity, this is seen negatively, separating the Jews from their peers.

It is the health exception that is the means by which ritual practice is accepted or rejected in Western Enlightened society and it impacts on the ritual practice and meaning of the procedure within religious communities. Within eighteenth-century European science, following the new scientific view of the inheritance of acquired characteristics, the assumption was that Jewish males could be born without a fore-skin—that they were often aposthetic. This marked them as inherently different from other groups and was part of the arguments that were eventually used to focus in on racial differences between Jews and other races. According to Johann David Michaelis, the noted Orientalist of the German Enlightenment, it is true that the Jew, like the ape, can be born circumcised. But Michaelis interpreted this anomaly in no way as a sign of the higher status of the Jew. Michaelis believed that the circumcision would only bring higher status if such a condition gave a specific advantage to those born circumcised. Michaelis, who lived in a society that firmly believed that masturbation was the origin of a myriad number of physical and psychological ailments, relied on the belief that circumcision had no curative powers to reverse or prevent ill-nesses due to masturbation as an argument against its conferral of any advantage. Circumcision, he states, is not a cure for masturbation. Those born without a prepuce are no better off than anyone else. Michaelis argues that nature would have made the act of masturbation, a source of sin as well as a source of illness, completely impos-sible rather than dealing with it through aposthia. The Jew, Michaelis notes, following Philo, takes those born circumcised for especially holy men since they have a dimin-ished sexual urge (1773, 94). We, he implies, know better. One must note here that Mohammad, according to the Hadith, the written accounts of Mohammed's life and observation, was born without a foreskin, which is seen as a sign of his perfection. For Muslims, infant male circumcision comes to be seen as one of the practices known as "fitra," acts considered to be those of a refined person. There is no detailed discussion of Islam in any of the Enlightenment discussions of the pitfalls of circumcision as this is a hammer used specifically to characterize European Jewry.

The liberal anthropologist Johann Friedrich Blumenbach argued for the existence of congenital circumcision in his study of the sexual drive in 1781. It is important to note that Blumenbach was a strong opponent of the polygenetic theory of the races, which saw the races as inherently different. (Although, he also believed that Jews [or, at least, their skulls] were immediately and incontrovertibly identifiable as dis-tinct.) But he was also a strong advocate (as were most of his contemporaries) of the view that acquired characteristics could be inherited. If Jews (and others) circum-cised their children, it was reasonable to expect that some "boys in the orient are born circumcised" (Blumenbach 1971, 69). That this marker was understood as a marker of Jewish identity in all cases can be seen in Friedrich Schiller's ironic treat-ment of his "Jewish" character Moritz Spiegelberg in his first play, *The Robbers* (1782). Schiller intends to show Spiegelberg's duplicity by having Spiegelberg deny his Jewish identity. The character is made to refer to himself as having been "miraculously born circumcised" (Schiller 1943, 22). His denial of the religious origin of his circumcision is a comment on the nature of the Jew, seen, at least by Schiller, as mendacious.[4]

Charles Darwin left the question of circumcision and identity open in his 1868 study of *The Variation of Animals and Plants under Domestication*. In asking the question of whether mutilations or injuries can be acquired, he observes: "With respect to Jews, I have been assured by three medical men of the Jewish faith that circumcision, which has been practiced for so many ages, has produced no inherited effect; Blumenbach, on the other hand, asserts that in Germany Jews are often born in a condition rendering circumcision difficult, so that a name is there applied to them signifying 'born circumcised'" (Darwin 1868, 23). Yet later Darwinians have a very specific take on this: Hastings Tweedy, President of the Section of Obstetrics of the Royal Academy of Medicine in Ireland in 1920, observed that he "had never satisfied himself that the craze for circumcision was justifiable. According the laws of evolution the foreskin must have been greatly needed by the human race or it would not have persisted" (Report 1920, 768). Circumcision is a "natural" (and therefore healthy) occurrence among the Jews—unless it is not.

This debate about the special relationship between Jews and ritual circumcision and the health exception is reflected in the Verein der Reformfreunde (Society for the Friends of Reform) in Frankfurt in 1843 which claimed that ritual infant male circumcision was neither a religious obligation nor a symbolic act. (Zunz 1844; Hoffman 1996, 2–9; Katz 1998, 320–356). This was in response to the February 8, 1843, finding of the Frankfurt Public Health authority that circumcision had to be carried out under medical supervision. With the expanding role of medicine came further opposition; certain ritual aspects of Jewish circumcision such as *metzitzah* (drawing the blood from the circumcision wound through sucking) were deemed unhygienic (Katz 1998, 337–402). Outbreaks of syphilis and tuberculosis from 1805 to 1865 were blamed on the ritual circumcisers. Reformers thus advocated modifying *metzitzah* using a sponge or a glass tube. But the end result of concerns over hygiene and deformation was that ritual circumcision was undertaken less often by acculturated Jews in Central and Western Europe.

The idea that the circumcised were inherently different because they were marked as Jewish dominated the nineteenth century discussion. Through the Enlightenment, discussions of such religious practices seemed to be colored by debates about their medical efficacy, but these were never neutral, as specific attitudes toward the Jews seem always to define the debate. As an anonymous author stated in the leading German pediatric journal *Journal für Kinderkrankheiten* in 1872: "The circumcision of Jewish children has been widely discussed in the medical press as is warranted with topics of such importance. But it is usually discussed without the necessary attention to details and the neutrality that it deserves. Indeed, it has not been free of fanatic

---

4. On Schiller and the Jews, see Oellers 1988.

anti-Semitism" (Anonymous 1872, 367–372). No discussion of circumcision within medicine is without an ideological perspective. This prefigures the discussion that James Boon has concerning Peter Charles Remondino's 1891 view of the "intolerant uncircumcision in a history of totalitarian prejudices too notorious to need reviewing" (1999, 66).

The reintroduction of the surgical reconstruction of the foreskin in the mid-nineteenth century is seen as a political act by Johann Friedrich Dieffenbach in his classic handbook *Die operative Chirurgie* (1845):

> One must understand me correctly. I present such methods only for their physiological-surgical principles and to illustrate Celsus' idea of the extension of the prepuce out of luxury, belief, shame, or politics. It would be a denigration of the art [of surgery] if in this manner bachelors are created like virgins through the reconstitution of the hymen, about which one writer so pointedly said: "a fine operation!" Both are a morbid mockery of humanity from the practice of the oriental slave trader. (Dieffenbach 1845, 517)

Here the negative health exception takes precedent: such operations are not medically necessary but rather serve to draw medicine itself into disrepute. Dieffenbach believed that doctors who performed this surgery were quite aware that they were indulging patients with an aesthetic procedure without medical value.

By the mid-nineteenth century the discussion of the practice of circumcision centered on the health exception. This was part of a more general medical debate about whether the Jews, by their ritual practice or eugenic selection, were healthier or sicker than other groups. Thus in 1890, John S. Billings, the head of the Surgeon General's Library in Washington, persuaded the Census Bureau to undertake a census (the only one ever) of the racial diseases of a specific group—the Jews. He asked: "Are these differences due to race characteristics, properly so-called, to original and inherited differences in bodily organization, or are they, rather, to be attributed to the customs, habits, and modes of life of the two classes of people?" (Billings 1891, 70). In his answer to this question, Billings noted that when Jews became integrated into American culture they showed their inherent racial degeneracy in spite of their ritual practices. In regard to circumcision the argument was made on both sides. In 1860 a London practitioner, Dr. Fowler, writing in *The Lancet* claimed the complete efficacy of circumcision in combating one of the most wide spread etiologies of illness of the time, masturbation:

> Has the operation of circumcision any effect in diminishing the habit or practice of onanism amongst the male children and the young lads of the Jewish community? Practising in a neighbourhood where this community abounds, I do not remember ever having had either a confessed or even a suspected case of this description amongst our Hebrew brethren. I wish I could say the same respecting juvenile Christians. (Fowler 1860, 382)

One of the only persistent factors in debates on circumcision is the coexistence of extreme opinions on its efficacy. Additionally, circumcision is often debated alongside issues of public health. Advocacy for the procedure in both cases is based on a positive health exception. Indeed, the American physician Peter Charles Remondino, so well discussed by Boon, projects his nineteenth century fascination with circumcision as hygiene into the world of the Egyptians: "In ancient Egypt . . . the nobility, royalty, and the higher warrior class seem to have adopted circumcision as well, either as a hygienic precaution or as an aristocratic prerogative and insignia" (Remondino 1891, iii). While arguments relying on the health exception to show the dangers of circumcision persist, the image of the health exception that Remondino successfully argues for in late ninetenth century America contributes to the creation of a climate that makes the United States into a circumcising culture. In the 1920s, a debate in the Royal Academy of Medicine in Ireland saw a Dr. Solomons defend the practice of circumcision: "most educated people ask to have their sons circumcised." It helps "in preventing masturbation." Circumcision is advised as "a real help to the weakest spot in the human character." The "ordinary schoolboy was not taught to keep himself clean." Solomons argued that the procedure did not require anesthesia: "In fact it was harmful." He also argued that syphilis was five times greater in the uncircumcised. Our Darwinian physician Hastings Tweedy argued the case against Solomons and stated that circumcision does not "reduce sexual desire." Dr. Tweedy also doubted Solomons's figures about prophylaxis against syphilis. He had seen fatal cases in circumcised patients, three caused by chloroform and one from hemorrhage (Report, 1920, 768). In the 1930s there was a debate in Great Britain on whether the government should require infant male circumcision, and arguments for medical intervention became central. One physician at the time held that "if the removal of the prepuce lessens the incidence of syphilis . . . then circumcision is surely a duty in all cases" (Darby 2005, 260). Such claims were regularly made throughout the nineteenth century, advocating circumcision as a preventative against a range of diseases from the evils of masturbation to sexually transmitted diseases. Infant male circumcision is valuable because it has a positive health impact unless—of course, it does not.

The debates about circumcision as a prophylaxis against syphilis (and other sexually transmitted infections/diseases, or STIs/STDs) had been a staple of the late nineteenth-century hygiene debates. Indeed, it lay at the center of why the United States became a medically circumcising culture (even with a decrease in rates today) while much of the rest of the Western world did not. These debates about circumcision were always countered with the claim that the very act of ritual circumcision actually transmitted syphilis and often caused death or impairment through the surgery itself. The clearest result after one hundred and fifty years of debates about the efficacy of circumcision as a prophylaxis against infectious disease is the determination both anecdotally and epidemiologically that such a procedure has little or no effect on

STI transmission in Western cultures. Indeed, the American practice of circumcision began during the late nineteenth century and continued with other medical rationales (for example, reduced cases of penile cancer and uterine cancer in sexual partners) after the introduction of antibiotics for the treatment of STIs. Indeed, it continues as a rationale for the reduction of cases of cervical cancer even after a specific vaccination protocol (Gardisil) is available for those forms of Human papillomavirus (HPV) that are antecedent to many of such cancers. Of course, the debate about what is in the best interest of the child resurfaces around this procedure, a three-course vaccination: does it place children at risk either from perceived or real side effects from the vaccine? Does it place the child at risk for increased promiscuity because of the absence of risk from HPV infection? (Gilman 2009, 1420–1421) The use of the vaccine is now generally accepted as a powerful force in reducing HPV infections in men and women, while the evidence for the efficacy of circumcision, considering the surgical risk, is more limited.

Health is the primary focus in debates over circumcision, but what defines health differs from advocate to opponent. By the 1950s, another rethinking of the health exception was undertaken as the impact of Anna Freud's idea of the "best interest of the child" came into contact with the articulation of the human rights that should be afforded the bodily integrity of the child (Schiratzki 2013). Infant (human) rights confronted another form of human right, that of communitarianism in the form of the rights of the religious community. (Here one must add that Anna's father, Sigmund, saw circumcision in terms of the health exception as a source of psychopathology in his account of the case of Little Hans in his "Analysis of a Phobia in a Five-year-old Boy" [1909].) Again and again, circumcision is attacked as the "rape of the phallus." The focus is on infant pain and bodily integrity, from the perspective of the best interest of the child (Schoen 1987, 128).

These negative medical evaluations of circumcision come to color its legal reception in Europe. A law on circumcision of boys was adopted in Sweden in 2001, in the aftermath of a 1997 Swedish Supreme Court decision holding "that ritual circumcision of a minor boy that was performed with parental consent was not punishable as assault" (Swedish Supreme Court 1997). This was the first law concerning circumcision passed in Europe following the end of the Third Reich (Schiratzki 2011, 35–53). The law is a set of medical directives and stipulates that only a licensed doctor may perform a circumcision on boys less than two months old and that a licensed doctor or certified anesthesiologist must be present; that the parents, if they share joint parental responsibility, must be in agreement about the procedure for the child; and "if possible, the boy himself should provide informed consent to be circumcised. The law states that regardless of age, a boy's wishes not to be circumcised should always be respected." While the question of agency seems to be paramount, the stated rationale was to reduce the risk of the procedure to the health of the infant.

Current discussions are no different. Opponents have continued to argue that male circumcision is bad because it violates the body, especially that of the infant, unless it has a medical rationale. Only when medically indicated is circumcision considered to be in the "best interest of the child." Conversely, the opposing argument goes: Infant male circumcision is good because it creates a powerful group identity, which is in the "best interest of the child." The latter argument is even more powerful when this group identity can also claim that circumcision confers positive health benefits. It is also the case that a negative impact on health can counter any communitarian claim. Thus the British National Health Service dropped newborn circumcision in 1949 in response to Douglas Gairdner who opposed it in a widely quoted essay. Gairdner noted that the procedure was linked to sixteen deaths annually, although these were from the general anesthetics employed, *not* the circumcision itself (Gairdner 1949).

When in 1999 the issue of parents' right to circumcise came before British courts, it was the Muslim practice that was seen as putting the child at risk:

> Re "J" (child's religious upbringing and circumcision) said that circumcision in Britain required the consent of all those with parental responsibility, or the permission of the court, acting for the best interests of the child, and issued an order prohibiting the circumcision of a male child of a non-practicing Muslim father and non-practicing Christian mother with custody. The reasoning included evidence that circumcision carried some medical risk; that the operation would be likely to weaken the relationship of the child with his mother, who strongly objected to circumcision without medical necessity; that the child may be subject to ridicule by his peers as the odd one out and that the operation might irreversibly reduce sexual pleasure, by permanently removing some sensory nerves, even though cosmetic foreskin restoration might be possible. The court did not rule out circumcision against the consent of one parent.[5]

In Britain as well as on the continent, the presence of a large and new Muslim community has meant that Muslims have now become the litmus test for bad communitarian practices instead of than Jews. The liberal consensus against "Islamic rituals" such as female genital cutting also easily extends itself to rituals such as infant male circumcision as a violation of human rights, as in the anti-Islam campaigner Hirsi Ali's 2004 short-lived opposition to the practice of infant male circumcision (*Rotterdams Dagblad* 2004).

Yet in the United States, it remains a Jewish practice and it continues to attract the attention of the health authorities. Recently in New York City, ritual metzitzah among

---

5. Press Release, Landesgericht Köln, Urteile des Amtsgerichts und des Landgerichts Köln zur Strafbarkeit von Beschneidungen nicht einwilligungsfähiger Jungen aus rein religiösen Gründe [Judgments of the Local District Court and of the Cologne Regional Court on the criminalization of circumcision of non-consensual boys for purely religious reasons], JUSTIZ-ONLINE [Landgericht Köln website] (June 26, 2012); Decision of May 7, 2012 [in German], Docket No. Az. 151 Ns 169/11, Landgericht Köln Cologne. Accessed September 14, 2012. http://www.loc.gov/lawweb/servlet/lloc_news?disp3_l205403226_text.

ultra-orthodox Jews was blamed for infant deaths from herpes. The New York City Board of Health passed a regulation on September 12, 2012, to require parental notification of risk, a demand that has been vociferously opposed by religious authorities, who note that the procedure is never the cause of any possible danger to the health of the infant. According to the Board of Health about 3,600 male infants are circumcised with direct oral suction each year and their risk of contracting herpes is estimated at roughly 1 in 4,000. The Centers for Disease Control and Prevention call the procedure unsafe and recommend against it. Indeed, some members of the Board of Health have said that they believe that requiring consent did not go far enough. "It's crazy that we allow this to go on," said Dr. Joel A. Forman, a professor of pediatrics at Mount Sinai School of Medicine. Again, the debates center on ritual as communitarian practice versus the health of the infant: "This process [demanded by the Board of Health] is being created without a shred of evidence," said Rabbi William Handler, one of a few ultra-Orthodox Jews who gathered in protest of the regulation. "The city is lying, and slandering compassionate rabbis" (Otterman 2012). "They feel that if their child doesn't have the metzitzah, he is not Jewish, so this, to them, is the most important act that they can do for their son in life," said Dr. Kenneth I. Glassberg, the director of the division of pediatric urology at Morgan Stanley Children's Hospital at New York-Presbyterian. "Medically, I don't approve of it," he added of the oral contact, "but if you're asking me, 'Does it cause harm?' I haven't seen enough proof that it causes harm" (Otterman 2012). This is the problem with the health exception: since it argues "theology" against "science" neither side can muster sufficient evidence to persuade the other.

It is the rather new concept of "health risk," rather than the transmission of infectious diseases, that is now evoked for and against the practice in New York. As Susan Bewley, Professor of Obstetrics, and Sarah Strandjord, Professor of Pediatrics, Kings College (London) argue:

> . . . if neonatal circumcision is beneficial, it should be recommended for all (accepting that parents do not have to take the advice). If it is not beneficial (or risky or harmful), then society can either allow some leeway for parents to harm their infants (with or without medical collusion), or disallow it until boys are of an age to make their own decisions. (Bewley and Strandjord 2012)

This is a rather bold re-statement of the role that the health exception plays in these arguments.

In other words health trumps group identity unless the group identity can draw on a health rationale. Sadly, this debate has never been separate from attitudes toward religious ritual. In the 1990s, the focus in Europe turned to Muslim ritual practice, especially in the British and German courts. Indeed the shades of Mantegazza's anti-religious liberalism have been echoed as opposition to practices such as female genital cutting have been extended to rituals such as infant male circumcision, and both have been defined as violations of human rights, as Hirsi Ali claimed in 2004. Only when the health exception is advocated can there be an argument for an elective surgical procedure for infants and that has never been done for female genital cutting even within Islam (Al-Sabbagh 1996).

Thus the advocacy of the American Academy of Pediatrics rests on an evaluation of a wide range of studies, but at its core are the CDC studies that argue that there is a radically reduced rate of HIV transmission in circumcised males in sub-Saharan Africa. But, as one recent study claims:

> ... sub Saharan studies of circumcision benefit used in support of "universal" circumcision in Africa including infant circumcision have been subjected to critical re-analyses which indicate the benefit has been overstated: reporting relative risk reduction rather than the absolute risk reduction of only 1.3% in female to male HIV transmission while ignoring the 61% increase in male to female HIV transmission posed by circumcised males. (Boyle and Hill 2011, 316)

And indeed the CDC Federal Register Notice proposal for "universal" circumcision in the US as advocated by Bewley and Strandjord was recently withdrawn from the web without explanation. This is not to say that circumcision may not reduce the risk of certain rates of disease, but as a rationale for its wider application, its efficacy in preventing the actual transmission of disease remains unproven. The counter argument focusing on the human rights of the infant is also flawed, for medical and forensic arguments for vaccination, surgical, and therapeutic intervention—as well as forced blood transfusions that run counter to the interests of parents—on religious grounds have been well documented over the past century. Indeed, European pediatricians argued that the changes were purely culturally biased:

> Seen from the outside, cultural bias reflecting the normality of nontherapeutic male circumcision in the United States seems obvious, and the report's conclusions are different from those reached by physicians in other parts of the Western world, including Europe, Canada, and Australia. In this commentary, a different view is presented by non–US-based physicians and representatives of general medical associations and societies for pediatrics, pediatric surgery, and pediatric urology in Northern Europe. To these authors, only 1 of the arguments put forward by the American Academy of Pediatrics has some theoretical relevance in relation to infant male circumcision; namely, the possible protection against urinary tract infections in infant boys, which can easily be treated with antibiotics without tissue loss. (Frisch et al. 2012)

Once you make the health exception, any communitarian argument against medical intervention is just as flawed (Kalichman, Eaton, and Pinkerton 2007; Sawires et al. 2007; Kalichman 2010).

Certainly the debates about this question, so substantially raised in the proposal to make it "unlawful to circumcise, excise, cut, or mutilate the whole or any part of the foreskin, testicles, or penis" of anyone seventeen or younger in San Francisco in the spring of 2011, aired a litany of "human rights" claims from freedom of religion to the question of bodily integration to the problem of informed consent when such practices are performed on infants. Underlying this attempt at legally barring circumcision is the stated assumption that such interventions harm the infant's body by severing nerves in the penis. The influential Los Angeles Rabbi David Wolpe read this as an anti-Semitic attack on religious freedom: "Some involved are simply opposed to religion (there are after all some misguided Jews arguing for the ban as well), some wish to target both Muslims and Jews. But can anyone doubt that there are anti-circumcision advocates who seize on this as a chance to hurt Jews and the Jewish tradition?" (Wolpe 2011). Others saw this law as a questioning of the Abrahamic religions. The National Association of Evangelicals published an announcement in the Baltimore Sun arguing "Jews, Muslims, and Christians all trace our spiritual heritage back to Abraham. Biblical circumcision begins with Abraham. No American government should restrict this historic tradition. Essential religious liberties are at stake. The proposed ban violates the First Amendment's guarantee to exercise one's religious beliefs" (Brown 2011). This was noteworthy because unlike Jews and Muslims, Christians are not religiously mandated to practice circumcision. As a result Governor Jerry Brown signed a bill into law that prevents California communities from banning the practice of circumcision on infant males. Assembly Bill 768, which was introduced after a San Francisco initiative on the topic of circumcision gained momentum, passed the state legislature in late August of 2011. The bill argued that anti-circumcision measures would infringe on the medical, religious, and personal freedoms of parents. Sadly, the complexity of these medical, religious, and human rights questions was ignored by the legislature.

The debate over legal measures that ban or allow circumcision took a different turn in Europe. According to a decision handed down by the Cologne regional court on June 26, 2012, circumcision of young boys is a criminal act, prohibited by law, even if parents have consented to the procedure.[6] The decision was grounded on the reasoning that such circumcisions cause "illegal bodily harm" to the children, and that the child's right to physical integrity supersedes parents' rights and the freedom of religion. The Jewish response was clear and immediate "Circumcision is absolutely elementary for every Jew," the organization's president, Dieter Graumann, said in an interview with the *Rheinische Post* newspaper. He warned that if the Cologne

---

6. Press Release, Landesgericht Köln, Urteile des Amtsgerichts und des Landgerichts Köln zur Strafbarkeit von Beschneidungen nicht einwilligungsfähiger Jungen aus rein religiösen Gründe [Judgments of the Local District Court and of the Cologne Regional Court on the criminalization of circumcision of non-consensual boys for purely religious reasons], JUSTIZ-ONLINE [Landgericht Köln website] (June 26, 2012); Decision of May 7, 2012 [in German], Docket No. Az. 151 Ns 169/11, Landgericht Köln, Cologne. Accessed September 14, 2012. http://www.loc.gov/lawweb/servlet/lloc_news?disp3_l205403226_text.

ruling were to become the legal basis for determining the legality of circumcision that "Jewish life in Germany might ultimately no longer be possible" (*Der Spiegel* 2012). The Conference of European Rabbis called an emergency three-day meeting in Berlin to discuss what to do. Its president, Rabbi Pinchos Goldschmidt, the chief rabbi of Moscow, called the Cologne ruling the "worst attack on Jewish life since the Holocaust." Citing France's ban on Muslim veils and Switzerland's ban on the construction of new minarets for mosques, Goldschmidt suggested that the Cologne decision is part of a wider trend of intolerance against religious traditions in Europe (*Der Spiegel* 2012).

The Cologne regional court upheld the lower court's ruling, but on different grounds; that the doctor believed he was acting lawfully in the context of an unclear legal situation surrounding the practice. While the court held that religious circumcisions were illegal because they violate the child's right to physical integrity and self-determination, it differentiated such acts from instances when a circumcision is medically necessary. On December 12, 2012, in an overwhelming vote (434 to 100 votes), the German parliament voted to keep ritual circumcision legal in Germany. There were four stipulations to the law:

1. Adequate training of the practitioners for non-medical circumcision during the first six months.

2. Does not specifically require the use of an "effective painkiller" as "according to the standards of medical practice" also covers the "necessary and effective treatment of pain in individual cases." (If no anesthesia the act remains bodily harm [*Körperverletzung*], but is not illegal [*rechtswidrig*].)

3. Parents are to be made aware of potential consequences.

4. The practice is not to be carried out on children who could be at risk of complications by non-medical circumcisers.

However, "the ministry specifically avoids making any special provisions for circumcision for religious reasons, choosing instead to anchor it in legislation governing the rights of children to avoid requiring steps to determine the motivation of a parents' decision to have their children circumcised" (Eddy 2012). It is clear that the six-month window established by the law allows for most Jewish and Muslim practices to occur legally (even though Muslims can and do circumcise up to the fourteenth year of life). What is evident is that the requirement for anesthesia violates some religious practices and the demands for a risk assessment, as we have seen in New York City, is seen as an anti-religious statement, no matter the desire of the ministry.

Why have the debates about infant male circumcision surfaced in the United States, in the UK, and in Germany (in very different forms) recently? In each instance, This certainly has to do with a contemporaneous surfacing of fierce public debates about Islam, Sharia law, and civic society in the public sphere—from the then Archbishop of Canterbury, Rowan Williams, views of Sharia law in 2008 to regional attempts to outlaw these laws in American states such as Oklahoma (with virtually no Muslim community). While in the past it was the ritual practice of circumcision among Jews that was the trigger for such debates, it is now Islam. Advocates evoke the health exception and public health authorities are placed in a position where they must either support or contradict such claims; opponents stress the violation of human rights and note the health risks. These ideological claims color the science in all directions: either blurring risk, making broader claims about efficacy, or providing rationales for the procedure. The vehemence of these debates seems in no way to be impacted by any evidence-based medical or epidemiological claims.

The health exception in the circumcision debates is analogous to the debates about the health exception in abortion: abortion is a right because women have a legal right to control of their bodies—unless you are opposed to abortion, where the rights of the fetus then trump all else. Unless (and this has recently been foregrounded in American discussions) the pregnancy is the result of rape or incest or endangers the health of the mother, the procedure is contraindicated on religious grounds. The most radical opponents to abortion dismiss the first two exceptions, but the health exception seems always to remain, even among those most opposed to the procedure. In the modern world, the health exception—argued on both sides of the circumcision debate—can in truth never be resolved, in regard to abortion or to circumcision. One observer's health risk is another's valid intervention; one observer's sense of the rights of any category may or may not be trumped by the health risk.

Over and over again, the health exception is used to argue for or against what is in its essence a religious practice. One could see in this a justification for advocating or for banning this practice if the use of science was autonomous. But in every case, including the most recent public health advocacy, there is the assumption that there is an essential relationship between circumcision and health even though what is defined as health is constantly shifting. James Boon stressed that circumcision is first and foremost a cultural practice. In the debates about the health exception it is clear that one of the cultures that reads circumcision is medicine, as its adversarial position for or against simply reflects again Boon's claim of its function "separating an 'us' from a 'them' [as] entangled in various discourses of identity and distancing."

References

Allan, Nigel. "A Polish Rabbi's Circumcision Manual." *Medical History* 33 (1989): 247–254.

Al-Sabbagh, Muhammad Lufti. "Islamic Ruling on Male and Female Circumcision." In *The World Health Organization Eastern Mediterranean. The Right Path to Health: Health Education and Religion*. 1996. Accessed September 14, 2013. http://www.emro.who.int/vip/PDF/female_male_circumcision_en.pdf.

American Academy of Pediatrics. *American Academy of Pediatrics Committee on Fetus and Newborn, Standards and Recommendation for Hospital Care of Newborn Infants.* 1971. Accessed September 14, 2013. http://www.cirp.org/library/statements/aap/#1971.

———. "American Academy of Pediatrics Task Force on Circumcision, Circumcision Policy Statement." *Pediatrics* 103, no. 3 (1999): 686. Accessed September 14, 2013. http://pediatrics.aappublications.org/content/103/3/686.full.

———. "Circumcision Policy Statement: Task Force on Circumcision." *Pediatrics* 130, no. 3 (2012): 585–586. Accessed September 12, 2013. http://pediatrics.aappublications.org/content/103/3/686.short.

Anonymous. "Die rituelle Beschneidung bei den Juden und ihre Gefahren." *Journal für Kinderkrankheiten* 59 (1872): 367–372.

Arrowsmith, William, trans. *The Satyricon of Petronius.* Ann Arbor: University of Michigan Press, 1959.

Bewley, Susan and Sarah Strandjord. "Letters." *Pediatrics* 130, no. 3 (2012): 585–586.

Billings, John S. "Vital Statistics of the Jews." *North American Review* 153 (1891): 70–84.

Blumenbach, Johann Friedrich. *Über den Bildungstrieb und das Zeugungsgeschäfte.* L. v. Kàrolyi, ed. Stuttgart: Gustav Fischer, 1971.

Boon, James A. *Affinities and Extremes: Crisscrossing the Bittersweet Ethnology of East Indies History, Hindu-Balinese Culture, and Indo-European Allure.* Chicago: University of Chicago Press, 1990.

———. *The Anthropological Romance of Bali, 1597–1972: Dynamic Perspectives in Marriage and Caste, Politics and Religion.* Cambridge: Cambridge University Press, 1977.

———. "Circumscribing Circumcision/Uncircumcision: An Essay amidst the History of Difficult Description." In *Implicit Understandings,* edited by Stuart B. Schwartz, 556–585. Cambridge: Cambridge University Press, 1994.

———. *Other Tribes, Other Scribes: Symbolic Anthropology in the Comparative Study of Cultures, Histories, Religions and Texts.* Cambridge: Cambridge University Press, 1982.

———. *Verging on Extra-Vagance.* Princeton, NJ: Princeton University Press, 1999.

Borgen, Peder. *Philo: An Exegete for His Time.* Leiden: Brill, 1997.

Boyle, Gregory J. and George Hill. "Sub-Saharan African Randomised Clinical Trials into Male Circumcision and HIV Transmission: Methodological, Ethical and Legal Concerns." *Journal of Law and Medicine* 19, no. 2 (2011): 316–334.

Brown, Matthew Hay. "Evangelicals Join Jews against Circumcision Ban." *The Baltimore Sun.* June 9, 2011. Accessed September 12, 2013. http://weblogs.baltimoresun.com/news/faith/christianity/.

Celsus, F. Marx. *De medicina.* Vol 1. In *Corpus Medicorum Latinorum,* Loeb Classical Library, translated by W. C. Spencer. Cambridge, MA: Harvard University Press, 1938.

Chebel, Malek. *Histoire de la circoncision: des origines a nos jours.* Paris: Balland, 1992.

Cohen, Shaye J. D. *Why Aren't Jewish Women Circumcised? Gender and Covenant in Judaism.* Berkeley: University of California Press, 2005.

Collins, John J. "A Symbol of Otherness: Circumcision and Salvation in the First Century." In *"To See Ourselves as Others See Us": Christians, Jews, "Others," in Late Antiquity,* edited by Jacob Neusner and Ernest S. Frerichs, 163–185. Chico, CA: Scholars Press, 1985.

Dann, Rachel, ed. *Current Research in Egyptology 2004: Proceedings of the Fifth Annual Symposium which took place at the University of Durham, January 2004.* Oxford: Oxbow Books, 2006.

Darby, Robert. *A Surgical Temptation: The Demonization of the Foreskin and the Rise of Circumcision in Britain.* Chicago: University of Chicago Press, 2005.

Darwin, Charles. *The Variation of Animals and Plants under Domestication.* Vol. 2. London: John Murray, 1868.

Deutsche Akademie für Kinder- und Jugendmedizin. "Stellungnahme zur Beschneidung von minderjährigen Jungen Kommission für ethische Fragen der DAKJ." 2012. Accessed September 12, 2013. http://dakj.de/media/stellungnahmen/ethische-fragen/2012_Stellungnahme_Beschneidung.pdf.

Dieffenbach, Johann Friedrich. *Die operative Chirugie.* Vol. 1. Leipzig: F. A. Brockhaus, 1845.

Eddy, Melissa. "Proposal Sets Circumcision Regulations in Germany." *The New York Times.* September 26, 2012. Accessed September 15, 2012. http://www.nytimes.com/2012/09/27/world/europe/27iht-circumcision27.html.

Fowler, Robert. "What Are the Effects of Circumcision?" *The Lancet* 75, no. 1911 (1860): 382.

Fox, Marie and Michael Thomson Fox. "The New Politics of Male Circumcision: HIV/AIDS, Health Law and Social Justice." *Legal Studies* 32 (2012): 255–281.

Frisch et al. 2012. "Commentary: Cultural Bias in the AAP's 2012 Technical Report and Policy Statement on Male Circumcision." *Pediatrics.* March 18, 2013. Accessed September 15, 2013. http://pediatrics.aappublications.org/content/early/2013/03/12/peds.2012-2896.

Gairdner, D. M. "The Fate of the Foreskin: A Study of Circumcision." *British Medical Journal* 2 (1949): 1433–1437.

Gilman, Marina, Sander Gilman, and Michael M. Johns. "Human Papillomavirus, Abstinence, and the Other Risks." *The Lancet* 373, no. 9673 (2009): 1420–1421.

Gilman, Sander L. "'Barbaric' Rituals?" In *Is Multiculturalism Bad for Women?* Edited by Joshua Cohen, Matthew Howard, and Martha C. Nussbaum, 53–58. Princeton: Princeton University Press, 1999.

———. "Comment on Marie Fox and Michael Thomson Fox. 2012. 'The New Politics of Male Circumcision: HIV/AIDS, Health Law and Social Justice.' *Legal Studies* 32: 255–281." *Global Discourse: An Interdisciplinary Journal of Current Affairs and Applied Contemporary Thought* 3, no. 2 (2013): 376–378.

Gollaher, David. *Circumcision: A History of The World's Most Controversial Surgery.* New York: Basic Books, 2000.

Grossman, Elliot A. *Circumcision: A Pictorial Atlas of Its History, Instrument Development and Operative Techniques.* Great Neck, NY: Todd & Honeywell, 1982.

Grossman, E. and N. A. Posner. "Surgical Circumcision of Neonates: A History of Its Development." *Obstetrics and Gynecology* 58 (1981): 241–246.

Harrison, Daniel M. "Rethinking Circumcision and Sexuality in the United States," *Sexualities* 5 (2002): 300–316.

Hoffman, Lawrence A. *Covenant of Blood: Circumcision and Gender in Rabbinic Judaism.* Chicago: University of Chicago Press, 1996.

Judd, Robin. *Contested Rituals: Circumcision, Kosher Butchering, and Jewish Political Life in Germany, 1843–1933.* Ithaca: Cornell University Press, 2007.

Kalichman, S. C. "Neonatal Circumcision for HIV Prevention: Cost, Culture, and Behavioral Considerations." *PLoS Med* 7, no. 1 (2010): e1000219.

Kalichman, S. C., L. Eaton, and S. D. Pinkerton. "Male Circumcision in HIV Prevention. *The Lancet* 369 (2007): 1597–1599.

Kant, Immanuel. "Religion within the Boundaries of Mere Reason." In *Religion and Rational Theology*, translated by Allan Wood, 32–192. Cambridge: Cambridge University Press, 1996.

Katz, Jacob. "The Controversy over the *Mezizah*: The Unrestricted Execution of the Rite of Circumcision" and "The Struggle over Preserving the Rite of Circumcision in the First Part of the Nineteenth Century." In *Divine Law in Human Hands: Case Studies in Halakhic Flexibility*, 320–402. Jerusalem: Magnes Press, 1998.

Lévi-Strauss, Claude. "Exode sur Exode." *Homme* 28 (1988): 106–107.

Mantegazza, Paolo. *The Sexual Relations of Mankind*. Victor Robinson, trans. New York: Eugenics Pub. Co., 1935.

Mark, Elizabeth Wyner. *The Covenant of Circumcision: New Perspectives on an Ancient Jewish Rite*. Hanover, NH: Brandeis University Press, 2003.

Michaelis, Johann David. *Orientalische und Exegetische Bibliothek*. Frankfurt am Main: Johann Gottlieb Garbe, 1773.

Morris, Desmond. *Bodywatching*. London: Jonathan Cape, 1985.

Oellers, Norbert. "Goethe und Schiller in ihrem Verhältnis zum Judentum." In *Conditio Judaica: Judentum, Antisemitismus und deutschsprachige Literatur vom 18. Jahrhundert bis zum ersten Weltkrieg*, edited by Hans Otto Horch and Horst Denkler, 108–130. Tübingen: Niemeyer, 1988.

Otterman, Sharon. "Board Votes to Regulate Circumcision, Citing Risks." *The New York Times*. September 13, 2012. Accessed September 13, 2013. http://www.nytimes.com/2012/09/14/nyregion/health-board-votes-to-regulate-jewish-circumcision-ritual.html.

Remondino, Peter Charles. *History of Circumcision from the Earliest Times to the Present*. Philadelphia: F. A. Davis, 1891.

"Reports of Societies from June." *British Medical Journal* 1, no. 3103 (June 5, 1920): 768.

Rotterdams Dagblad. "Hirsi Ali wil verbod besnijdenis jongens." *Rotterdams Dagblad*, October 4, 2004.

Rubin, Jody P. "Celsus's Decircumcision Operation: Medical and Historical Implication." *Urology* 16 (1980): 121–124.

Sawires, S. R., S. L. Dworkin, A. Fiamma, D. Peacock, and G. Szekeres, et al. "Male Circumcision and HIV/AIDS: Challenges and Opportunities." *The Lancet* 369 (2007): 708–713.

Schiller, Friedrich. *Werke*. Vol. 3. Weimar: Hermann Böhlaus Nachfolger, 1943.

Schiratzki, Johanna. "Banning God's Law in the Name of the Holy Body—the Nordic Position on Ritual Male Circumcision." *The Family in Law* 5 (2011): 35–53.

———. "Best Interests of the Child." In *Oxford Bibliographies in Childhood Studies*, edited by Heather Montgomery. New York: Oxford University Press, 2013.

Schoen, E. J. "Ode to the Circumcised Male." *American Journal of Disease of Childhood* 141 (1987): 128.

Schwartz, Howard Eilberg. *The Savage in Judaism: An Anthropology of Israelite Religion and Ancient Judaism*. Bloomington: Indiana University Press, 1990.

Silverman, Eric Kline. *From Abraham to America. A History of Jewish Circumcision*. Lanham, MD: Rowman & Littlefield Publishers, 2006.

Der Spiegel. "The World from Berlin: Circumcision Ruling Is 'a Shameful Farce for Germany.'" *Der Spiegel*. July 12, 2012. Accessed September 15, 2013. http://www.spiegel.de/international/germany/german-press-review-on-outlash-against-court-s-circumcision-ruling-a-844271.html.

de Spinoza, Benedikt. *A Theologico-Political Treatise and Political Treatise*. New York: Dover, 1951.

Swedish Supreme Court. NJA 1997 s. 636. Accessed September 14, 2013. http://www.notisum.se/rnp/sls/lag/20010499.htm.

Tacitus. *The Histories*. Books IV–V. In *Tacitus in Five Volumes III: The Histories, Book IV–V. The Annals, Books I–III*, translated by Clifford H. Moore. Cambridge, MA: Harvard University Press, 1969.

Trachtenberg, Moisés. *Psicanálise da circuncisâo*. Porto Alegre: Sagra, 1990.

Trachtenberg, Moisés and Philip Slotkin. "Circumcision, Crucifixion, and Anti-Semitism: The Antithetical Character of Ideologies and Their Symbol Which Contain Crossed Lines." *International Review of Psycho-Analysis* 16 (1989): 459–471.

Waszak, S. J. "The Historic Significance of Circumcision." *Obstetrics and Gynecology* 51 (1978): 499–501.

Whiston, William, trans. *Works of Josephus: Antiquities of the Jews*. Philadelphia: The John C. Winston Company, 1954.

White, Andrew Dickson. *A History of the Warfare of Science with Theology in Christendom*. 2 Vols. New York: D. Appleton & Company, 1896.

Wolpe, David. "Circumcision Ban Another Attack on Judaism." *The Washington Post*. June 6, 2011. Accessed September 15, 2013. http://www.washingtonpost.com/blogs/on-faith/post/circumcision-ban-another-attack-on-judaism/2011/06/06/AG1oVJKH_blog.html.

Zunz, Leopold. *Gutachten über die Beschneidung*. Frankfurt am Main: J. F. Bach, 1844.

4
Inimical Friendships?— Eugen Rosenstock-Huessy, Franz Rosenzweig, and Dialogue between the West and Islam

Wayne Cristaudo

> Our formula "Respondeo etsi mutabor [I respond although I will be changed]" reminds us that human society has outgrown the stage of mere existence which prevails in nature. In Society we must respond, and by our mode of response we bear witness that we know what no other being knows: the secret of death and life. We feel ourselves answerable for life's "Renaissance." Revolution, love, any glorious work, bears the stamp of eternity if it was called into existence by this sign in which Creator and creature are at one. "Respondeo etsi mutabor" a vital word alters life's course and life outruns the already present death.
>
> —Rosenstock-Huessy 1938, 753

Perhaps the most anti-natural injunction of the New Testament—in a religion that many have, not wrongly, defined by its anti-natural character—is the commandment to love one's enemies. Enemies are naturally those who threaten our very existence— the extinction of the enemy is thus the most natural thing in the world.[1] By contrast, loving the enemy is one of the hardest.

Loving the enemy is valuable even if, or precisely because, it involves a number of transformations. First, it involves striving to *see* or know the enemy. For how can one love what one does not know? Of course, just as we are mysteries to our very selves, the seeing and knowing is not an exhaustive act. Indeed to know something completely is a threat to our capability to love it; for loving is a transformative relationship that is an energizing encounter. Love activates—and to activate there must be some vitality. Routine is comforting up to a point, but when comfort no longer activates, recuperates, or energizes, it anaesthetizes, dulls, and depletes us. This was why so many political philosophers from Machiavelli to Hegel argued that the greatest danger to freedom was not warfare, but a surfeit of the pleasures that come with peace.

The enemy endangers us, but it also activates. In an undergraduate lecture, Eugen Rosenstock-Huessy once reminded his students to be wary of friends because

---

1. When Carl Schmitt defined the political in terms of friends and enemies he had merely rearticulated a definition of justice that Plato had considered as one of the most elementary ideas people have about justice—doing good to friends and harming our enemies.

they put us to sleep, but to be grateful for our enemies because they wake us up.[2] The enemy demands a response from us, and whether that response is militarily or verbal, we must gather our resources. The choice between survival or perishing forces a response—no matter how heinous—that in times of peace we would never need to search for or deploy.

An enemy changes us—and this is true individually or collectively. That Goethean/ Nietzsche formulation "become who you are" contains a thrilling message about the latent potentials that we harbor, and both Nietzsche and Goethe knew that the unleashing of those potentialities require resistance and engagement more akin to viewing life as a battlefield than anything that a life devoted to mere consumption and satiation could offer.

In sum, then, the injunction to love the enemy may be counterintuitive, but if it is an injunction that is contrary to our nature, it is contrary in the same way that the Copernican revolution was anti-natural. That is, it awakens us to a reality that is contrary to what *appears* to be the case.

To be sure, that such an injunction emerges out of a particular socio-historical-cultural narrative that is part of a dominant creative narrative or current within the West can easily lead people to dismiss this insight as irrelevant because it finds itself articulated by Jesus Christ. But the fact is that love and enmity are among the most universal of tendencies. As I write this, an Israeli couple, Ronny Edry and Michal Tamir, have launched an online initiative under the first posting of their "Israel Loves Iran" blog—and a number of responses have arisen under the banner "Iran Loves Israel." The people involved in this act of goodwill are responding to their neighbor—irrespective of their political and traditional religious hostilities, and certainly irrespective of the injunction having once come from Jesus Christ. That the origins of a truth neither validate nor discredit it was, of course, a basic insight of Aristotle's. And it is true today that culture has become such a fetishized term of appeal that, all too frequently, it is a means of concealment of the fallacy of origins. We are never one thing, and we are certainly not merely an expression of some bedrock we designate as "culture"—if, in this paper I still use the word, I do so in a very loose sense.

Our sources of nourishment are many. And all of us today live in a world composed of such multiples origins, sources of appeal, conflicting narratives, symbols, and sacred codes that an appeal to simplicity is very appealing indeed. But when it comes to life's most serious questions—How do we survive? What future do we make? Whom or what authority do we obey?—the value of a simple answer easily lends itself to oversimplification and tempts us to delude ourselves about the nature of the reality that constitutes us and within which we participate; I choose the term "us" deliberately because we now live in a time that, in spite of the vastness of cultural

---

2. Rosenstock-Huessy 2005. See also the section "'Love Thine Enemy' in Politics," in Rosenstock-Huessy 1969, 459–462.

differences, we are very much, however involuntarily, bound to a common reality. Nevertheless, delusion has its reasons and its appeal—but it remains delusion none-theless. If someone insists that his or her delusions are sacred then there is nothing that can be done.

Dogma is a powerful and invaluable means of community building and it is an indispensable component of every revealed faith, but even dogmas have some extrin-sic source of recognition which enables peoples to live under their labels, and thus to live off their power: and these are the achievements and triumphs of the lives lived according to them. Dialogue takes over from dogma wherever the unexpected extrinsic matters so much that a dogma cannot suffice to escape those matters or materializations. The refusal to respond to the implacability of the unaccounted for—the contingent and extrinsic—is the refusal of the fanatic who refuses to participate in a dimension of reality, and by so doing might as well not be alive. It is another formulation of the fanatic: the fanatic prefers the purity and certitude of a reality already attained even to the point of death, and would have others die with him or her rather than participate in life's mysteries, uncertainties, fecundities, and the potencies it bestows upon us, which are activated by experience and imagination.

The problem is compounded by the apt expression provided by Shakespeare: "We are such stuff as dreams are made on." We are all complicit in world-self-and-"other" making. This simple fact is why the Enlightenment view of reality and human beings (so vociferously defended by Richard Dawkins and the recently deceased Christopher Hitchens) largely misses the point. For being symbolic, gestural, and speaking creatures, we make ourselves through the non-natural and we make unnat-ural realms, and in so doing display a nature in which nature but furnishes materials for actions and modalities of being and play and serious actions undreamt of within earlier ages. This was, in spite of their metaphysical conceits, the basis of modern idealism and voluntarism.

One striking feature about "naturalists" such as Dawkins is that they repeat the same failure that was committed by the first naturalistic metaphysicians of the seven-teenth century who held that to cure human beings of their delusions about the world and themselves, they would have to bring the imagination under the control of the understanding. In other words, the "cure" for human folly lay in tapering the faculty of the imagination so that it would follow our correct understanding of the order and sequence of nature. Spinoza already had grappled with the complexity of ethics, but once Kant had identified an unbridgeable fissure between *is* and *ought*, naturalism had shrunk considerably. But the problem, as Kant only partially realized, was far bigger than that. Nothing so obviously shows us that our world and vocabulary are not simply a hit and miss (badly imagined/ badly understood) amalgam of successful and failed observations about nature than our cultural artifacts—our architecture, arts, forms of play and design, and the like. For these employ materials found within nature, but they do not correspond to anything *within* nature. Kant grappled with this problem by deploying a facultative logic, what he would call a transcendental psychology, whose preliminary version Descartes and Spinoza had deployed to erect their metaphysical naturalism. But that facultative logic collapsed with Kant, and although he belatedly recognized, and only in a limited way, art's importance, the next philosophical generation (not to mention those movements of the twentieth century with the exception of the Analytic tradition which has never moved beyond naturalism) saw that reason could only be saved if it were liberated from the straightjacket of mechanism. Twentieth-century philosophy had to bid adieu to reason itself whenever reason became mere naturalism (thus the philosophical need for phenomenology), or an abstraction over and above our existence (thus the philosophical need for existentialism), or was seen to be but a specific means for forming social fabrications and discourses (thus the need for post-structuralism). That this could so easily be reduced to the tiresome stupidity of a metaphysical "discourse" about "truth" versus "relativism," which seems to have been endlessly played out in the 1980s and 1990s only indicated that many disputants in that particular game were totally clueless to the philosophical journeys that had been going on since the naturalist metaphysical revolution which was the foundation of modern philosophy.

Forgive my lengthy aside about the history of modern Western philosophy, but it is deeply relevant to the discursive situation that is at the basis of any inter-religious dialogue. For religious dialogue is not a dialogue that exists between two simply superstitious groups (the Hitchens/Dawkins/Enlightenment secularist certainty), but rather a dialogue that is taking places between contrary ways of peoples having been made and contrary ways of world-making—a dialogue between contrary worlds and selves, and I am tempted to use a naturalistic metaphor and say contrary trajectories. That is, groups have been "transported" by cultural memories, institutions, languages, sacred codes of appeal, and so on, which certainly still push, still provide authority, and still create types of people who stand for very different things. Yes, as I indicated above the world is still the world, and no group can exist in hermetically sealed isolation. All attempts to do so are delusory, but that does not matter unless the deluded come to see themselves as deluded and are willing to respond on the basis of their experience and realize that the life they are making is no longer worth making. To be sure, some people are willing to continue making the life they make even at their own life's expense—but the suicidal act is not that uncommon for collectives, just as it is not uncommon for individuals.[3]

None today, then, can be sure that their ultimate source of appeal is unproblematic. Though in the West, it tends to be the thoughtful person of faith who concedes

---

3. See David Goldman's provocative *How Civilizations Die (And Why Islam Is Dying too)* (2011). See also his *It's Not the End of the World: It's just the End of You* (2011).

this rather than the atheist—for, in my observation, the atheistic imagination generally portrays believers as deluded idiots—while atheists are "brights," a term coined by Daniel Dennett that manages to show allegiance to the spirit of Enlightenment as well as an existential assuredness of the atheist's intellectual superiority and honesty.

I do not believe that the atheist any more than anyone else lives (to use Camus's famous formulation) without appeal. And if the atheist believes in ethics, or basic human goodness, one must simply ask on what basis? Where is this bedrock? There is no small army of moral and ethical philosophers who have a stake in (us) accepting (their) moral or ethical reason(s)—though their lack of agreement about what that might be exactly simply alerts us to what philosophers such as Schopenhauer, Kierkegaard, and Nietzsche had been shouting from rooftops in the nineteenth century. And if Kant has not managed to demonstrate exactly that reason is, he at least called moral reason by its proper name—an "idea." But the idea is no less a wisp than God, which Kant also left as a "mere idea." Our ethics committees are all over the place in Western institutions, but anyone with the slightest knowledge of ethics knows that they rest on authority, not on reasons that are philosophically fail-safe. And the fact that ethicists publish paper after paper, tome upon tome, trying to come up with a foolproof ethical grounding should only alert us to the fact that the object of ethics is no more reasonable than theology (which, albeit for different intents and purposes, is what a number of logical positivists said almost a century ago).

The reasons I came to be unable to take atheism seriously were anthropological and linguistic, not metaphysical. The point is well made by Rosenstock-Huessy's argument that a "god" indicates a name implored and appealed to as an ultimate power and authority within a dominion. The "gods" allude to the powers we serve through our actions. Concomitantly, the "god" is not a *substance* open to philosophical exploration. (Among other instances too numerous to list, see Rosentock-Huessy 2013, 7, 39–43; Rosenstock-Huessy 1956.) Polytheistic societies are catalogues of the living powers that peoples have served; monotheistic societies are societies in which there is a faith in some singular originating source of creation; and atheistic societies are societies whose vocabulary tend to either mask the divinizing behavior of people, or compartmentalize their semantic fields so that certain academic (originally, for the most part, Greek) modes of classifying the world and ourselves have ultimate authority.

All of this, I think, is to different degrees understood by philosophically literate people of faith today. To this extent we might even say that the very fact that there is this shared anthropological understanding is symptomatic of a certain form of friendship. It is the kind of friendship we might say that manifests itself in the fused group (to use Sartre's term) that was behind the "interfaith" meeting that engendered this volume. Our mutual encounter, our common participation, will also make us "enemies" of those for whom dialogue itself is already a communion with the devil, an encounter too risky for those who believe that dialogue may seduce those away from the true faith and lead them into the vortex of nihilism.

To participate in a dialogue with those who do not share one's faith is indeed something that has the potential to shake certitudes. For to share faith is largely to accept boundaries and sufficiently stable meanings so that solidarity can be formed on the basis of shared convictions; the boundaries guard against the entrance of information or narrative flows opening up new appeals. But dialogue with other faiths has the potential to let those flows in. Moreover, once the dialogue is a genuine dialogue in which the purpose is not only to establish the value of one's past, but also the possibility of a concordant future, the discussion must move to an assessment of the comparative resources that are latent within the contrary traditions. Such a comparison inevitably introduces a realm of appeal that is lacking within the required frame of reference of those sharing convictions. To simply call that realm of appeal the realm of reason would be to enter into another labyrinth of endless inquiry—and here I would simply invoke Franz Rosenzweig's post-Nietzschean line—reason is not something outside of the world but something we use within it (Rosenzweig 2005). And just as it would be unreasonable for a scientist to simply appeal to the Bible rather than experimental data, or a long distance runner preparing for the Olympics to smoke five packets of cigarettes a day, or for someone to jump off a cliff, flap their arms, and think they will fly, it is unreasonable not to take account of the fact that reason is not its own authority, that it works in conjunction with other powers, and that in any dialogue the range of considerations demanding our attention varies considerably and requires a great wealth of knowledge about history, culture, society, human nature, and philosophy among other things. In this respect the decision to enter into dialogue is to take a risk—it is to enter into a new way of thinking about things, a new semantic field, a new frame of reference. And to return to my previous point—the risk is that in fraternizing with the enemy one may be won over to the ways of the enemy, or to put it another way, one may no longer be so sure about the value of one's sacred code and the worthiness of the future one is trying to build.

A common way to avoid this danger is to make sure that a dialogue does not get too difficult and that the dialogical participants agree (often without actually having made this agreement explicit) to only look for what they hold in common. To be sure this may build friendships of a sort, but I cannot help thinking that this way—which I have to say I see as the primary dialogical model discernible in books and conferences—is one that leaves too much untouched. The problem is the same problem I see as plaguing the various Rousseauian forms of radical politics (including Marxism): it assumes a natural harmony (in the case of Marxism within the industrial working class) that one can tap into once impediments to that harmony are torn down. The problem of politics, however, is to build harmony where it does not exist. This is why starting with the concept that is latent in so much interfaith dialogue—"we are all friends here"—actually impedes the harder work of the creation of bonds of solidarity where they do not yet really exist. To be sure the willingness to speak is already to establish a bond of sorts—but the bond is only real if the speech is real—if people speak of their fears and differences. There is no guarantee that dialogue will lead to common ground, but we can be sure, if I may rephrase Wittgenstein, when we pass over in silence of what we cannot speak, the presence that looms within the silence will not disappear.

Today, in my view, the urgent dialogue is between Islam and the West. The very terms are fraught with problems that do not undo the urgency of the dialogue. For of course, there is not one Islam just as there is not one West, and what dialogue could be representative? Of course, this can also be said of every collective noun that refers to living collectives. And the point should not obscure the fact that the trajectory of the West and the trajectory of Islam are very different indeed, although they may at times intersect, and the differences are conspicuous in the social mores of their respective societies. From the vantage point of the West, what has been striking is how the presence of Islam has only been noted because of a collection of violent statements and acts commencing in Europe with the Rushdie affair and more recently, and at the time this essay was being written, with the murders committed by Mohamed Merah. What is less appreciated by the West is how, from diverse Islamic vantage points, the West itself is also defined as a violent intrusive power—the establishment and support of the State of Israel being the ultimate violation which manages to unite groups whose own internal enmity is considerable to say the least. But the one great difference is that the West contains many Muslim immigrants and, for a number of reasons, is either adapting or reacting with anti-immigration parties and its own violent young men such as Anders Breivik. Breivik, we might recall, is now serving time in prison in Norway for politically motivated mass murders undertaken in July 2011. Amongst his victims were eight people who had been working in government buildings that he bombed and sixty-nine people (mostly youth) shot down at a Worker's Youth League camp on the island of Utøya. The murders were committed in conjunction with the publication of his electronically uploaded political manifesto *2083: A European Declaration of Independence*. Breivik believed that his actions were a declaration of war against those responsible (and more specifically their children) for Europe's Islamification.

If dialogue at a geopolitical level is desirable, the nature of geopolitics is such that the international arena is not a forum where dialogue occurs—enmities remain entrenched and action and interests rule. And no interfaith dialogue is going to bridge the geo-political divides between the Saudis, Iran and Turkey, and Al Qaeda. (Indeed the notion that there are many forms of Islam is often made by the more liberal-minded wanting to stress liberal wings of Islam, but a more geopolitical eye can take little comfort from the factions and fractures of Islam today, where the more liberalized Muslims outside of Europe do not seem to be winning anything.) But this does not change the fact that dialogue with this vague and amorphous cluster of energies and peoples who are followers of Mohammad must take place in Europe—in an unpublished conference paper I have argued why the dialogue in Europe takes place in a very different context and has an urgency that makes it very different from the United States (Cristaudo 2012). The dialogue in Europe is urgent because in Europe inimical neighborliness is a far greater reality than in the United States. The reality comes with all manner of pressures of the sort referred to above, which all impact upon the kinds of dialogues already taking place.

One fact should be noted from the outset. As with the United States, Europe (in no small manner because of the role of the US in European post-World War II reconstruction) has undergone a range of social transformations in public and social policy that have generally created a far more "liberal" set of policies and social attitudes than were widely held when, in the post-World War II period, Muslim immigrants peacefully entered Europe on a scale heretofore unknown. Who would have guessed then that Catholic Spain and Portugal would follow Norway and Sweden in allowing same sex marriages? Policies such as these have steadily accumulated—and although Europe, like everywhere else in the Western world, has had significant legislative expansion in the workplace, the environment, the family, schooling, etc. The emancipation movements of the 1960s and early 1970s have drastically transformed the social fabric of Europe.

The transformations certainly changed the "speech-scape" of Europe, but it can hardly be said that the transformations were the result of dialogue between those who wanted radical change and those who did not. On the contrary, the transformations were due to a group whose social attitudes were formed around a consensus of the importance of personal freedom and choice, a common hostility to the values that heretofore presided, and their entry into positions of social and political authority where they were able to form alliances with the like-minded and change the institutions to fit their ideas of justice. For the sake of convenience we might call this the consensus of the '68 generation. And one of the reasons the consensus was so successful was because that generation having gone into positions of teaching at school and university levels taught the generation below them, transformed curriculum, and basically won what has been described elsewhere as "the cultural wars."

The gains made by the consensus coincided with massive changes in university curriculum and compartmentalization in the humanities, and a plethora of intellectual currents challenged the previously widely accepted narratives and behaviors and social and political constructions of policies and attitudes dealing with matters of race, class, gender, and ethnicity. Underlying this was a very clearly discernible set of common convictions about the shamefulness of the West's colonial and fascist past, the importance of social equality and freedom, and a more general animosity or sense of shame about Western societies. There was also an extraordinary sense of confidence in the ability to change social institutions. Social institutions were, after all, socially constructed. Habits and sentiments could be changed swiftly with new styles of teaching about gender, for example, being put in place. Racism could be cured by teaching children to value and respect each other.

This was part of a longer pedigree of ideas coming out of Europe and the United States that preceded the Second World War. European artists and writers, mindful of the dangers of the loss of our animality, and the horrors of rationality that had culminated in the First World War, along with anthropologists in the 1920s and 1930s had been questioning any notion of Western triumphalism and were driven by a sense of loss and mourning at the level of dehumanization that was accompanying modernity. In spite of such ideas impacting upon the '68 generation, it was the Holocaust and the Second World War that provided the most important impetus for the radical reaction against more traditional European mores, which could be seen as having facilitated the horrors Europe had just emerged from. Moreover, the Holocaust and Second World War, unlike the Great War, could be interpreted in bipolar terms. Scouting out fascism was a relatively easy intellectual affair provided one already had a certain commitment to the Western trajectory of liberalism and socialism, freedom and rights/socialism and welfare, and, of course, secularism.

All of this is important to the backdrop or what might be called the "mindset" of contemporary progressive Europeans, who unexpectedly found themselves forced to think about peoples whose values simply did not fit a template that had been successful in so many ways.

The lack of fit is conspicuous in the fact that the '68 generation had little sense of the model not being universally applicable—even though ironically the model also represented itself as distinctly not universalist and it eschewed metanarratives and celebrated "difference." But the kind of difference that post-structuralism celebrated had to be construed in terms of its own making. This was evident when Foucault went to Iran to celebrate the revolution that had taken place. He wrote about it in terms, redolent of Sorel and Parisian Maoism, of revolutionary energy, but completely ignored the specifically Islamic factor of the revolution (which did not stop him chastising some Iranian women living in Paris, who feared what Khomeini would do, for not being clever enough to realize that Islam is not just one thing!) (Afray and Anderson 2005). What generally was crucial to the diversity championed by the '68 generation mindset was that difference could be cast in terms of gender, ethnicity, race, etc. That is, that difference could be rendered to comply with the real code of '68, which was all along nothing more nor less than freedom and equality, which were ever the twin pillars of the modern liberal-socialist political mindset (now neatly entwined in the EU).

It is then important to note that Islam became a noticeable presence in Europe when that society was undergoing a transformation of institutions, habits, and sentiments of enormous magnitude, and the swiftness of the transformation was extraordinary. Not surprisingly given the shift that had taken place in social attitudes and given how successful at least at an institutional level the transformation had been it is perhaps not surprising that Islam would not be seen for what it is—whatever that may be—and that much of the discussion about how to make sense of Islam really had very little to do with Islam, and much more to do with the continued insistence that any problems involving Islam were of the same order as other social problems that were in the process of being solved. That is to say, in the context of social policy, Islam was not primarily viewed as a problem having to do with the presence of groups bringing into Europe a different set of appeals that were related to a different sacred code and very different social memories. Likewise, there was generally a conspicuous failure to recognize that Islam could not readily be represented in terms of the same struggles for power that members of the '68 generation had experienced with their parents and grandparents. In the main, and this is very evident in most social science literature dealing with the social problems of Muslim communities in Europe, Islam had to be understood in terms of economic and social disadvantage and racism and ethnocentrism.

What, then, is noteworthy about this is not only that in spite of all talk of alterity, all this ostensible good will only contributed to the subaltern remaining invisible. Indeed the widespread use of such generic terms as "alterity," "subaltern," and "the Other" place all attention on the one who is not the Other, the one who has power, authority, etc. But this only masks what is truly unique about the various "members" united by nothing other than their "alterity." The all-important matters of diverse and contrary or contradictory appeals and sacredness were hidden by the hue of the more generically radical liberal appeal. It is not the radical liberal appeal as such that I have such a problem with as the manner in which it fails to see that it too makes a world that threatens to extinguish more traditional life-ways of the "subaltern." And this is most definitely the case when the subaltern is a group whose needs and interests, appeals and social preferences are not only alien to traditional Europeans, but even more alien to the power brokers of the society whose educational thought-ways, sentiments and appeals are of '68.

There is also another part of the problem and I might use the example of Michel Foucault whose work belongs to the more emblematic representatives of '68 generational thinking. Foucault had argued, in a way that combined Marxism with Nietzsche's will to power, that all our social and professional narratives, "the discursive regimes" of modern society are really ciphers of power. But neither Foucault nor his followers who have made their project the identification of the flow and formation of power within our social institutions have paid much attention to how they have inserted themselves into the power structures being analyzed, and what the larger social and economic meaning of their will to power might be. Although Foucault pilloried Husserl's idea of phenomenology as the preservation and deployment of the transcendental subject, his own role and that of his followers is precisely that of the transcendental subject. This works hand in hand with the fact that Foucault also insisted that he was interested in the productive nature of power and thus his work was not to be construed in terms of power being reduced to mere oppressor-oppressed terms. In fact, though, this claim of Foucault's was extremely disingenuous—on the one hand he did indeed want to provide an outlet for the production of emancipatory power-complexes of those like himself engaged in social resistance (and this was in part his riposte to those, invariably Marxists, who claimed that his vision of social struggle was one of hopelessness); on the other hand, he and his followers all held the high moral ground because they always sided with the relatively powerless against the more powerful (in spite of Foucault's rather disingenuous gesture of eschewing moral authority, a gesture made with great flare in a famous debate with Chomsky).

In the Foucauldian project and in its self-representation we see the entire ideology or tactic of the '68 generation (and ideology functions by being an unconscious set of self-serving operations and appeals of those who deploy it)—its condemnation of all motivations involving the erection of a power complex other than its own. Thus as it increasingly becomes a powerful group it generally refuses to apply the very modalities of critique which had become so intrinsic to itself. That this generation has had enormous gains in social and personal wealth is undeniable—the debt crisis in Europe is, not completely, nevertheless partly but one manifestation of this generational grab for private property—but there is a deafening silence from itself about its own power. Again I might refer to the tremendous changes that have taken place in the class basis of leaders of social democratic parties in Europe (it is also true of Australia and New Zealand). This does not mean—as conservative critics often hold—that the conservative side of politics is the more pure. On the contrary, ideological differences within the mainstream are completely insignificant when it comes to these issues.

One more issue should be mentioned about the mindset of this generational group who have in the main been so successful at holding political power that they have set the value of consensus, which has authoritative articulation in Europe today. This is not to say that there is not significant dissent. There is. But that dissent is invariably "constructed" as extremist, and now that ideas of the '68 generation are mainstream, the rights of critique which were so essential for this group's acquisition of power is largely denied to its critics.

Further, in keeping with the model of historical and social representation in which the past of Europe is fundamentally a heritage of malevolency, it should not be surprising that the '68 generation has had little interest in acknowledging Europe's larger heritage. A good example of this was in the discussion around the now discarded European Union Constitution and the discussion of whether the Christian roots of Europe should be acknowledged in the constitution. The idea was supported, *inter alia*, by Angela Merkel (who having grown up in East Germany was largely immune to the '68 paradigm), but it was rejected because it was seen as unnecessarily insensitive to non-Christians. Irrespective of whether the decision was right or wrong, the statement that for so long Europe and Christianity were deeply intertwined, and that European institutions had spent centuries nurturing Christian habits and sentiments is so obviously true it barely is worth mentioning. That European habits and sentiments are no longer recognized as predominantly Christian is also the case. But Europeans are post-Christian rather than non-Christian, and the importance of that cannot be underestimated, especially when the society must now find a way to engage in genuine discussion with Islamic people.[4]

But how can this engagement be done if one of the parties of the dialogue is a social amnesiac. Indeed, this is precisely what most Europeans today, including educated ones, are. A simple test could be given to demonstrate this—ask most Europeans about Christianity and the Churches that are everywhere on their landscape. How many Europeans can "read" a Church? Probably about as many who can make sense of the trinity, which would be about as many as could speak with some knowledge on the Arius controversy. Why do these things matter? If I said that to understand European institutions one would need to understand the great upheavals that have taken place in Europe in its wars and revolutions, I would hardly be saying something controversial. But there is not a revolution (and this is true of many wars as well) prior to the French revolution—which is characterized *inter alia* by being the first anti-Christian revolution on European soil—in which appeals to some aspect of the Christian faith or Christian institutional features were not entwined.[5] This seems so obvious it barely warrants mentioning. Yet after the Second World War politics and society were (with some few exceptions) almost entirely discussed in ideological and economic terms. And now that Islam is an unavoidable topic for the future of Europe the idea that it is essential to have some fundamental understanding of the values and

---

4. One particularly important post-Christian legacy is the widespread appeal to social improvement and inclusion on the basis of a variant of the principle of universal solidarity for the suffering; this very appeal was the original "glue" of the Church.

5. Jules Michelet and Alphonse La Martine both thought it essential to ask the question to what extent the French revolution was a Christian event. Michelet opens his work with the question "Is the Revolution Christian or anti-Christian?"(1857, 13), answering that it is "the tardy reaction of justice against the government of favour and the religion of grace" (1857, 23). Alphonse de Lamartine (1856) writes in the opening book of his three-volume classic, "All that could then be seen of the French Revolution announced all that was great in this world, the advent of a new idea in human kind, the democratic idea, and afterwards the democratic government, This idea was an emanation of Christianity." For Lamartine it was the cultivation of sensibilities and hope that made the revolution a providential act carried out by fanaticism and fear—virtue filtered through corruption as it is made actual.

core doctrines of Islam as well as the roots of the European tradition is still a minority point of view. There is still an overwhelming tendency to construct debates in terms of posits and tacit appeals that have so "successfully" transformed European society. But as I have been suggesting, contemporary European consensuses, nevertheless, make it particularly difficult to identify the concerns and actions of people who come with different consensuses, and who are simply not part of the consensus formation that has occurred in European-based societies over the last forty to fifty years.

The '68 consensus was not derived dialogically but strategically and politically. I would also say that not only does it not equip those immersed in it to dialogue, but that it has cultivated a thoroughly un-dialogical even anti-dialogical set of habits and gestures—dialogue is restricted to those who are already like enough to be *appropriately* different. Like all radical movements, subversion is encouraged until power is achieved, then the term extremism is deployed to silence dissent, and order, once mocked or denounced, is invoked as *responsible*—though the very anodyne language of condemnation as exercised today on behalf of the "community" by social and political power brokers is the epitome of bourgeois civility and invocations and appeals which sustain it. Indeed, I find nothing so striking about the trajectory of bourgeois habits and sentiments as its tendency to hide its bourgeois character behind a discourse that purports to detest the bourgeois as philistine.

The unintended consequence of that has been to engender the kind of "extremist" reactions that it has hoped to curtail. When Anders Breivik argues incessantly in his manifesto about what he calls "political correctness" his point should be noted, for he is but one of a far larger group of angry disaffected youth reacting to a consensus they do not identify with. Of course no consensus can or should accommodate the completely wicked and delusory—and Breivik's actions make him part of that category. But the consensus has spawned hostilities from people who would never do or approve of what Breivik did, but will organize politically because they believe that the world is being made more rather than less dangerous because of a consensus they do not feel part of.

I have been arguing that the way in which Islam has become a problem in Europe is itself indicative of deep problems within European society. Introducing immigrants for economic purposes alone without considering a larger array of needs (other than mere economic welfare) has been disastrous because people do not live by bread alone. Many post-World War II Europeans, having witnessed their traditions culminate in catastrophic ideological collisions, simply thought that traditions did not matter that much, and if they did they would be more or less similar in day-to-day interests and habits. This was an easy way to do nothing. Multiculturalism then added to the problem by also making social virtues of the tribalism and ghettoization that were unfortunate consequences of a host nation failing to find real means of social solidarity with their new "neighbors" who had come to do jobs few of their own citizens wished to do. Multiculturalism may have facilitated political management of migrant communities to enable "efficient" policy formation, but it did not build a greater sense of communal spirit of the nation as a whole— as is all too evident by the rising number of anti-immigration parties in Europe.

Further, European society, like all Western liberal democratic societies, is suffering from a surfeit of problems which one may plausibly argue are created by liberal democracy itself—widespread social atomism and fragmentation, an excess of litigation, and rules, a rather selfish and infantile social ethos, generationally unbalanced property acquisition and dispossession, a plague of abstract relations at the expense of substantive relations, institutional dysfunction, a news media so driven by economic interests that it has not only seriously blurred the boundaries between entertainment and information, but, as in the UK with its scandals over phone tapping, has become so seriously compromised that one may seriously wonder if it can recover. The problems are intensified by a thoroughly instrumentalized education system which blunts the talents of judges, lawmakers, journalists, teachers, and civil servants by having an education that has been spawned out of a witches' brew of formalism, compartmentalization, over-politicization, and economic rationalization.

Indeed the problems of liberal democratic societies are massive, and the '68 generation's solution of us all being more politicized (this mantra has been repeated ad infinitum in material coming from Arts faculties for two generation), far from being a remedy, may well be part of the larger problem of the corrosion of civil society. As bad as this all is there is no obvious alternative but to try and fix what is breaking, though it may be irreparably broken.

In sum, then, Islam is a problem within a society that is riddled with problems and one could well make the point that Islam is the least of Europe's problems. Unfortunately, if that is true it does not change the fact that Europe is contributing to the radicalization of some Islamic youth. For it seems clear that younger people of Islamic origins are more likely to hold so-called more "extreme" views than the earlier generations of Muslims who came looking for work and a new life in Europe. It is also true that anti-Islamic movements are also rapidly gathering force. Under such circumstance one might say Islam is perhaps a gift in the way that Derrida spoke of Plato's *pharmakon*—for Islam may pose a serious threat to Europe if the tensions between the two worlds are not solved—but it has undoubtedly also forced Europeans to consider the pathologies of their own culture, and finally it is possible that Islam's presence in Europe may be valuable for Europe's future. And finally— as the '68 generation—never thought—if there is to be a genuinely global peace, then peace between the different faiths of the world must take place. And such peace requires dialogue. This means there needs to be a more dialogical climate within Europe's own post-Christian "community," and that requires a general preparedness within it to listen and respond to points of view emanating from the very different life-experiences of different groups that are outside the more acceptable consensus that has institutional articulation but is not widely held by the group that is potentially the most dangerous of all, viz. young disaffected non-tertiary educated white males who are unemployed, or in low skilled jobs. They are among the most likely to build up resentment and turn their energies and frustrations on migrants. Of course the irony is that sociologically, at least, they are the group that are most like the young radical Islamists whom they will often pit their bitterness against. Not finding more ameliorating political pathways and speech-ways for this group helps the Breiviks of the world become their spokesmen.

Nevertheless, it is a fact that it is the educated elites who are power brokers of ideas and that even though that group needs to factor in the fact that politics is about steering forces, and not merely laying down a moral platform and preaching. I have already suggested that this group is now being forced to take into account a more thorough and complicated account of the historical and theological narratives of peoples—and that theological narrative cannot simply be the preserve of specialists who are simply one more example of the instrumentalized and compartmentalized intellectual fragmentation of modern Western societies. But it now must also engage with the contrary historical and theological narratives of Muslims.

Having thus far identified what I take to be significant philosophical and social obstacles to dialogue, in what remains of this paper, I want to propose that the speech thinking model provided by Eugen Rosenstock-Huessy and Franz Rosenzweig provides an important example of how such a dialogue as must take place between Islam and the West may be conducted.

First, the dialogue took place between friends. And it is highly questionable whether any dialogue can take place between peoples who are not willing to know each other and to *become* friends. Ironically, this also means dropping the idea that we must all respect each other irrespective of what we believe. For fifty years, the '68 generation has shown little respect for those within their own culture who do not see the world like them—to have made a fiat of respect for cultures radically different from European culture merely because they are different was a piece of political maneuvering that has only created social acrimony from those who do not believe they have been consulted about what matters. The idea of respect is an abstract idea and the idea that respect is something that should take place between different peoples is the kind of abstraction that is just as likely to spawn its opposite and to keep relationships abstract. Respect breeds tolerance, but even when tolerance does not breed antipathy, it breeds indifference.

A large part of the pathological nature of modern liberal democratic societies is predicated on the fact that solutions to social problems tend to be dealt with at one step removed from the natural alliances and relationships that people evolve over time which bind communities. In part this is because of the acceleration of time that is (as Marx perceptively noticed) part of capitalist (which is to say modern commercial) economies. The problem is compounded by the political capitalization by party interests, and managerial style "performance indicators." Respect is an important element on relationship formation but it is something that is earned—once it is laid down as a right it becomes meaningless.

Secondly, the dialogue was based upon inimical points of view. In this instance it was the inimical ends of the Jewish and Christian faiths. Like so many Germans of his generation Rosenzweig had been born into a liberal Jewish household—though his closeness to a devout uncle played an important part in inspiring him about the Jewish life. But that was not until he met Rosenstock-Huessy, who had also been born into a liberal Jewish household but entered the Christian faith as a teenager, he did not really know how to reconcile his intellectual side with the emotional sensitivity he harbored for the religious heritage he knew was his, but which he did not know how to connect with. So impressed was he by Rosenstock-Huessy and his cousins, the Ehrenbergs, who had also converted to Christianity, he himself was on the verge of converting to Christianity. Deciding to attend Yom Kippur just prior to his intended baptism he had an epiphany and decided to "remain a Jew."

Let us pause here on the fact of *remaining*—and link this to the situation of Muslims in Europe. Being modern is to sever roots, to choose forms of community that one wants to participate in, thus at every turn Muslim immigrants in Europe are confronted with (tacit) invitations to leave their traditions—the act of remaining means to value something of a heritage sufficiently to decline the invitation. But at the same time to participate in a world made by another tradition is already to have accepted the invitation up to a point. Economic and technological progress do not come without a heritage or a price—and the price of being on European soil is already to participate in an environment where certain modalities of communal bonding, such as traditional penalties, considered divinely sanctioned, for apostasy or, different gendered legal weights (which many Europeans may still argue are not sufficiently eliminated in Europe) must be forgone. Although modernity arose out of a series of crises which took place on Christian soil and would breed anti-Christian/secularist responses the Christian Churches have been forced to adapt to a particularly secular social environs. Thus the means and ways of being a member of one's Church have changed fundamentally. The same is inevitable for Jews and Muslims. When Rosenzweig said he was remaining a Jew he was also saying—as Rosenstock-Huessy would underscore via the title he chose for the English translation of their publication some fifty years after they were first written: Rosenzweig chose *Judaism Despite Christianity*. The "despite" meant that Rosenzweig acknowledged that he was a member of a world that had been made the way it was because of its Christian heritage. And that was something that could not be changed. Rosenstock-Huessy's work has been primarily devoted to demonstrating this—and the point is not that this achievement has occurred because of the mere superiority of one religion over another. On the contrary the explosions that have made Europe and that then took ideas—such as the nation state—around the world and forced the remaking of the globe in accordance with an institutional array that first evolved in Europe (and European colonies such as America and the American revolution) occurred because of cruelty and injustice which for the most part its faith was implicated in. Thus it was that Rosenzweig had wished to revive a Jewish sense of identity in a world that he had observed had been thoroughly Christianized. Now one great difference between Judaism and Islam, if viewed from Rosenzweig's perspective (and *The Star of Redemption* provides an elaborate comparison of the two faiths, and he is very critical of Islam), is that Judaism, unlike Islam or Christianity, is a matter of blood rather than conversion, and does not need its own political form or state.

Christianity has always differentiated between the Church and the secular, between priest and prince, but there have been protracted times when the power of the Church has completed infiltrated the secular—and for its success it had to pay the belated price of having its property periodically stripped away by secular powers. Islam operates from within another framework entirely and the dualism of religion and state is not endogenous—but Islamic people are no less members of nation states—and no less plagued by the problems nation states bring with them. Indeed the problems that the nation state has bought into the Islamic world are frequently worse because of the arbitrary lines imposed by Western imperial powers and the clan/tribal disputes unsolved by Islam, particularly in much of central Asia and the Arab world. On the other hand, it is also true, that nation states, if relatively well run, have the potential to provide certain benefits for its members—representation within the international arena, the securing of trading agreements etc., a centralized and (potentially) representative political, legislative and administrative system, and the means for mediating ethnic, tribal, religious differences. (Of course like all powerful systems, a nation state gone mad and bad is a curse.)

Being in the world requires sacrifice of tradition merely by virtue of being in the world—and that sacrifice has had to be made by Christians and Muslims alike. This does not mean that the world for which the sacrifice is made is the best of possible worlds—but extrication from that world is not a matter of mere good will. It is an uprooting on such a massive and destructive scale that it is surely not wrong to call those who would undertake it "fanatical"—for the extrication from a world requires such brutality of will and action that the most fundamental acts of civility must be violently severed. What I am suggesting then is that being a Christian, Jew, or Muslim today involves a certain *despite*, and that the purity of position is not an option. All coreligionists are inextricably impure.

A genuine dialogue must start, then, not only from a willingness to enter into relationships, to *become* friends *despite* fundamental differences concerning what is most important in the way the world and self are made, but also to accept that we are in a world of impurity and adaptation, of compromise and politics, and shared heritages. We now, for better or worse, all inhabit a world which contains forces unforeseen by religious founders, at the very least unarticulated by them. Between Muslims and (post-)Christians and Jews in Europe there is the fact of contiguity—contiguity, unlike distance, forces responses, if not always resolutions, and while contiguity may exacerbate hatreds, it also provides opportunities for friendships. For at least people must mingle and cannot escape encountering Others by retreating totally into their representations of the Other. In their mingling they see each other's faces, their fears and hopes. And lines of communication become possible because experience (potentially) breaks in upon our pictures and representations. We are confronted with a certain sameness—a rawness of common humanity revealed in small gestures and acts of everyday kindness and vulnerability and cruelty. The differences, though, do not simply dissipate because of the encounters—indeed new tragic possibilities arise, and real difference appear as real to those whose romanticization of the Other breaks down. As in families, though, tolerance is always a trial and it involves the tolerable burden of hearing each other's cries and screams—which is to say it has little to do with the anodyne liberal abstract variant of the same.

Dialogue is not like table manners. And the example of the dialogue between Rosenzweig and Rosenstock-Huessy was frequently heated, and at times very vitriolic. Both men were uncompromising about who they were and what they held sacred, though both were critical of each other's choices, neither was interested in converting the other (though Rosenzweig scholars frequently make this mistake of thinking Rosenstock-Huessy wanted to take Rosenzweig away from the Jewish faith, while the fact is that once Rosenzweig chose to remain a Jew, Rosenstock-Huessy not only had no interest in converting him, but was delighted that he had learnt so much from Rosenzweig now being a genuine "prophetic Jew"[6]). The passionate encounter transformed each of them—they learnt from each other. They became more than they would have been had they not met each other, and had they simply shared the same faith. They both devoted their lives to their faith, and to the explication of its meaning. That explication became more real and more powerful because a dimension of their respective faiths had undergone illumination precisely because of the encounter of the difference.

A people is a path; and the greatness of a faith is heritage, and heritage is accentuation and specification of accumulated potencies. One of the problems with humanism is that it generally overlooks this—for it discards and discounts the means by which people make themselves. The encounter of peoples on different paths is fascinating and intriguing because we are exposed to possibilities that we may not be yet we

---

6. See especially his enthusiastic review in 1921 of Franz Rosenzweig's *Der Stern der Erlösung* in Eugen Rosenstock-Huessy, "Zwolf Bücher," item 111, reel number 2, 2005. *Collected Works on DVD*.

may still esteem, and thus be touched by. This does not mean that criticism between religions should cease—on the contrary criticism is a means of eliciting response, a means of testing and trying the value of someone or something. I have found it astonishing how Rosenzweig's North American admirers are all embarrassed by his criticism of Islam. I have defended his criticisms of Islam elsewhere, and have argued that in his discussion of Islamic doctrine he says nothing that any Muslim would disagree with—his arguments have generated embarrassment to the radical liberal sensibility because of the critical appraisal of those doctrines, rather than his identification of their content. But why should a Jew not criticize a Muslim, or a Muslim a Jew or a Christian, or a Jew a Christian, or a Christian a Jew. Criticism is not an appeal to extermination; Nazism did not "criticize" Judaism. Rather it authorized a particular narrative in order to do as much harm as possible to a people. In order to guarantee the deed of harm it eliminated the political prerequisites for any genuine critical encounter between any bodies of faith. Likewise, the Holocaust did not come from theological dispute, but the insistence on the inhumanity of a group expressed by a group that was willing to bid goodbye to its humanity so that it could act on a scale of savagery that was all too human in the worst sense of its possibilities.

It is a great pity that no Muslim has yet to engage with Rosenzweig's challenge. Indeed, I would suggest his challenge should be engaged with, just as Rosenstock-Huessy engaged with Rosenzweig's challenge to Christianity—and all too few Rosenzweig scholars have recalled that it was Rosenzweig who woke Rosenstock-Huessy from his Christian slumber by demanding that Rosenstock-Huessy answer his provocations.

But because of his provocations, an inimical friendship was formed. In the end both walked away with respect for the other's faith—even though at another level something in the other's faith also made them feel sick (Rosenzweig said he felt nauseous around Christians, and Rosenstock-Huessy did not like being around religious Jews). It would be easy to chastise both for how they felt—for not being bourgeois enough to cure their uncivil thoughts—but the point was that they formed an alliance. Their alliance was against the mechanization and spiritually crippling modes of modernity and it was formed by the desire to reactivate traditions which they were part of. Muslims today are reacting to the same spiritless forces, and it is all too understandable why people want substantive forms of solidarity in a world that is increasingly without substance. In saying this we might recall Augustine's very definition of evil as a privative, and say that our world's lack of substance is a world that is full of evil.

Just as Muslims are changed along with everyone else by modernity, they will be changed by entering into dialogue. But that dialogue will only occur once European peoples engage in serious questions, including provocations about Islamic faiths. The West knows one big thing—it has been formed by centuries of shameful acts. In the main, the enduring and valuable legacy of the '68 generation has been to force us to confront much that is shameful within the Western heritage. But it is perhaps also fair to say that we can only build a future in solidarity when we see not only Ourselves, but each Other in their beauty and their shame. The Islamic world has yet to examine its own shameful history, but that too will be required if a real peace between peoples can be created. Presently in the West there is a minor flood of books reminding Europeans how good Moorish Spain and the Ottoman Empire were. Such revision-ism suggests that the West is trying better to understand its historical connection to Islam. Romanticism may be a start, but ultimately romanticism requires suspension of the more important truth that all peoples are mired in pasts of shame and cruelty. If Islamic peoples cannot confront the shamefulness of their imperial projects, con-quests and the cruel components of their histories how can friendship and growth take place with peoples who want to resolve themselves to make a world in which gender, race, ethnicity and the like are not opportunities for political suppression?

Further, just as the sacred codes of Jews and Christians have long been subjected to hermeneutical tools and historical modes of inquiry, this too is inevitably the case for Islam.[7] Such subjection changes all those who participate in it. The history of the West is one where violence and censorship have also been part of its Christian heritage, but presently the threat of violent retaliation is sufficiently a serious reaction among Muslims believing they must defend their faith with violence that critics such as Hirsi Ali require bodyguards or, like Ibn Warraq, anonymous identities. Likewise publishers tread warily when it comes to publishing explosive books. Presently much of Europe has accepted a paradigm of politics over dialogue, and now that an alien faith is sufficiently strong to demand to be engaged with that will not work.

Ultimately, we are facing the fact that there will no longer be pure Jew, pure Christian, or pure Muslim (indeed if ever there were)—we can either retreat into delusions and fail to accept this and create untold further damage in the attempt to find purity, or we can accept that all of us are being transformed and that this too might, theologically speaking, be part of a divine plan. To be sure, how we all come to understand the God who reveals Himself in the future might be more than any of our Abrahamic traditions, as well as non-Abrahamic traditions, have heretofore fath-omed. That may fill us with fear or wonder. This we know, though: our different paths have led us here. And talk we must in order to find opportunities and new things unimagined, or else we remain locked in speech no longer living, and yet we will continue to "live" with the most familiar and stale of all things—death and stagnation.

---

7. See Abdel-Samad 2010, who argues that the inability to adapt to such procedures will destroy Islam. Abdel-Samad, in contrast to Hirsi Ali, still sees value in Islamic tradition, but like her he does not want to be silenced about what is completely contrary to the procedures which provide a basis for the most fundamental human right of all—to be allowed to change and respond to what one feels is right while not wishing to deny this to others.

References

Abdel-Samad, Hamed. *Der Untergang der islamischen Welt*. München: Droemer, 2010.

Afray, Janet and Kevin Anderson. *Foucault and the Iranian Revolution: Gender and the Seductions of Islamism*. Chicago: Chicago University Press, 2005.

Cristaudo, Wayne. "The 'Problem" of Islam in the Context of the USA and Europe: Contrary Experiences—Contrary Problems—Contrary Solutions?" Unpublished paper presented at the Conference on Islam at Hong Kong Baptist University, April 18–19, 2012.

Goldman, David. *How Civilizations Die (And Why Islam Is Dying Too)*. Washington D.C.: Regnery, 2011.

———. *It's Not the End of the World: It's just the End of You*. New York: RVP, 2011.

de Lamartine, Alphonse. *History of the Girondists: Vol. 1. Personal Memoirs of the Patriots of the French Revolution*. Book 1, Vol. 1. H. T. Ryde, trans. London: Henry Bohn, 1856.

Michelet, Jules. *History of the French Revolution*. C. Cocks, trans. London: Bohn, 1857.

Rosenstock-Huessy, Eugen. "Four Disangelists"—1954 Vol 10—Lecture 2—Dec 1. 1954, Lecture (number-page) 2–023, Item number: 635, Reel number: 16. In DVD *The Collected Works of Eugen Rosenstock-Huessy on DVD*. Norwich, VT: Argo Books, 2005.

———. "'Love Thine Enemy' in Politics." In *Out of Revolution: Autobiography of Western Man*, 459–462. Oxford, England: Berg Publishers, 2013.

———. *Out of Revolution: An Autobiography of Western Man*. Norwich, VT: Argo, 1969 [1938].

———. *Soziologie, Bd. 1, Die Übermacht der Räume*. Stuttgart: Kohlhammer, 1956.

———. *Speech and Reality*. Introduction by Clinton Gardine. Norwich, VT: Argo, 2013.

Rosenzweig, Franz. "Meta-Logic" and "Meta-ethics." In *The Star of Redemption*, translated by Barbara Galli. Madison, WI: University of Wisconsin Press, 2005.

5
Collaborating and Conflicted

Being Jewish in Secular and Multicultural Hong Kong

Zhou Xun[1]

Hong Kong's Jewish Film Festival (HKJFF) is Asia's only Jewish festival. Its current trailer begins with an image tracking a man wearing a Djellaba-style long robe and hat across the desert. On his journey he is first met by a Chinese girl, then a black man wearing a kippah, an Indian woman, and finally a Caucasian looking male joins the group. The trailer ends with all of them dancing together. This trailer is based on a story by HKJFF founder, Howard Elias, a Toronto-born Jew who is now the warden of the Hong Kong Jewish cemetery. It sets out to capture the Jewish experience in Hong Kong and is a reflection of the multifarious natures of the Hong Kong Jewish communities, as well as Hong Kong society in general. Today there are between six and ten thousand Jews living in this densely populated cosmopolitan city. While the beautiful Edwardian free-baroque style Ohel Leah Synagogue is hailed as one of Asia's oldest synagogues, Hong Kong is now arguably the center for Jewish life in Asia and the Jewish Community Centre (JCC), in a tall luxury modern apartment tower in central Hong Kong, is its focal point. This essay examines the conflicts and collaborations amongst different Jewish groups in Hong Kong from the second half of the nineteenth century to the years following Hong Kong's handover to the People's Republic of China (PRC) in 1997. In examining this former British Colony, now a Special Administrative Region (SAR) of the People's Republic of China, this essay adds a new dimension to the parallel discussions of intra-communal Jewish life in Europe and North America.

A Short History

Depicted as "diverse, welcoming and interesting," Hong Kong's Jewish community consists of members from all over the world: India, South Africa, the United States, Canada, Britain, Germany, Israel, Iraq, and many other countries. Some of their families have been in Hong Kong since its founding as a colony in the second half of the

1. I am grateful for the generous helps from Brenda Yi, the librarian of JCC library, and Judy Green, the Chairwoman of Hong Kong Jewish Historical Society, and Elizabeth Sinn who introduced me to them. I am also grateful for the many conversations I had with Sander Gilman while writing this chapter.

nineteenth century, and they alongside the Chinese population in Hong Kong, as well as the Indians, the Muslims, the Parsees and the British, have helped to transform this small *outpost* on the Eastern periphery of the British Empire into a cosmopolitan city and the financial center of Asia.

The first group of Jews arrived in Hong Kong in 1842 after the First Sino-British War—better known as the First Opium War. Most of them came via the then British Bombay and Calcutta. A number of them had already been trading in nearby Canton, now Guangzhou. Initially, almost all the Jewish traders in Hong Kong were involved in the opium trade, though the Jewish community has always tried to underplay this fact. After making a fair amount of money in the opium trade, Jacob Phillips, the son of Rabbi Isaiah Phillips of Birmingham, decided to abandon this diseased jungle (as Hong Kong was known at the time) and returned to Britain to take up a profession in public service. Others, all of them Sephardi merchants who had previously been living in British India, stayed and some became the richest men in the Far East. As the history of modern China is inextricably entwined with that of opium, those Jewish traders in Hong Kong—including the Sassoons and the Kadoories, who had made much of their money through opium—were part of the making of that history.

The Sephardi textile merchant David Sassoon (1792–1864), originally from Baghdad, had already been selling opium to the Chinese for a number of years prior to the Opium War. During the Opium War, with the support of the British army, he sent his oldest son Elias David Sassoon to Hong Kong to cash in on the opium trade. In the aftermath of the Opium War, the Treaty of Nanking in 1842 forced China to open five ports to foreign trade. Three years later in 1845 the Sassoons opened a branch of their commercial operations in Shanghai, one of the five treaty ports. As the anti-opium campaign intensified in China and international pressure to stop the opium trade increased, the opium trade became highly contested but even more lucrative. When the Chinese government imposed a ban on opium, the Sassoons and other opium traders, many of them Jewish, seized the opportunity and began to control the price of opium. By 1870, David Sassoon, Sons & Co. was indisputably the largest opium importer in China (British Parliament 1880, 215). The firm dominated more than one third of the total Indian opium trade to China (British Parliament 1870, 21). Besides their branches in Shanghai and Hong Kong, the Sassoons opened another branch in Zhejiang province, in eastern China, and later in the nearby Anhui province. In the meantime, the outbreak of the Civil War in the United States in 1861 caused a serious shortage of cotton supply to the Lancashire mills in Britain and forced the British to look for alternative suppliers (Arnold 1864). This created a real opportunity for the Sassoons in Bombay. As opium brought them greater capital for investment, they quickly overtook the Parsis to dominate the British textile trade. Together, opium and cotton created the massive fortune of the Sassoons.

With the money their forefathers had made on opium, the younger generation of the Sassoons, as well as other Jewish merchants such as the Kadoories and Silas Hardoon, were able to widen their business interests into shipping, banking, and land speculation in Hong Kong as well as in Shanghai. Arthur Sassoon, the fifth son of David Sassoon, in partnership with the Scotsman Thomas Southerland, took the lead in forming a provisional committee of Hong Kong Shanghai Bank Cooperation (HSBC). The idea was to provide a full banking service to meet the needs of the local business community as the prosperity of trade with China and India was attracting an increasing numbers of British investors. The bank also sought to combine banking with the tremendous business opportunities in shipping and trade between Hong Kong and Shanghai (Ji 2003, 45–49). The cooperation was formally incorporated in spring 1865, in Hong Kong and Shanghai, and Arthur Sassoon became one of its eight board members. In the meantime the Sassoons continued in the opium business. It was only in the early twentieth century, after the British government had imposed stricter control over the trading of opium, that the younger generation of Sassoons began to detach themselves from the trade.

As the number of Jews in Hong Kong increased gradually over the years, a formal Jewish life began to establish itself. In 1855, a Jewish cemetery was laid out behind the Chinese village Wong Nei Chong (in today's Happy Valley), and two years later the first Jew was buried here at the same time that the Crown Lease was granted. By the 1860s, more Jews moved to Hong Kong as employees or partners of David Sassoon, Sons & Co. and its rival firm, E. D. Sassoon & Co. The latter was an enterprise of Elias David Sassoon, the second son of David Sassoon. As the Jewish population grew, it also became necessary to have a regular place of worship for the expanding community. From 1867, the community began to lease a premise on Hollywood Road in central Hong Kong Island. This was the earliest synagogue in Hong Kong. Fourteen years later, it was relocated to the north side of Staunton Street, not far from its former location.

As the Jewish community grew in size, tensions within the community grew as well. According to Carl T. Smith, by the end of the nineteenth century, "class as well as religious division had become a feature of the community" (Smith 1996, 400). In the 1880s and 1890s, pogroms brought an influx of Jewish refugees from Russia and Balkans. Unlike their Sephardi counterparts, these Ashkenazi Jews from Europe were mostly poor. They found employment in badly paid jobs as barmen, inn keepers, cleaners, and so on. A number of women resorted to prostitution. There were also regular police reports showing some Ashkenazis were involved in street brawls, assaults, and using indecent language. These incidents caused a great deal of embarrassment to the well-established and fairly wealthy Sephardi community. The newcomers were of different social, cultural, language, religious, and economic background. They did not find it easy to adjust to the Sephardi traditions and were not willing to be identified with the Sephardis. This conflict within Jewish groups was not unique to the Jews of Hong Kong. In New York, at exactly the same moment, the established and wealthy German-Jewish community of the Guggenheims and the Schiffs were dealing with the influx of Eastern European Jews, with much the same anxiety and antipathy. In Hong Kong, some of the Ashkenazis hired a hall and formed a temporary congregation of their own. The Ashkenazi congregation mostly met on Jewish holidays such as the New Year and Yom Kippur. According to Emmanuel Raphael Belilios, another successful Jewish opium trader from Calcutta and then a senior member of the Jewish community, when the Ashkenazi could not form a *Minyan* (the quorum of ten Jewish males necessary for communal prayer) amongst themselves, they did join with the Sephardis.

Being the oldest member of the Sephardi synagogue, E. R. Belilios took an active part in its management. Venetian by origin, he did not always see eye to eye with other Sephardis who had originally come from the Arab lands and for whom Arabic was their *lingua franca*. (Until 1925 Arabic remained the main language spoken by the majority of Sephardis in Hong Kong, and these Sephardi merchants were sometimes referred to at the time as "merchants from Arab lands.") One major conflict was over the building of the new synagogue. Belilios wanted the new synagogue to welcome their Ashkenazi brothers from Europe. But even the location he had chosen was not acceptable to other members of the Jewish community. Desperately wanting to be identified with the British elites, Belilios had purchased a lot on the prestigious Kennedy Road with the intention to build a residence for himself. He proposed to sell the remaining portion to the synagogue trustees. But when Belilios presented his proposal to Jacob Elias Sassoon in Bombay, he refused to go along with it. In the meantime, other members of the Jewish community in Hong Kong also opposed Belilios's proposal arguing that the Kennedy Road location was inappropriate as the shabby appearance of the poor Jews from Europe would disgrace the community in this wealthy neighborhood (Smith 1996, 400–401). Failing to win support, Belilios resigned as one of the managers of the funds for a new synagogue and devoted his time and energy to the social and political life of Hong Kong.

Despite its internal conflicts and multifaceted character, the Hong Kong Jewish community remained close-knit, and over the next century the community flourished. As the employer of some forty Sephardis, the younger Sassoons became the natural leaders of the community. In 1881, David Sassoon's grandsons Jacob, Edward, and Meyer donated a section of the Sassoon estate between Caine Road and Robinson Road, above the city center, to the Jewish community. (Prior to that, the Sassoon brothers leased the property to the British colony government to house British troops [British Parliament 1866, 355].) In addition to the land, they also gave money for the building of the new synagogue. In return they requested that the synagogue be named in memory of their mother, Leah Gubbay, the late wife of Elias David Sassoon.

The foundation stone was laid in May 1901 and Leigh & Orange, a Hong Kong–based international architect practice, won the task of building the synagogue. While the interior followed Sephardi style, the exterior of the synagogue was built in the Edwardian free-baroque style that was fashionable at the time. The establishment of the Ohel Leah Synagogue marked an end and a beginning of an era for the Hong Kong Jewish community: it gave the community a sense of permanence and an established institutional life. Alongside the Sassoons, Elly Kadoorie, a former employee of the David Sassoon, Sons & Co., and his brother, Ellis Kadoorie, also took up active leadership roles in the community.

The Hong Kong Jewish Recreational Club (JRC) was started in 1905 as a modest association. Initially a one-bedroom building that was put up by means of a debenture issue, it was turned by Elly Kadoorie into a Victorian club fit for the Hong Kong colonial life. Having been married in England to Laura Mocatta, an English Sephardi, Kadoorie was attracted to the Victorian English life and wanted to introduce the English club to Hong Kong Jewish life. He gave money to expand the JRC on the condition that the debenture be dropped. The new club building opened in 1909 and became a central focus of Jewish social life in Hong Kong for the greater part of the twentieth century. In 1920, Israel Cohen, a British Jew and Communist traveling through Hong Kong, noted that the JRC was "the finest Jewish institution" and was "equipped with something of the comfort characteristic of a social or political club in the West End of London. There was a large and tastefully furnished room with a grand piano, . . . a reading room . . . ; a billiard-room that was seldom neglected, and a bar presided over by a white-jacketed Chinese mixer who could dispense you any cocktail that you chose" (*Bulletin* 2010, 88–89). Besides a billiard room, the JRC also brought tennis, bowling and croquet—other Victorian games—to the Hong Kong Jewish community (Wilson and Swan 2008).

Under the leadership of Lawrence Kadoorie, Elly's son, a major innovation was introduced to Ohel Leah Synagogue. At the New Year Services in 1938, a certain number of prayers were read out in English as well as in Hebrew despite oppositions from some members of the synagogue. The movement of Hong Kong Jewry into the world of British Jewry became inscribed on the *minhag* (liturgy) as well as the social practices of the Jews of Hong Kong.

Jews as Builders of Hong Kong

The relatively small Hong Kong Jewish community for the most part of the twentieth century, as noted by Israel Cohen during his journey there in the 1920s, was "nevertheless strong and creative enough to impose upon an impression of their own" (*Bulletin* 2010, 88). By the turn of the twentieth century, the Kadoories and Sassoons were amongst the most prominent families in Hong Kong's economic and civic culture. Even today, their names are enshrined in streets, buildings, and institutions across the territory. While the Ohel Leah Synagogue has certainly become a part of Hong Kong's historical and cultural heritage, the Kadoories are also behind one of Hong Kong's most famous landmarks, the Peninsula Hotel. As the founders of China and Light, the Kadoories were also responsible for illuminating the streets of Hong Kong and supplying electricity for 80 percent of the territory's population. The company's Castle Peak Power Station, first built in the 1980s, was and still is one of the largest and most modern coal fired power stations in the world.

Alongside the Kadoories, Sir Matthew Nathan (1862–1939), a British Jew, was one of Hong Kong's most able governors under the British and a key player instrumental to Hong Kong's future development. It was Nathan who initiated Hong Kong's urban planning and the development of the city's infrastructure. During his tenure, the construction of Kowloon-Canton Railway, Hong Kong's most important railway and the only railway built during the entire British rule, began. And Nathan Road, Kowloon's major and most famous road, also known as Hong Kong's Golden Mile, was named after him to honor his monumental achievements and contribution to Hong Kong. Sir Reginald Antrobus, Nathan's superior at the Colonial Office praised him as a "first rate official" (Antrobus 1906). Despite his achievements, Nathan remained an outsider: he was a Jewish bachelor who lacked a university education. He was loathed by the British ruling class in Hong Kong and was not a welcome figure at their regular Victorian tea parties and charity balls. One of his faults was that as the governor he was the titular head of St. John's Cathedral but, being a professing Jew, he did not attend the Church of England Sunday services. It was real relief to him when he was spared laying the foundation stone for an Anglican cathedral in Hong Kong, but this event further diminished his popularity amongst the Hong Kong British society (Haydon 1976, 109). He also became a constant target for gossip because he was a bachelor in an age that had grown more and more anxious about homosexuality after the Oscar Wilde trials in the 1890s. Given the hostile social atmosphere, he was forced to leave Hong Kong after three years and moved to South Africa as the Governor General of Natal where his career of public service continued. In 1911, Asquith moved him to the Board of Inland Revenue and then, in 1914, appointed him Under-Secretary of Ireland. Nathan fully recovered from the setbacks he experienced in Hong Kong.

As key players in the city, the Jews, in particularly the Kadoories, were famous for their philanthropic works that benefitted the non-Jewish population of Hong Kong, and they left lasting legacies. In the 1910s, the Kadoories opened a school for the Chinese and another for the Hindus, as well as Helena May, a home for English girls working in Hong Kong. In 1890, after he withdrew from being an active member of the Jewish community, E. R. Belilios, who later became the chairman of HSBC, donated much of his energy to strengthen his social and political position in Hong Kong. After a number of failed attempts to establish a tie with the British Prime Minister

Benjamin Disraeli, Belilios gave money to the Hong Kong colonial government to build the Central School for Girls. The School was later renamed Belilios Public School (BPS) in honor of him, and is still standing today. In 1879, Belilios gave £1000 to the British governor of Hong Kong to erect a statue of Disraeli in Hong Kong, but his offer was rejected by Disraeli himself. Instead Belilios used the money to set up a medical scholarship named after him and also helped to establish the Alice Memorial Hospital (Eitel 1895, 563–564). The hospital served as one of the major teaching hospitals for students of the Hong Kong College of Medicine for Chinese, the earlier incarnation of the Faculty of Medicine at the University of Hong Kong, today one of the most prestigious medical schools in the world. Dr. Sun Yat-sen, the "Father of the Chinese Nation" was one of the first graduates of the college. Belilios was also famous for his philanthropic work to promote the welfare and education of Chinese girls who were driven to crime and prostitution by poverty, and he set up a fund to build a probation home for girls. In 1893, he was made a Companion of St. Michael and St. George for his significant contribution to Hong Kong society, becoming the first Hong Kong resident to receive this honor (Choa 2000, 58). Between 1881 and 1900, Belilios served on the Hong Kong Legislative Council.

Despite their accomplishments and the efforts of some prominent members to become Anglicized, the Hong Kong Jews were never wholly accepted by the British elites in Hong Kong. Their not being "British enough" in a way helped them to maintain their Jewish identity in the British colony (as it had done in their British "homeland"). Matthew Nathan, Hong Kong's only Jewish governor (1903–1907) can be seen as an example of this. During his tenure, he took active part in Hong Kong Jewish life and helped the community to secure the lease to extend the Jewish cemetery. After Hong Kong, where his being Jewish clearly contributed to the rejection he received from the elites of society, he briefly explored the Anglican faith, but in the end he rejected it. During his assignments in South Africa and Ireland, he made an effort to attend the Anglican Church regularly, but remained absent from all Easter services. Throughout the rest of his life, he remained a professing Jew (Chasin 2008, 47).

Jews Living in the Twentieth-Century Hong Kong

Hong Kong's Jewish community, like the Chinese, the Muslim and other communities in Hong Kong, has been inevitably influenced by the political and historical environment. The Sino-Japanese War in the 1930s and 1940s cast a shadow on the life of Hong Kong and impacted Hong Kong Jewish life.

On Christmas Day 1941, the Japanese army marched into Hong Kong and occupied the thriving British colony. Civilian nationals of countries that were at war with Japan were kept in POW camps. As many Hong Kong Jews had acquired British nationality, they did not escape this fate. After occupying Hong Kong, the Japanese authority implemented a policy aimed at restoring "Asia value" in Hong Kong and returning the city to the East Asians. In the process of eradicating "the poisonous remains of British cultural leftovers," the Victorian-style JRC was badly damaged (Hong Kong Broadcasting Office 1942, 107–108). Apart from a plaque at Ohel Leah Synagogue commemorating the Jews who died trying to defend Hong Kong, documents housed at the Hong Kong Heritage Project—commissioned by Michael Kadoorie—note that the Jewish Recreational Club provided entertainment to the British force that were fighting the Japanese in Hong Kong. Lawrence Kadoorie also helped form the Jewish Ladies' Committee with the intention to provide entertainment for those "soldiers with Jewish persuasion." In the meantime, with a commitment to helping Jewish refugees, the Hong Kong Jewish community once again stood together with a common goal.

The Jewish refugees escaping the war in Europe began to pass through Hong Kong as early as 1938 after China entered the war with Japan. The long established Jewish Benevolent Society was the first to take up the responsibility of taking care of them. As the Jewish community leader, Lawrence Kadoorie appealed to Hong Kong Jews to unite together and lend their hands to help these refugees: "Today more than ever is it the duty of every Jew to realize his responsibilities." But in fear of increased anti-Semitism, he warned the community that "In trying to help those of our people who have lost their all, we must remember that to take work from others in order to fulfill this object will cause that very anti-Semitism that we must try at all costs to avoid" (Kadoorie 1939).

As soon as the war ended in 1945, the life and social structure of Hong Kong returned more or less to normal as it was before the war. Many of those who had escaped during the war returned as soon as the war ended. By 1947, the population in Hong Kong grew to 1,750,000. Refugees crowded into Hong Kong, and many of them were Jewish refugees from Europe who found refuge in China and were now waiting for their passage to Palestine, North America, or Australia. Many of them however lacked the necessary paperwork to stop in Hong Kong, which had returned to British rule. The American Jewish Joint Distribution Committee (JDC) was then sponsoring and coordinating transportation for these refugees. During the war years, they had worked closely with Horace Kadoorie to provide relief work for the Jewish refugees in Shanghai. Now, once again, they coordinated with Lawrence Kadoorie, Horace's brother, in Hong Kong, using the Kadoories' British connections to try to obtain the proper authorization for the refugees to stay in Hong Kong while in transit. The Kadoories regularly visited the Hong Kong Immigration Department to ensure those Jewish refugees due to arrive had their necessary visas ready for resettlement to Israel, North America, Europe, and Australia. As Hong Kong was already crammed with displaced persons as well as the British being repatriated, there was a concern that the influx of Jewish refugees would compete for the city's limited resources. This meant that even transit visas were difficult to obtain. The Kadoories wrote thousands of letters to governments, NGOs, and individuals to guarantee successful repatriation. The Kadoories, as the guarantors of the Jewish refugees, housed them in the grand Peninsula hotel—owned by the Kadoorie family—as they waited for the next ship. This was the Kadoories' effort to assure the colonial government that these Jews would not be a burden to Hong Kong and to avoid anti-Semitism. There was even an attempt to build a Jewish hostel for the refugees. But it was, according to Lawrence Kadoorie, a difficult task. The decision was taken by JDC not to send any more refugees via Hong Kong "except on definite shipping facilities, because we realize the difficulties which will be created by such people having to remain in Hong Kong for indefinite periods of time . . . " (Hong Kong Heritage Project Archive).

For those who did secure their transit visa through Hong Kong, the grand Peninsula hotel served only but temporary shelter. In July 1946, some two hundred and fifty Jewish refugees arrived in Hong Kong on their way to Australia. To accommodate them, the ballroom at the Peninsula was turned into a huge dormitory. For these refugees, life at the Peninsula was by no means luxurious. It was like being back in the refugee camp all over again with very strict routines.

In addition to the Kadoories, the Hong Kong Jewish community, while still readjusting to postwar life after returned from Japanese war camps, worked closely alongside the National Jewish Welfare Board in helping their fellow Jews in transit. Just as Primo Levi, the Italian Sephardi, embraced Yiddish as the language for Jews after his experience in the concentration camp (Gilman 1991, 293–316) one could argue that after a half century of conflicting interests, World War II brought the Sephardi and the Ashkenazi Jewish groups in Hong Kong together. Their common effort during and after the war marked the beginning of their ongoing collaboration. Many individuals from the existing Jewish community offered their hospitality and friendship to their refugee brothers. A makeshift synagogue was set up at the Peninsula, and the Hong Kong Jewish Women's Association, a larger reincarnation of the earlier the Jewish Ladies Committee, was formed to help distribute goods to the refugees.

As more and more refugees departed Hong Kong, the Hong Kong Jewish community began to devote its energy to rebuilding Jewish life in the British colony. In 1949, the Kadoorie family once again made a generous financial contribution for the reconstruction of a new Jewish Recreational Club. Besides those older Sephardi members, a growing number of Ashkenazi Jews began to take an active role in the Club and in Hong Kong Jewish life as whole.

But the community's postwar effort to rebuild Jewish life was soon interrupted. In 1966 and 1967, when China was experiencing the upheaval of the Cultural Revolution, Hong Kong was also in chaos. Anti-British riots were a regular feature. Extreme leftists, many of them Communist supporters closely linked to the PRC, were bombing cars, killing people, and engaging in all kinds of destructive activities.

These riots also caused tremendous financial damage to Hong Kong. According to estimates, the damage caused by the 1966 riot alone was HK$20 million. These events affected Hong Kong's Jewish community as well as individuals within the community. Some four months after Michael Kadoorie was appointed to the Board of China Light & Power Co., Ltd (CLP), another leftist riot took place that intended to immobilize Hong Kong's industry in order to deprive the Hong Kong government of its sources of revenue and eventually get rid of the British rule (Cheung 2009, 63). About 70 percent of employees at CLP went on strike. Joining with many other prominent businessmen, Michael Kadoorie stood firmly on the side of the British and sacked many CLP employees and employees of other Kadoorie owned enterprises who had joined the strike. At the height of the riot, Michael's father, Lawrence Kadoorie, deliberately "instituted night-shifts for the construction crews working on his projects, their flood-lights demonstrating Hong Kong's defiance of the mainland's threats and his own faith in the future" (*Independent* 1993). A few years later, Lawrence Kadoorie was knighted by the Queen for his contribution to the British Empire. As the leaders of the Hong Kong Jewish community were preoccupied by the political events taking place at the time, Hong Kong's communal Jewish life was very much neglected. David Buxbaum, a Jewish student living in Singapore, visited Hong Kong at the time. He noted that the Hong Kong Jews were "a community without much Jewishness. Having come from Singapore, we were surprised at the lack of school, a shochet, a kosher mikva, a rabbi, or a regular minyan service." And according to him, even the much-lauded JRC was poorly maintained (*Jewish Asia Times* 2010).

Things began to pick up as Hong Kong entered the 1970s and individuals grew wealthier. Members of Jewish community felt a need to bring Jewish culture and religion back to Hong Kong Jewish life. To provide Jewish children their Jewish education became a pressing topic for the Hong Kong Jewish community. Prior to the World War II, the community sent their children to Jewish schools in Mainland China. As the majority of Jews left China after the war and with the Communist seizure of power in 1949, all Jewish schools in China ceased to exist. (All religions were banned and the Jews were not one of the ethnic groups recognized by the new Communist state.) In 1969, a Hebrew school finally opened its doors to promote Jewish education in Hong Kong. Some three years later, Judy Diestel, an active member of the Jewish community who had lived in Shanghai during World War II, became the principal of the school. Under her leadership, school attendance grew and it quickly became a focal point of the community. Here, children of Sephardi and Ashkenazi families attended and their parents worked together to support the school in many of its activities. As Diestel put it, "the community evolved around the school, sharing in its spirit, its events and in the mutual need for a Jewish environment" (Maynard 1995, 25).

Toward the end of the 1970s, Hong Kong, by then the world's third largest financial center became more cosmopolitan. This cosmopolitanism also became a characteristic of the Hong Kong Jewish community. Prior to 1997, the Ohel Leah congregation consisted of some 200 families who came from the United States, Israel, the Netherlands, and fourteen other countries. This demographic change was partly due to the gradual opening of the PRC, which was beginning to economically engage the rest of the world. Hong Kong, being so close to China, became a regular and popular stopping point for those wishing to do business with or in China. Jewish business people from all over the world flocked to Hong Kong. In the 1990s, as Israel became China's second biggest trading partner, Israelis also flooded into Hong Kong. Besides bankers and businessmen, there were also a number of journalists and students. Some were long-term residents, and many more were on temporary assignments. This was markedly different from the members of the older Sephardi community, most of whom were permanent residents of Hong Kong. These "new" Jews added new dimensions and challenges to the existing Hong Kong Jewish life. Faced with these changes, the Jewish community in Hong Kong adopted "cosmopolitanism" as their "new" identity in line with the rest of the Hong Kong population. Services at Ohel Leah Synagogue, for example, began to follow the Ashkenazi form. A student from an Orthodox Ashkenazi Yeshiva was appointed the Rabbi of the synagogue in 1986, and a couple of years later he went on to open the first Chabad house in Hong Kong. Around the same time, the United Jewish Congregation was formed catering to the needs of the Reform-Liberal group. Being relatively small in size yet very diverse, the Hong Kong Jewish community developed some unique arrangements: Ohel Leah and the Jewish Community Centre are maintained by an Orthodox trust, which also sponsors the United Jewish Congregation—the only example in the world of a Reform congregation being funded by an Orthodox one.

The religious restrictions imposed by the Communist government on the mainland population presented further opportunities for the Hong Kong Jewish community, especially as the 1984 Joint Declaration between Britain and China over Hong Kong's handover guaranteed Hong Kong the freedom of "religious belief." For a while, Hong Kong's Jewish Community Centre and Ohel Leah Synagogue provided material and educational support for Jewish communities on the mainland. For instance, until very recently, Jewish communities in China went to Hong Kong for Passover supplies, and as a result Hong Kong acquired the role of the center for Jewish life in Asia.

Being Jewish in Post-1997 Hong Kong

In 1997 the British handed over Hong Kong to the Communist government in China, and Hong Kong became a Special Administrative Region of China. This event profoundly affected Hong Kong society. It in turn impacted on the Jews of Hong Kong. Prior to the handover, Hong Kong residents, including Jews, wondered to what degree the Communist Party would want to control Hong Kong as the 1984 Joint Declaration between Britain and China made no specific provisions for how Hong Kong's social and economic systems would be preserved or how the transition to Chinese rule would be made. At the time only 3 percent of Hong Kong residents were ethnically non-Chinese, and the Jews were among this small minority. There were then only about 2,500 Jewish residents in Hong Kong. A few members of the elder generation who came to Hong Kong in 1949 after the Communists took over China were troubled by the uncertain future. Some saw "bedlam in Shanghai [in 1949] and it could happen here." "The Age of Pacific is upon us," but "things could turn sour." While many of the younger Jews had foreign passports, quite a few elderly members of the Jewish community did not. This was another factor they worried about. "I have never felt isolated or rootless as a Jew in Hong Kong," lamented one elder member of the Jewish community. "For years there has been a vital Jewish community here and elsewhere in Asia, and I pray there always will be" (Tarnapol 1986, 35).

Wealthy and middle-class ethnic Chinese flooded Canada and Australia to purchase properties at very high prices with the hope of gaining foreign citizenship; those expatriates with foreign passports stayed in Hong Kong to wait and see what would happen. The Diestels were among them. Having moved to Hong Kong from Shanghai after World War II, they were by then the leaders in the Jewish community. Living in the same luxury apartment block as Hong Kong's new chief executive, Tung Chee-hwa, the Diestels were full of optimism. A number of well-to-do Jews in Hong Kong shared the Diestels' optimism. It is said that money was and is the religion of Hong Kong. Five years prior to the handover, the trustees of the Hong Kong Jewish community leased half of its property on Robinson Road in the Mid-Levels district, originally owned by the Sassoon brothers, to Hong Kong's biggest property developer. This deal made the Hong Kong Jewish community one of wealthiest Jewish communities per capita in the world. This wealth was seen by many as a guarantee of the community's future. In addition, the "Eisenberg connection" added another layer of warranty for the community. Shoul Eisenberg, a World War II Jewish refugee from Europe who lived briefly in Shanghai, was one of the most influential China brokers for world trade since the 1950s. He was also instrumental in re-establishing the diplomatic and trading relation between China and Israel in the early 1990s. At the time of the Handover, his protégé Avishay Hamburger was in charge of the local Israel Chamber of Commerce in Hong Kong. With Eisenberg behind them, many members of the Jewish community were certain that Beijing would be unlikely to do anything drastic to harm the ever-thriving China-Jewish tie.

By 2000, the PRC government had done very little to change Hong Kong except to turn it into an even greater money making machine. As the wealth of Hong Kong SAR grew, many Hong Kong Chinese who had fled before 1997 returned Hong Kong. Joining them were thousands of expatriates from other ethnic backgrounds, including Jews. Although the SARS crisis in 2003 initially impacted the expansion of Hong Kong, the region quickly recovered, and there followed an even greater sense of optimism. As a result Hong Kong's economy grew at a remarkable rate. The optimism that nothing can beat Hong Kong continued during the 2008 worldwide economic recession, and many more Jewish businessmen, bankers, and young entrepreneurs seeking opportunities and employment moved to this financial center of Asia as Asia came to represented the future in this gloomy time. In 2010, Hong Kong's Jewish population grew to 5,000, literally doubling in size since 1997. Though it remains small compared to those in Europe and North America, this community is remarkably active and diverse. There are Jews "from every-where, even from countries where I didn't know there were Jews, like Zaire," said Asher Oser, Ohel Leah's newly appointed rabbi (DeWolf 2010). This multicultural-ism is matched by five congregations: in addition to the Ohel Leah Synagogue, there is now a United Jewish Congregation on Hong Kong Island, three Chabad Houses covering all of Hong Kong, two Sephardi Orthodox congregations covering Kowloon and Hong Kong Island. While Jews from different backgrounds and region have choices to go to different congregations, they are also brought together by the Jewish Community Centre, a Jewish Day School, a Jewish newspaper and magazine, and Asia's one and only Jewish film festival.

The Hong Kong Jewish Film Festival was first launched in 2001 by the Canadian businessman Howard Elias and his friend as a small screening party. Over the years it grew to become one of highest rated film festivals in Hong Kong. In an interview with CNN, Elias claims the festival to be "non-partisan":

> Even if someone is not active in the Jewish community, they come to the festival, which is great. There's no religion to it, except the fact that we're kosher. It's just a big party. We're the only Jewish film festival in Asia—there's nothing else between Jerusalem and Sydney. We've had people come from Shanghai and Beijing, and the Israeli ambassador to Myanmar came a couple years ago. (DeWolf 2009)

In 2009, according to Elias, about a third of the festival audience was local Chinese, and they "absolutely loved the festival" (DeWolf 2009).

While the Hong Kong Jewish Film Festival is comfortably becoming increasingly secular, other secular aspects of Hong Kong life have proved problematic for observant Jews. One challenge has been maintaining Jewish dietary restrictions that prohibit the consumption of pork, shellfish, and other popular Hong Kong foods that have not been judged kosher by a rabbi. For years the Jewish community in Hong Kong remained an "almost secular community," according to Michael Green, the commit-tee chair of the Jewish Historical Society. For a long time, the community lacked a permanent rabbi and the restaurant inside the Jewish Club was only "kosher-style" until the late 1990s (DeWolf 2010). In 1995, the new JCC replaced the former Jewish Recreational Club. Besides providing recreational facilities to the Hong Kong Jewish community, the center also houses a dairy restaurant, a meat restaurant, and, more recently, a kosher supermarket catering to observant Jews. The kosher products served or sold are all imported. Those from the USA and Canada bear printed *hasgachot* while products from Australia and England are listed in Kashrut Guides. Besides the JCC, there are now a number of kosher restaurants throughout Hong Kong, and one can even find kosher products in Hong Kong's major supermarket. Today a number of the larger hotels in Hong Kong, such as the Langham Hotel in Kowloon, serve Passover dinners. Langham Hotel's Main Street Deli was one of the first to start the trend. It has been importing kosher food from the United States since 2005. Keeping Kosher is no longer a problem in Hong Kong.

Another issue many Jewish families have faced is their children's education: specifically, findings ways to give their children a Jewish education but at the same time maintaining a highly competitive international standard. Carmel School's Elsa High School, Hong Kong's first Jewish high school, tries to bridge these goals. Its curriculum combines the best elements of religious and secular education with a firm foundation in an internationally recognized syllabus. While Jewish students love the Jewish experience they get at Elsa High, students from other religious or secular backgrounds enroll in the school because it extends their awareness and understanding of various economic, political, historical, and geographical perspectives (DeWolf 2010).

Elsa High offers a Jewish perspective to non-Jewish students in Hong Kong; Hong Kong Jewish residents also benefit from the multicultural experience of living in Hong Kong. Jews become part of the Hong Kong experience along with (and indeed acoustically merging with) religious practices. Thus South African born Judy Green, the chairwoman of Hong Kong Jewish Historical Society, recalls that during her many visits to the Hong Kong Jewish cemetery, which is right behind a Buddhist monastery, "You can hear the nuns chanting. It's very peaceful."

For Rabbi Asher Oser, the current Rabbi of Ohel Leah Synagogue, being Jewish in secular and multicultural Hong Kong is what Jewish life is about because Judaism tries to make sense of those contradictions. In a way, the secular and multicultural nature of Hong Kong life helps to moderate conflicts within the Jewish community. Rabbi Oser predicts that there will eventually be an "Asianization of Judaism," but he does not quite know what that will entail. Like many members of the Hong Kong Jewish community, Rabbi Oser has lived in a number of countries: he was born in Australia, educated in Canada, and most recently served as the rabbi for a congregation in Providence, Rhode Island. "There are few Jews here, and it's a transient place, yet there are deep roots," he says. Being rooted in this transient place summons up not only Hong Kong Jewish life, but life in Hong Kong in general. For the Hong Kong Jewish community, their deep roots can be found in their shared Jewish identity no matter where they are originally from.

References

Arnold, R. Arthur. *The History of the Cotton Famine: From the Fall of Sumter to the Passing of the Public Works Act*. London: Saunders, Otley and Co., 1864.

British Parliament. "Commercial Reports from Her Majesty's Consuls in China: 1879." British Parliamentary Papers (Trade reports) [C.2718] China. No. 3 (1880): 215.

————. "Further Memorials Respecting the China Treaty Revision Convention." British Parliamentary Papers, 1870 [C.80] China. No. 6 (1870): 21.

————. "Index to the report from the Select Committee on Mortality of Troops (China)." British Parliamentary Papers, 1866 (442) (442-I): 355.

Chasin, Stephanie. *Citizens of Empire: Jews in the Service of the British Empire, 1906–1940*. Los Angeles: University of California Press, 2008.

Cheung, Gary Ka-wai. *Hong Kong's Watershed: The 1967 Riots*. Hong Kong: Hong Kong University Press, 2009.

Choa, G. H. *The Life and Times of Sir Kai Ho Kai: A Prominent Figure in Nineteenth Hong Kong*. Hong Kong: Chinese University Press, 2000.

Colonial Office Papers, Public Record Office, London 446/50, minutes by Sir Reginald Antrobus, January 28, 1906.

DeWolf, Christopher. "Interview: Howard Elias, Founder of Asia's Only Jewish Film Festival." CNN.com. November 12, 2009. Accessed February 12, 2014. http://travel.cnn.com/hong-kong/play/interview-howard-elias-founder-asias-only-jewish-film-festival-963969.

————. "Keeping Kosher." *China Daily*. December 8, 2010. Accessed February 21, 2014. http://www.chinadaily.com.cn/hkedition/2010–12/08/content_11666891.htm.

Eitel, E. J. *Europe in China*. London: Luzac & Co.; Hong Kong: Kelly and Walsh, 1895.

Gilman, Sander L., "To Quote Primo Levi: If You Don't Speak Yiddish, You're Not a Jew." In *Inscribing the Other*. 293–316. Lincoln: University of Nebraska Press, 1991.

Haydon, Anthony. *Sir Matthew Nathan: British Colonial Governor and Civil Servant*. Brisbane: University of Queensland Press, 1976.

Hong Kong Broadcasting Office. "Cultural Activities in the New Hong Kong, a special article from the Hong Kong Broadcasting Office." *The New East Asia*, September (1942): 107–108.

Independent. "Obituary: Lord Kadoorie." *Independent*. August 26, 1993.

Jewish Asia Times. "A Brief Sojourn in Asia and the Flourishing of Jewish Life." *Jewish Asia Times* 5, no. 1 (April 2010): 20.

Ji, Zhaojin. *History of Modern Shanghai Banking: Rise and Decline of China's Financial Capitalism*. New York: M. E. Sharpe, 2003.

"The Journal of a Jewish Traveller." In *Bulletin Igud Yotzei Sin*, LVII, no. 402 (August–September 2010): 88–89.

Kadoorie, Lawrence. "Lawrence Kadoorie's speech at Jewish Recreational Club." February 1939. From Hong Kong Heritage Project Archive.

Maynard, Debra in association with George Ngan, "A History of the Jewish Community in Hong Kong." In Anon., *A Vision Fulfilled*. Hong Kong: The Jewish Community Centre, 1995.

Smith, Carl T. *A Sense of History*. Hong Kong: Hong Kong Education Publishing, 1996.

Tarnapol, Paula. "Pondering the Future Under Chinese Rule." *The Jewish Monthly*, March (1986): 35.

Wilson, Pamela F. and John M. Swan. *Glenferrie Hill Recreation Club: A Memoir 1907–2001*. Hawthorn, Australia: J. M. Swan, 2008.

6
Terrorists in the Village?

Negotiating Jewish-Muslim Relations in South Asia

Yulia Egorova

In 2010, Pakistani-Canadian writer and journalist Tarek Fatah published a book under the title *The Jew Is Not My Enemy: Unveiling the Myths that Fuel Muslim Anti-Semitism*. The book aims to explore why Judaism and Islam are polarized in the contemporary world and offers a provocative critique of anti-Jewish and anti-Zionist rhetoric in Muslim communities. Fatah was prompted to embark on his project examining Muslim anti-Semitism by the Mumbai attacks of 2008, when the Chabad-Lubavitch Jewish Center was taken over by members of a Pakistan-based extremist organization, and an Israeli-born rabbi, Gavriel Holtzberg, and his wife, Rivka, were murdered together with other hostages. Fatah asks why Muslims who are not involved in the conflict in the Middle East would resent Israel or the Jews and suggests that in the late 1940s and 1950s there was no anti-Semitism in Pakistan, where the Jewish communities of Peshawar and Karachi had enjoyed peaceful relations with their Muslim neighbors (Fatah 2010, 175–177). To support his position, Fatah quotes a former officer in the Pakistan army who is adamant that even the establishment of the State of Israel did not cause local Muslims to change their attitudes toward local Jews: "Of course, we were on the side of the Arabs, but it did not cross our minds to target the Jews of Peshawar" (Fatah 2010, 176).

These words reminded me of a conversation I had in Mumbai with a member of the Bene Israel Jewish community who knew the rabbi assassinated in 2008. "These attacks were committed by terrorists from abroad who saw the rabbi as a symbol of Israel," he said. "This is no reflection on the relations that we have here with local Muslims who have always been friendly toward the Bene Israel. In fact, the local Jews of Mumbai have never been targeted." And yet, a few months later, the leaders of another Indian Jewish community, the Bene Ephraim of Andhra Pradesh chose to seek police protection in case Islamic terrorists were to attack their synagogue and instructed community members to wash off Jewish symbols from the walls of their houses. The idea that South Asian Jews have never been the target of Muslim violence was also challenged by Bene Israel commentator Levi Sankar from Toronto who, commenting on Fatah's statement about the absence of anti-Semitism in the early history of Pakistan, stated that local Jews felt threatened and after the Partition had to leave for India, Israel, and other countries. Referring to the experiences of his family, he argues that "in the late 1940s the Jew-hatred spread from the Middle East to Pakistan and the Pakistani Jewish community became refugees fleeing persecution or assimilated" (Sankar 2010).

Who is right in this debate? Did anti-Zionist sentiments of Pakistani Muslims develop into "Jew-hatred," as it is suggested by Levi Sankar, or were they just perceived as such by his community? Did the Mumbai attackers see Rabbi Holtzberg and his family purely as a symbol of Israel and not of Judaism? Were the fears of the Bene Ephraim leaders regarding possible hostility from either "Islamic terrorists" or local Muslims completely justified or were they based on Islamophobic prejudices propagated by the mass media?

This paper seeks to call attention to the fluid, processual, and context-dependent nature of Jewish-Muslim relations. I will focus on a number of historical and ethnographic episodes pertaining to the mutual perceptions of Jews and Muslims in South Asia to explore tropes of collaboration and conflict that are present in the accounts of both communities of the subcontinent and to reflect on the intricate and complex ways in which issues in local and global politics, such as Indian caste relations, the rhetoric of the "war on terror," and the conflict in the Middle East, affect these relations.

In doing so, I will engage with wider debates about the meanings of anti-Semitism and Islamophobia—two notions that have acquired a wide range of meanings and have not been immune from controversy. As Andrew Shryock has observed, Islamophobia has become a unifying concept bringing together differing and diverse sentiments and practices into one framework. Acts of violence directed against Muslims or legislature criminalizing particular forms of Islamic practice have been variously conceptualized as racist, secularist, nationalist, or anti-immigrant (Shyrock 2010, 2). Writing specifically about the context of Europe and North America, Shryock points out that oftentimes people who exhibit anti-Muslim prejudices have only minimal knowledge of Islam, and he suggests that we can hardly be sure that Islamophobia is ultimately about Islam at all (2010, 3).

Anti-Semitism is an equally complex concept the meanings of which have been discussed by scholars from a wide range of disciplines. The issue that has produced particularly heated debates both in public and academic domains is that of the relationship between anti-Semitism and anti-Israeli/anti-Zionist attitudes. As Matti Bunzl observes in his discussion of anti-Semitism and Islamophobia in Europe, anti-Semitic violence has resurfaced in recent years, which gave rise to a debate about what became to be known as the "new anti-Semitism." On one side of this debate, Bunzl argues, is a group who has been labeled by some as the "alarmists." They see recent resurgence of anti-Semitism as a situation where Israeli policies toward the Palestinians are used as a new pretext to openly express resentment of Jewish populations. For the alarmists, Bunzl argues, any criticism of Israel carries the baggage of time-worn, anti-Jewish hatred. Their opponents in this debate, called by some the "deniers," reject the idea that criticism of the Jewish State is inherently anti-Semitic and draw attention to the relatively comfortable life that Jewish communities lead in Europe. They recognize that individual Jews and Jewish organization are increasingly becoming target of abuse, but they tend to view them as part of the larger trend of violent attacks directed against Europe's minorities (Bunzl 2007, 1–3).

The question of Jewish-Muslims relations looms large in the debate about the new anti-Semitism with the alarmists calling attention to those cases of anti-Semitic violence where the perpetrators are Muslims, and the deniers focusing on the anti-Semitism of the extreme right (Bunzl 2007, 25). Bunzl suggests that as far as the anti-Semitism of the extreme right is concerned it does appear to be a continuation of the old project of excluding the Jews from the national body of Europe. However, when we consider the Islamic component of recent violence directed against Europe's Jews, we have to admit that it is based on a very different idea. Bunzl argues:

> When young, disenfranchised Muslims attack French Jews, they do not do so in the interest of creating an ethnically pure France. Nor are they asserting that French Jews do not belong in Europe. On the contrary, they are attacking Jews precisely because they see them as part of a European hegemony that not only marginalizes them in France, but, from their point of view, also accounts for the suffering of the Palestinians. In the Arab world, Israel, after all, is understood first and foremost as a European colony. (2007, 26–27)

Bunzl suggests that to explain attacks on the Jews as an example of anti-colonial struggle is not to offer an apology for this phenomenon, but to highlight the difference between the realities of the old and the new anti-Semitism: "While the former sought to exclude Jews from the nation-states of Europe, the latter targets Jews precisely because of their Europeanness" (Bunzl 2007, 27). Brian Klug argues in a similar vein that though anti-Semitism is indeed becoming more visible in the public discourse on Israel, "whether in the salon, on 'the street', in the mosque, in the UN or in the media" (2003, 121), it has to be recognized that anti-Semitic propaganda and attacks directed at the Jews intensify when the situation in the Middle East worsens, and "the longer Israel is at loggerheads with the rest of the region, the more likely it is that anti-Semitism will take on a life of its own" (Klug 2003, 134). Indeed, this phenomenon has been well documented historically. Thus Bernard Lewis suggests in his discussion of published anti-Jewish materials circulating in the Arab world that anti-Semitism in the Middle East significantly intensified following the Sinai War of 1956 and the Six-Day War of 1967 (Lewis 1991, 349). Drawing on the example of contemporary Arab interpretations of the Quranic references to the Jews, Suha Taji-Farouki demonstrates how the political climate of confrontation with Israel influenced the way

Quranic constructions of the Jews were discussed by authors from the Middle East (Taji-Farouki 1998).

The argument about the impact of Arab-Israeli conflict on the emergence of anti-Semitism in certain Muslim circles is supported ethnographically by studies in the social sciences. For instance, Paul Silverstein argues in his discussion of anti-Semitism and Islamophobia in France and North Africa that the younger generation of French Muslims draws parallels between such phenomena as the occupation of Iraq and of Palestinian Territories and their own condition of discrimination in France, and that their response to the French state can take on the form of both anti-Zionism and anti-Semitism (2010, 143–144). At the same time, he problematizes the nature of Jewish-Muslim relations in contemporary Europe even further by demonstrating that while in some cases the state oppression that North African immigrants and their children encounter in France is responded to with violence directed against the Jews, in other cases Muslim populations in France and North Africa, such as Berber activists, identify with persecuted Jews and espouse "philo-Semitic" and pro-Israeli attitudes, which shows that the mutual animosity of Jews and Muslims in France as differently positioned subjects is not by any means inevitable (2010, 144).

This chapter continues academic discussions about Jewish-Muslim relations in the contemporary world by looking at the example of South Asia, where, like in Europe, Jews and Muslims constitute "minority" communities—Muslims representing the largest and Jews being one of the smallest. The histories of their formation as well as relationship patterns that the two communities developed with their neighbors in South Asia are rather different from those of Jewish and Muslim diasporas overseas. In Europe, the Jews have had a long and difficult history of being perceived as the "ultimate other" (Gilman and Katz 1991, 1); in India, they have always constituted only a tiny, though very diverse, community, one among many other religious groups. Muslims, on the contrary, have for a long time represented a numerically strong population in South Asia, but within Europe became numerically and politically significant only in the second half of the twentieth century. I argue that an analysis of Jewish-Muslim relations in South Asia can illuminate a number of nodal points in Jewish-Muslim collaboration and conflict in the contemporary world, such as the impact of the situation in the Middle East and of the local structural settings on the two communities' mutual perceptions and attitudes, and the interaction of complex and conflicting processes which are at work in the production of such phenomena as anti-Semitism/philo-Semitism and Islamophobia/Islamophilia.

The remainder of this chapter consists of two parts. In the first part, I highlight the main themes in the mutual perceptions of Indian Jews and Muslims as they were reflected in the printed sources of the Bene Israel Jewish community of the Konkan coast.[1] These sources, which come from the later British period (end of the nineteenth

---

1. Konkan coast is a section of the western coast of India in what is now the state of Maharashtra.

through the first half of the twentieth century), index key issues in the relationship between the two communities, such as the impact of the Zionist movement and the situation in Palestine, and tropes of Jewish-Muslim cooperation in a country where both communities constitute a minority. In the second part of the chapter I focus on an episode from my recent fieldwork conducted among the Bene Ephraim of Andhra Pradesh to demonstrate how the issues mentioned above continue to inform Jewish-Muslims relations in India today having incorporated discourses on Israel's defense, elements of Dalit activism, and the rhetoric of the "war on terror."

Jews, Muslims, and India

The Jewish communities of India consist of three main groups: the Jews of Cochin, the Bene Israel, and the Baghdadi Jews.[2] The Jews of Cochin, resident in the Indian state of Kerala, represent the oldest Indian Jewish community, whose documented history dates back to the Middle Ages. The Baghdadi Jews comprise the descendants of Arabic-speaking Jews who came to India in the eighteenth and nineteenth centuries and settled mainly in the cities of Bombay and Calcutta. The Bene Israel, at the same time, became known to some Western audiences only in the eighteenth century. According to a Bene Israel legend, their ancestors arrived on the Konkan coast of western India in 175 BC after they fled ancient Palestine to escape the persecutions of Antiochus Epiphanes. Their community originally resided mainly on the Konkan coast, where it was "discovered" by a Christian missionary back in the eighteenth century. Their early practices were reminiscent of Judaic ones, and in the course of the nineteenth century the Jews of Cochin, the Baghdadi Jews, and Jewish visitors from Europe gradually introduced the community to a wider spectrum of the Jewish religion. After the establishment of the State of Israel the majority of Indian Jews made an *aliyah*.[3] At the moment there are about four thousand Jewish people left in India, most of whom belong to the Bene Israel community resident in and near Mumbai. The second half of the twentieth century witnessed the development of two Judaizing movements[4] on the subcontinent—that of the Bene Menashe (also known as Shinlung), who emerged in the early 1950s from the Christianized tribes settled in the Indian states of Mizoram, Manipur, Assam, and the plains of Burma, and of the Bene Ephraim of Andhra Pradesh, who come from the community of Madiga Dalits (untouchables) and established their first synagogue in 1991.[5]

---

2. For research on the Bene Israel, Cochini and Baghdadi Jews of India, see, for instance, Isenberg 1988; Katz 1999; Katz et al 2007; Roland 1999; and Weil 2002; 2005.
3. *Aliyah* (Hebrew for ascent)—immigration of the Jewish people to the State of Israel.
4. For a wider context of Judaizing movements, see Parfitt and Trevisan Semi 2002.
5. For more information on the Bene Menashe, see Samra 1996 and Weil 2003; for the Bene Ephraim, see Egorova and Perwez 2012.

The community that has had the closest documented contacts with Indian Muslims is probably that of the Bene Israel. Community sources from the later British period suggest that the relations between the two groups had been good and involved instances of cooperation. Moreover, according to one narrative, the very first synagogue of the Bene Israel community owes its existence to an Indian Muslim. Thus, D. J. Samson writing in a Bene Israel periodical in 1919 observes the following:

> It is very important to note that the Mohomedans in India have treated the Bene Israel with great consideration; in fact they have all along looked upon them as brethren. Such treatment was very noticeable in the native regiments of the British in India. From personal knowledge gained in my early days I can vouch for the correctness of the above statement. It is also important to point out that Mohomedans have allowed the Bene-Israel dead to be buried in a portion of their cemetery in town where no separate Bene-Israel cemeteries existed. (Samson 1919, 33)

The trope of cooperation through ritual appears to be an important theme of South Asian Jewish-Muslim relations throughout the past century. Caste Hindus in India cremate their dead, which, in part, distinguishes them from Indian Christians, Muslims, or Jews. Use of the Muslim cemetery when the Bene Israel did not have one of their own was likely to create a bridge of collaboration and to draw attention to the similarities of the two traditions. The author then goes on to remind the reader about how the first Bene Israel synagogue emerged (Samson 1919, 33–34).[6] According to the community's narrative, the synagogue, constructed in Bombay in 1796, was founded by Samuel Ezekiel Divekar, a commander in the British Native Infantry regiment. During the Second Anglo-Mysore War (1780–1784) he (and, according to some versions of the story, a number of other Bene Israel soldiers) was captured by the forces of Tippu Sultan, the Muslim ruler of the Sultanate of Mysore. Divekar made a vow that if he survived captivity he would build a synagogue. The story goes that when Tippu Sultan's mother learnt that one of the prisoners was a Bene Israel, she asked her son to free him on the grounds that his community was often referred to in the Qur'an.[7] As a result of this intervention, Divekar was set free and returned to Bombay, where he constructed the first Bene Israel synagogue.[8]

This narrative shows that the Muslim community of the subcontinent was an important reference point for the Bene Israel. At the same time, community sources from the later British period point out that local Muslims viewed the Bene Israel differently from other Jews. For instance, D. J. Samson finishes his story about Divekar's rescue in the following way: "This incident shows that the Mohomedans in India have

6. Ibid., 33–34.
7. There are 43 references in the Qur'an to Banu Israel (Arabic for The Children of Israel), one of the Arabic names used to describe the Jews.
8. For a discussion of different versions of this narrative, see Roland 1999, 309–310.

always treated the Bene-Israel with great consideration. In fact Mohomedans make a distinction between the Bene-Israel and the Yehudies."[9]

Other Bene Israel sources of the same period corroborate that some Indian Muslims were not entirely free from anti-Jewish prejudice and that one of the reasons why they treated the Bene Israel well was precisely because they categorized them differently from other Jews. For instance, a Bene Israel historian Haeem Samuel Kehimkar[10] observes at the end of the nineteenth century that in 1882 a Muslim periodical *Kassid-i-Bombay* published an article accusing the Jews in Persia of killing a Muslim boy and using his blood for ritual purposes. According to Kehimkar, following this publication, some Muslims "had commenced murmuring at the Bene-Israel" (Kehimkar, 1937).

Blood libels have a long and tragic history involving extreme violence toward the Jews, and their history is firmly rooted in the European anti-Jewish discourse. Sander Gilman and Steven Katz have observed that "[t]he role of the Jew as the essential Other in the Christian West . . . must be raised in any discussion concerning the history of anti-Semitism" (1991, 2). Blood libels are one vivid example of European anti-Semitic imagery transferred to other parts of the world. As Lewis notes, blood libels were not known to Muslim history until the Ottomans learnt about them from their Christian subjects, and European consular and clerical missions played a part in the propagation of these ideas as well (1991, 348). The accusation of ritual killing published in *Kassid-i-Bombay* is an example of age-old European anti-Semitic propaganda finding its way into a Muslim publication, but its consequences, which could have turned out to be disastrous, appear to have been mitigated by the generally peaceful nature of Jewish-Muslim relations in Bombay. A representative of the Bene Israel community requested the editor of *Kassid-i-Bombay* to apologize and the latter expressed his regret for the publication (Kehimkar 1937, 96–98).

At the same time, it is noteworthy that both sides in this brief dispute distinguished between the "Jews" and the "Bene-Israel." Kehimkar notes that this event generated "every possibility of a riot being raised against the Jews and Bene-Israel." The editor of *Kassid-i-Bombay* writes in reply, "We are indeed sorry if the feelings of the Jews and Bene-Israel community are thereby offended; and if, with reference to this, a Jew or Bene-Israel should be pleased to forward any correspondence we will gladly publish it in our Journal" (Kehimkar 1937, 97–98).

What caused this distinction? Kehimkar observes elsewhere in his book that the ancestors of the Bene Israel took this name "during the time when the Mohamedan power prevailed in India," precisely out of fear of being persecuted by the Muslims

---

9. Samson 1919, 34. Yehudi is Arabic and Urdu for Jewish.
10. Haeem Samuel Kehimkar (1831–1908) completed his manuscript on the Bene Israel in 1897, but was unable to publish it during his life-time. The manuscript was eventually published by Immanuel Olsvanger in Palestine.

who supposedly were prejudiced against the name Yehudi. The historian even argues that in the course of time the members of his community "made it a point to deny that they were 'Yehudim' [Hebrew, pl.] or Jews and felt insulted if any one called them by that name, for a reproachful rejoinder, such as the word Kufree (heretic) was sure to follow the use of this word" (Kehimkar 1937, 74–75).

However, it appears from the same sources that though local Muslims may have had negative perceptions of the Jews in general, these attitudes were never directed at the Bene Israel. Indeed, as we saw above, the blood libel accusation never resulted in anti-Jewish riots in Bombay and the editor apologized for the publication. Gilman and Katz suggest that in Europe different and seemingly separate episodes of anti-Jewish prejudice built upon a common perception (Gilman and Katz 1991, 5). The episode described above illuminates both the continuous and context-dependent nature of anti-Jewish prejudice. On the one hand, it builds upon a medieval European myth. On the other hand, local Muslim attitudes toward the Jews appear to have bifurcated into prejudices directed against the "Jews" in general and a much more positive perception of the Bene Israel community, who were their immediate neighbors. Klug has suggested that anti-Semitism could be described as "the process of turning Jews into 'Jews,' a category of people with a set of stereotypes associated with them" (2003, 124). It may be suggested that for the editor of *Kassid-i-Bombay* the Bene Israel were Jews as a people, while other Jews—particularly those based abroad—were "Jews" as a category, and he clearly distinguished between the two.

How did the Bene Israel relate to instances of anti-Jewish prejudice like the one involving the blood libel? The fact that these negative sentiments that some local Muslims may have harbored against the Jews never led to any violence was probably one of the reasons why Indian Jewish sources from the turn of the twentieth century were so positive about local Muslims and tended to emphasize the good aspects of this relationship and to stress the similarities of ritual between Judaism and Islam. The same sources indicate that the Bene Israel identified very strongly as Jews, however, they were ready to invoke the specificity of their Bene Israel rather than general Jewish background when describing local Jewish-Muslim relations. On the one hand, as the incident with the blood libel publication demonstrates, they were prepared to challenge anti-Jewish prejudice. On the other hand, they were happy to build upon a narrative that distinguished them favorably from the rest of the Jews in the eyes of their Muslim neighbors.

In the first half of the twentieth century Indian Muslim attitudes toward the Jews and Judaism were affected by the Palestine issue when many Muslims adopted a negative attitude toward Zionism. After the First World War, M. A. Ansari and the Ali brothers launched the Khilafat movement, which argued that Palestine must remain under Muslim rule (Roland 1999, 84). The movement disintegrated in 1924, but the tradition of anti-Zionist sentiments among Indian Muslims survived. For instance, in 1933, the twenty-third session of the All-India Muslim League, a political party which advocated the establishment of an independent Muslim nation on the subcontinent, passed a resolution criticizing British policy in Palestine and requesting the Viceroy of India to convey to the British government the demand of Indian Muslims that the Balfour Declaration be rescinded (Pirzada 1970, 225–226). In the 1930s, the anti-Semitism associated with Muslim sentiments about the situation in Palestine was exacerbated by Nazi propaganda. Hitler's Germany made a concerted effort to promote its ideology among the Muslims in the Middle East (Lewis 1991, 348) and the Muslim community of India appears to have become targeted by this campaign, too. In this respect, one could quote a letter sent to the Indian Jewish periodical *Jewish Tribune* by an Indian Muslim sympathetic to the Jews urging support for the victims of Nazism. He observed with regret that many Indian Muslims had turned out to be susceptible to Nazi propaganda and were "happy to hear that the Jews were being persecuted in Germany and Austria" (*Jewish Tribune* 1938, 23).

To return to the theoretical debates about the relationship between anti-Zionism and anti-Semitism with which I started the chapter, it can be suggested that the negative attitudes toward the Jews described in this episode appear to intersect with anti-Zionism and may have partly been produced by the conflict in Palestine. It is clear that they were directed against the Jews—the victims of Nazi persecutions in Europe—rather than specifically against Zionism.[11] However, it also seems that they did not affect the local Jewish communities. Interestingly, almost foreseeing current debates about the nature of the "new anti-Semitis," a contemporary Bene Israel commentator suggested that it could only be expected that the situation in Palestine would have a negative impact on Jewish-Muslim relations in the diaspora. In 1923, the *Israelite* published an article observing that "in countries ruled by Islam, autonomous existence of aliens has not often been disturbed" and that Christendom had produced more outbursts of faith-infused violence that the Muslim world. Writing about local Muslims, the author revisits the main narratives of Indian Jewish-Muslim relations and suggests that the Palestine issue is likely to adversely affect them:

> . . . for us in India our Muslim neighbours have proved particularly kind. No distinction has ever been shown and help has been rendered even at burials wherever we happened to be few and isolated. It is yet fresh in memory, that some of our ancestors, to whom is partly due our status in India, owed their lives to the mother of Tipoo Sultan. . . . Will the Muslims of India be the same to us, as they have been, if our brethren in Palestine irritate their brethren there! (*Israelite* 1923, 103–104)

For the author of this quote, an anti-Jewish backlash aimed directly at the Bene Israel would be an expected and almost justifiable reaction to the conflict in Palestine.

---

11. For an in-depth discussion of the Indian attitudes toward the Holocaust, see Sareen 1999. For the Indian responses toward European Jewish refugees in India, see Weil 1999.

He suggests that anti-Semitism may become an unavoidable outcome of the structural tensions to be produced by the Zionist effort if the interests of the Muslim population of Palestine were not safeguarded. By reminding the reader about the Divekar episode and the help that the Bene Israel had received from local Muslims in matters of burial, the author also explicitly promotes the idea of a special connection between the two communities. As we will see in the following section, nowadays, almost a century later, the trope of Jewish-Muslim similarities is still supported by Indian Jews; however, it has to share space with images produced by global discourses of Islamophobia.

Caste between Judaism and Islam

When I first visited the village of Kothareddypalem in the Guntur district of coastal Andhra in 2001, Sadok Yacobi, the leader of the Bene Ephraim—a small community of former Madiga Dalits—took me to the local mosque to talk to his friends. Both Sadok and his Muslim companions stressed that the two communities had a special connection and that, in the conditions of India, where both represented "minority" communities, this connection was particularly important.

Nine years later, during Shahid Perwez's fieldwork in the village, he noted that Sadok's Muslim friend provided catering for the festivals in the synagogue. When we later interviewed this person and asked him what he thought about the Bene Ephraim tradition, he replied that he had a lot of respect for their leaders and did not object to them practicing Judaism, but that he was not convinced that they had always been Jewish. When we inquired about what in his opinion had prompted them to embrace Judaism he laughed and said, "Israel needs people to fight for her."

This brief statement contains a number of implicit assumptions about Judaism, Jewishness, and the relationship between the Jews and the State of Israel. It suggests a denial of agency for the Bene Ephraim, and an implicit denial of the possibility of a community embracing Judaism on its own accord, without interference from Israel and without a promise of material gain. Such assumptions, which are not limited to the Muslim discourse but are demonstrated by a number of local commentators, build upon age-old anti-Semitic stereotypes about perceived Jewish wealth. What comes here anew is a reference to the conflict in the Middle East and an explicit suggestion that if the Bene Ephraim were to succeed in their attempt to immigrate, they would be fighting Israel's neighbors. Here the Jewishness of the Bene Ephraim, which in one context—the reality of Judaism and Islam being "minority" religions in India—is seen as a positive identity marker, in the context of the conflict in the Middle East is construed as a threat.

Similarly, the Bene Ephraim perceive Indian Muslims as friends in the general course of Indian religious life and as a potential threat in the context of synagogue security. In 2004, the community made headlines when the police of Hyderabad (the capital of the state of Andhra Pradesh) uncovered a plot by alleged agents of a militarist organization based in Pakistan Lashkar-e-Tayyiba (later implicated in the Mumbai attacks of 2008) to attack Americans in Hyderabad and the Jewish families in Guntur. According to the *Times of India*, it was the first time that anybody in Andhra Pradesh realized that there were Jews in this district (*Times of India* 2004). After this incident and subsequently after the Mumbai attacks, the community applied to the police to increase security measures for them in the village of Kothareddypalem where they built a synagogue.

When I visited the community a few months after the Mumbai attacks, I was shown faint traces of the Star of David and other Jewish symbols on the huts of the Bene Ephraim that had to be washed off for some period of time. This was explained as a strategy to avoid a possible terrorist attack on Jewish houses. I also witnessed the community leaders, Sadok and Shmuel Yacobi, communicating with local newspaper reporters and stressing their need for more protection.

When talking about their fears of terrorists, community members kept stressing that their relations with the Muslims in the village were exceptionally good, as their religious traditions were similar. They said that they respected the Muslim religion, but at the same time were fearful about the possibility of Islamist terrorist organizations attacking the synagogue. In a different episode, the leaders of the community associated the perceived threat of terrorism with Islam much more explicitly. When Shahid Perwez, who conducted fieldwork among the Bene Ephraim, first met the Yacobis face-to-face, the latter initially expressed concern about his Indian Muslim background. Shahid had to offer a long explanation regarding the nature of this research, as well as his attitude toward terrorism, after which the Yacobis granted him a permission to continue with our work and welcomed him into the community. Once Shahid settled in the village, the Jewish signs and symbols reappeared on the Bene Ephraim homes. He was fully accepted in the community and doubts about his intentions were never raised again.

What caused the community to apply for enhanced protection and make their concerns known to the mass media? The Bene Ephraim were of course bound to feel that the Mumbai attacks, which involved what was probably the first organized violent attack carried out on Indian soil against Jewish people on account of them being Jewish or Israeli, were too close to home. However, their perception of the community's security issues also appears to be intertwined with their experiences and accounts of discrimination. The Judaization of the Bene Ephraim could be seen as a protest against caste inequality, in the process of which the community developed narratives comparing their condition of discrimination to that of the Jewish people. It is not surprising then that for the Yacobis portraying their community as victims of international terrorism meant re-asserting their Jewishness and establishing a connection with the Jewish communities worldwide. It was also supposed to attract the attention of the Israeli government and of international Jewish organizations. That is not to say that their fears of potential attacks on the synagogue are unfounded, but to highlight the very special nature of the community's discourse on "Islamic terrorism" which in an unusual interplay of collective historical memories reflects both the reality of anti-Jewish attacks worldwide and the character of the Indian social system.

It is noteworthy that their inclination to describe caste discrimination in terms which would be more familiar to wider audiences mirrors the attempts of other Dalit groups to internationalize their condition. To give one such example, some Dalit leaders have tried to equate caste discrimination with racism. They argued that the severity of their oppression is comparable to, if not worse than, that of Black communities in the West. This issue was debated in the preparations for the World Conference against Racism, Racial Discrimination, Xenophobia and Related Intolerance, which was held in 2001 in Durban. The Dalits argued that caste discrimination should be considered racism and put on the agenda of the conference, while the Indian government insisted on it being unconnected to race (Sabir 2003; Hardtmann 2009).

In the case of the Bene Ephraim, emphasizing the possibility of becoming victims of Islamist terrorist attacks was also a way of attracting the attention of the wider international community and establishing an extra link with the Jewish State. Just like the Dalits who participated in the preparations for the conference in Durban and felt that they could not succeed in their fight against discrimination without support from overseas, the Bene Ephraim are more hopeful about the possible support of Israel and Jewish communities worldwide than about getting help from the local authorities or the Indian government. Shmuel Yacobi once explicitly told me that the only hope for the Dalits to improve their social position was to seek help outside of India. It is not surprising then that the community's self-representation as victims of caste domination had to give way to expressions of concern about the possibility of becoming victims of terrorist attacks. Or, to draw on Shryock's insight, the Islamophobic sentiments that the community exhibited in relation to Indian Muslims ultimately has very little to do with Islam, and is embedded in the wider problematics of caste discrimination, the reality of security issues facing Jewish communities around the world and the politics of Jewish identity arbitration in the State of Israel.

Conclusion

In the episodes described above Indian Jews and Muslims appear to be going beyond simplistic constructions of "bad-Jews/Muslims" versus "good-Jews/Muslims."[12] The Bene Israel of Bombay of the turn of the century had to take up the issue of the blood libel with an Indian Muslim editor and admit that they preferred to call themselves

---

12. For a discussion of this dichotomy in respect of Muslims, see Shryock 2010.

Bene Israel as opposed to Jews for fear of persecution, but they nevertheless described their relations with local Muslims as very positive. A contributor to the *Israelite* suggested that though Muslims were very supportive of the Bene Israel, they could be expected to turn against them if the situation in Palestine exacerbated. The Muslim friend of the Bene Ephraim leaders sees the community as a potential threat to the Muslims of the Middle East, and yet, he respects their religious beliefs and helps the Bene Ephraim during synagogue functions. Andrew Shryock suggests in his discussion of the relationship between Islamophobia and Islamophilia, that what presents a real challenge in countering Islamophobic sentiments is the danger of reinforcing them by cultivating images of the opposite: "When friendship is subordinated to the demands of sameness—whether conceived in national or human terms—it can be just as coercive, just as prone to misrecognition, as the sentiments of hostility it is meant to correct" (2010, 9). In the examples considered here, the relationship between Jews and Muslims has witnessed tropes of sameness sharing space with images of uncompromising difference, and the realities of local social organization intersecting with issues of international politics.

To paraphrase Brian Klug, both parties turn Jews into "Jews" and Muslims into "Muslims" in some contexts, but still relate to them as individuals or groups not associated with any stereotypes in other contexts. Moreover, as we saw in the examples from Andhra Pradesh, even when local Jews and Muslims engage in using stereotypes which are explicitly anti-Jewish or Islamophobic, they carefully negotiate the boundary between a Jewish or Muslim person as a person and as a symbol of the perceived threat associated with their religious affiliation. The "Jews" and "Muslims" that they fear are categories produced by the realities of Indian and international politics and on many levels both communities make an effort to ensure that their attitude toward these categories does not affect the actual relationships between the people. However, it is not hard to see how under different circumstances their hostility toward "Jews" and "Muslims" as symbols can develop into hostility toward Jews and Muslims as people. As we know only too well, animosity toward the State of Israel has resulted in numerous instances of anti-Jewish violence, and the Bene Ephraim may not be immune from it. Similarly, though the numbers of Indian Jews and Muslims are such that it would be hard to imagine an anti-Muslim riot organized by the Jews, their rhetoric of the "war on terror" contributes to the general vilification of Islam, which may lead to anti-Muslim communal violence of which independent India has a well-documented and tragic history.

References

Bunzl, Matt. *Anti-Semitism and Islamophobia: Hatreds Old and New in Europe.* Chicago: Prickly Paradigm Press, 2007.

Egorova, Yulia, and Shahid Perwez. "Old Memories, New Histories: (Re)discovering the Past of Jewish Dalits." *History and Anthropology* 23, no. 1 (2012): 1–15.

Fatah, Tarek. *The Jew is Not My Enemy: Unveiling the Myths that Fuel Muslim Anti-Semitism.* Toronto: MacCleland & Stewart, 2010.

Gilman, Sander, and Steven T. Katz. "Introduction." In *Anti-Semitism in Times of Crisis*, edited by Sander Gilman and Steven T. Katz, 1–19. New York: New York University Press, 1991.

Hardtmann, Eva-Maria. *The Dalit Movement in India: Local Practices, Global Connections.* New Delhi: Oxford University Press, 2009.

Isenberg, Shirley Berry. *India's Bene Israel: A Comprehensive Inquiry and Source Book.* Bombay: Popular Prakashan, 1998.

Israelite 7, nos. 7–8 (1923): 103–104.

Jewish Tribune. September 1938, 23.

Katz, Nathan. *Who Are the Jews of India?* Berkeley: University of California Press, 2000.

Katz, Nathan, Ranabir Chakrabarty, Braj M.Singh, and Shalva Weil, eds. *Indo-Judaic Studies in the Twenty-First Century: A View from the Margin.* New York: Palgrave Macmillan, 2007.

Kehimkar, Hayim Samuel. *History of the Bene-Israel of India.* Tel Aviv: Dayag Press, 1937.

Klug, Brian. "The Collective Jew: Israel and the New Anti-Semitism." *Patterns of Prejudice*, 37, no. 2 (2003): 117–138.

Lewis, Bernard. "The Arab World Discovers Anti-Semitism." In *Anti-Semitism in Times of Crisis*, edited by Sander Gilman and Steven T. Katz, 342–352. New York: New York University Press, 1991.

Parfitt, Tudor, and Emanuela Semi. *Judaising Movements: Studies in the Margins of Judaism.* London: Routledge Curzon, 2002.

Pirzada, Syed Sharif Uddin, ed. *Foundations of Pakistan, All-India Muslim League Documents, vol. 2.* Karachi: National Publishing House, 1970.

Prashad, Vijay. "Afro-Dalits of the Earth, Unite!" *African Studies Review*, 43 (2000): 189–201.

Quigley, Declan. *The Interpretation of Caste.* Oxford: Clarendon Press, 1993.

Reedy, Deepa S. "The Ethnicity of Caste." *Anthropological Quarterly*, 78 (2005): 543–584.

Roland, Joan G. *The Jewish Communities of India: Identity in a Colonial Era.* New Brunswick: Transactions Publishers, 1999.

Sabir, S. "Chimerical Categories: Caste, Race and Genetics." *Developing World Bioethics*, 2 (2003): 170–177.

Samra, M. "Buallawn Israel: The Emergence of a Judaising Movement in Mizoram, Northeast India." In *Religious Change, Conversion and Culture*, edited by L. Olson, 106–132. Sydney: Association for Studies in Society and Culture, 1996.

Samson, D. J. "The Purity of Descent of the Bene-Israel." *The Israelite* 3, nos. 3–4 (March–April 1919): 33.

Sankar, Levi M. "Anti-Semitism: Why It Is Not an Issue in Pakistan." *National Post*, October 16, 2010. Accessed November 1, 2012. http://fullcomment.nationalpost.com/2010/10/16/todays-letters-i-stand-guilty-with-capt-semrau/.

Sareen, Tilak Raj. "Indian Responses to the Holocaust." In *Jewish Exile in India, 1933–1945*, edited by Anil Bhatti and Johannes H. Voigt, 171–183. New Delhi: Manohar, 1999.

Shryock, Andrew. "Introduction: Islam as an Object of Fear and Affection." In *Islamophobia/Islamophilia: Beyond the Politics of Enemy and Friend*, edited by Andrew Shyrock, 1–28. Bloomington: Indiana University Press, 2010.

Silverstein, Paul A. "The Fantasy and Violence of Religious Imagination: Islamophobia and Anti-Semitism in France and North Africa." In *Islamophobia/Islamophilia: Beyond the*

Politics of Enemy and Friend, edited by Andrew Shryock, 141–171. Bloomington: Indiana University Press, 2010.

Taji-Farouki, Suha. "Jews in the Qur'an: A Review of Muhammad Sayyid Tantawi's Banu Isra'il fi al-Qur'an and al-Sunna and 'Afif'Abd al-Fattah Tabbar''s Al-Yahud fi al-Qur'an." In *Muslim-Jewish Encounters: Intellectual Traditions and Modern Politics*, edited by Suha Taji-Farouki and Ronald L. Nettler, 15–37. Newark, NJ: Harwood Academic Publishers, 1998.

Weil, Shalva. "Dual Conversion among the Shinlung in North-East India." *Studies in Tribes and Tribals* 1, no. 1 (2003): 43–57.

———. "From Persecution to Freedom: Central European Jewish Refugees and Their Jewish Host Communities in India." In *Jewish Exile in India, 1933–1945*, edited by Anil Bhatti and Johannes H. Voigt, 64–84. New Delhi: Manohar, 1999.

———. *India's Jewish Heritage: Ritual, Art, and Life Cycle*. Mumbai: Marg, 2002.

———. "Motherland and Fatherland as Dichotomous Diasporas: The Case of the Bene Israel." In *Les diasporas: 2000 ans d'histoire*, edited by Lisa Anteby-Yemini, William Berthomière and Gabriel Sheffer, 91–100. Rennes: Presses Universitaires de Rennes, 2005.

7

The Damascus Affair and the Debate on Ritual Murder in Early Victorian Britain

David Feldman

The Damascus Affair in History

On February 5, 1840, two men disappeared from the streets of Damascus. One was a Capuchin monk, Padre Tommaso, the second his servant, Ibrahim Amara. The double-disappearance and possible murder required an investigation that was undertaken by the Ottoman governor-general of Syria, Sherif Pasha, and the French consul, Count de Ratti-Menton. The consul's involvement arose from the capitulatory agreement between the French government and the Porte, under which the Roman Catholic clergy in the Ottoman Empire enjoyed the protection of France. Within ten days Sherif Pasha had arrested, tortured, and interrogated three Jews. One died, but the two others confessed their knowledge of the murders, disclosed they had been committed to procure human blood for "Passover dough," and implicated other wealthy and prominent local Jews in the crime. Further arrests, tortures, and confessions followed. By March, ten men were sentenced to be hanged. At this point, Sherif Pasha paused. He was obliged to await confirmation of the executions from his superior, the Viceroy of Egypt, Mehemet Ali.[1]

The timeworn calumny that Jews use the blood of Christians in their rituals might appear a counterintuitive starting point for an exploration of co-operation as well as conflict between Christians, Muslims, and Jews. However, accusations can be opposed as well as upheld, cast into the rubbish heap of discarded superstitions, as well as elevated into truths universally acknowledged. The "Damascus Affair" is an episode that ended happily for the Jews. On September 6, orders to set free the Jewish prisoners reached the city, and two months later the Sultan issued a *firman*, declaring the ritual murder accusation to be without foundation. In Britain, the episode concluded with the Jews' public exoneration. Journalists and correspondents to newspapers who had been prepared to give the accusation credence or serious consideration

I am grateful to Julie Kalman for her comments on an earlier version of this chapter.

1. There is a large literature on the Damascus Affairs but I am principally indebted to Jonathan Frankel's magnificent account and analysis in *The Damascus Affair: "Ritual Murder", Politics and the Jews in 1840* (1997). See also the report by George Wildon Pieritz in Salomons 1840.

were silenced. This essay focuses on British responses to the Damascus accusation and why the Jews were vindicated.

In spring 1840 the situation looked bleak for the Jews. Most obviously this was the case in Damascus but it also appeared to be so on the island of Rhodes where there was a contemporaneous but shorter lived blood libel (Frankel 1997, 68–72, 162–163). Moreover, these events in the Ottoman Empire reverberated in West and Central Europe. In Britain, the charges received wide attention, not least in Parliament and the press. The issue, it seemed, carried implications for Jews and Judaism everywhere, and not only in the Ottoman lands. If the allegations were true, the *Times* proposed, "The Jewish religion must at once disappear from the face of the earth." If, on the other hand, the Jews were vindicated, then the cause of Jewish emancipation would be strengthened and Jews would then "appeal to all Europe for a final remission of those disabilities to which in countries still calling themselves civilized they are still exposed."[2]

In his magisterial account of these events, Jonathan Frankel counsels against an excessively optimistic narrative. This was not, as many contemporaries and the great nineteenth-century German Jewish historian, Heinrich Graetz, mistakenly believed, a triumph for Western "toleration," "civilization," and "progress" over a "despotic," "barbarous," and "fanatical" East. Graetz, Frankel argues, underestimated the degree to which the Damascus accusations were treated as an open question in Europe and became a lightning rod for opponents of the established order, from Catholics legitimists in France to radical nationalists in Germany. Moreover, it was the representatives of the French liberal monarchy, both in Paris and Damascus, who numbered among the Jews' most dangerous opponents and it was from the illiberal Hapsburg Empire that Jews received their staunchest support through the crisis. The optimistic narrative, Frankel points out, appears still less convincing once we notice that 1840 did not mark an end to claims that Jews murder Christians and take their blood. The decades that followed witnessed an increase in such accusations across Central and Eastern Europe (Frankel 1997, 436–442).

Yet Frankel's revisionism becomes muted once he turns to Britain. In this respect he keeps faith with Graetz's emphasis on Britain as the fount of enlightened public opinion. He writes, "to leave continental Europe and examine the stance adopted by the English press in 1840 is to enter not simply another country but another world" (Frankel 1997, 143). One aim of this chapter is to reassess British responses to the Damascus affair. In doing so we have one advantage earlier scholars did not enjoy: the digitization of large parts of the Victorian press. This allows us to make a wide survey of what was written about the affair as well to reassess more familiar material.

If the Damascus affair can no longer credibly be construed as one moment in the longer history of the triumph of tolerance over prejudice, how then should we

---

2. *Times*, June 25, 1840, 12.

regard it? This chapter proposes that, in part, it can be seen as an episode in the history of knowledge and belief: specifically, in the history of the knowledge and beliefs Christians had about Jews. In early nineteenth-century Europe, observant Jews remained mysterious, a people apart. Even in Britain, where there had been some desacralization of Jewish life, the Jews' patterns of work, residence, sociability, marriage, and worship meant that to a considerable degree they were simultaneously visible and opaque (Endelman 1979). In the midst of the Damascus crisis, one magazine reflected, "We know nothing about the Jews except as bill brokers, money agents and old clothesmen. They marry among themselves, and keep their secrets to themselves. Nobody knows what their religion may be."[3] The comment prompts a significant question. How could Britons in the early nineteenth century know that Jews did not kill Christians and use their blood in religious rites? It is this question that the present study takes as its starting point.

False and Atrocious Charges

As early as March 18, 1840, the *Times* carried a report that deplored the "barbarous prejudice and persecuting spirit" which had led to accusations of ritual murder, arrest and torture on the island of Rhodes and in Damascus.[4] West and Central European Jewish elites mobilized slowly in response to this and other reports. In France, the dire position of the Jews in Damascus was publicized by Adolphe Cremieux, a lawyer and vice president of the *Consistoire Central des Israelites*, in a letter published in two newspapers on April 8. In London it was not until April 21 that the Board of Deputies of British Jews gathered for a "special meeting," held at the home of Sir Moses Montefiore, to discuss the ritual murder case in Damascus. That meeting was attended not only by representatives of the London synagogues, but also by other leading figures from the Anglo-Jewish elite and by Cremieux (Frankel 1997, 109–110).[5]

The London meeting generated four resolutions. One offered thanks to Cremieux, but the others confronted the blood libel in terms that characterized the language used by prominent Jews and their supporters until November, when the controversy subsided. The resolutions expressed the meeting's "extreme concern and disgust" at the "false and atrocious charges" lately revived against Jews in the East. These charges had been "so frequently brought against the Jews during the Middle Ages" and "repeatedly had served as a pretext for the robbery and massacre of persons of the Jewish faith." Happily these charges had "long since disappeared from this part of

3. *The Satirist or, The Censor of the Times*, June 26, 1840, 201.
4. *Times*, March 18, 1840, 3.
5. London Metropolitan Archives, Board of Deputies of British Jews, Minute Book, Acc/3121/A5/A, April 21, 1840, Special meeting of the Board held at the residence of Sir Moses Montefiore.

the world, with the fierce and furious prejudices that gave them birth." Other resolutions highlighted the imprisonment of Jewish children and the torture of adults.
The accusations leveled in Damascus were thus presented as necessarily false. They
were characteristic of an age surpassed "in this part of the world."[6] The detail of the
charges, therefore, did not receive attention: their dishonorable provenance, as well as
the manner in which they were brought, were evidence enough that they were untrue.

The resolutions were not only for the edification of the small number who had
assembled at Montefiore's house. They were advertised in twelve London and seventeen provincial newspapers. In this way, the Board of Deputies tried to shape public
opinion. The elite of British Jewry flattered the British public at the same time that
it narrated the atrocities inflicted on Jews in Damascus. The similarity between the
treatment of Jews in the distant domestic past and in the contemporary near East
served to confirm that Britain was now a civilized, modern, and tolerant nation. The
Pasha's disregard for children and for the principle that physical punishment should
follow rather than precede conviction reinforced the same point.

The meeting also gave rise to a burst of activity. Not only did the Board broadcast the resolutions it had passed unanimously, it also arranged for the publication
of letters received from Constantinople and Rhodes. These provided pitiful accounts
of the sufferings of the Jews in those places. More than this, Joseph Henriques, the
president of the Board, sent the resolutions and letters to Her Majesty's Secretary of
State for Foreign Affairs, Lord Palmerston.[7] Results followed swiftly. Over the following two weeks the letters from Constantinople and Rhodes were carried or reported
in numerous additional publications the length breadth of the United Kingdom: from
the *Caledonian Mercury* and *Newcastle Courier* to the *North Wales Chronicle* and the
Hampshire Telegraph and Essex Chronicle. The accounts appeared not only in the
Times, a self-consciously Tory publication, but also in the *Northern Star*, the pre-emi-
nent voice of the radical Chartist movement.[8] Palmerston, moreover, proved sympathetic. His disdain for the accusations laid against the Jews in Damascus chimed with
his desire to diminish the upstart Viceroy, Mehmet Ali, whom the French supported,
and to return greater Syria to direct Ottoman rule. On April 30, he received a deputa-
tion of leading British Jews and assured them the influence of the British government
would be exerted to put a stop to the atrocities (Frankel 1997, 126).

This set the pattern of activity and rhetoric for the Jewish elite and their Christian
allies over the next weeks. In mid-May a "petition presented to the Pasha of Egypt by

---

6. Board of Deputies of British Jews, Minute Book, Acc/3121/A5/A, April 21, 1840, Special meeting of the
    Board held at the residence of Sir Moses Montefiore.
7. Board of Deputies of British Jews, Minute Book, Acc/3121/A5/A, April 21, 1840, Special meeting of the
    Board held at the residence of Sir Moses Montefiore.
8. *Times*, April 25, 1840, 5; *Morning Chronicle*, April 25, 1840, 3; *Caledonian Mercury*, April 27, 1840,
    4; *Newcastle Courier*, May 1, 1840, 2; *Northern Star*, May 2, 1840, 6; *Hampshire Telegraph and Essex
    Chronicle*, May 4,1840, 2; *North Wales Chronicle*, May 5, 1840, 3.

his Jewish subjects on behalf of their oppressed brethren" received wide newspaper coverage.[9] A month later the leader of the Conservative Party, Sir Robert Peel, introduced a debate in the House of Commons. He had been asked to do so, he explained, "by persons of the highest character belonging to the Jewish persuasion." He deplored both the "prejudice" against the Jews in Damascus and the use of torture which had given rise to the confession of an incredible crime and he asked Palmerston to use British influence to secure "a full investigation of the matter" (*Hansard's Parliamentary Debates* 54 [1840], col 1383). The Foreign Secretary reiterated the opposition between western civilization and eastern barbarity and, moreover, confirmed that the Consul at Damascus, Nathaniel Werry, had been asked to make a detailed report and that Colonel Hodges, the Consul-General in Alexandria, had been instructed to bring the matter to the attention of the Pasha and to urge him to punish the guilty and make atonement to the "unfortunate sufferers" (*Hansard's Parliamentary Debates* 1840, col 1383–1384).

This was little more than a gesture, however. Britain's support for direct Ottoman rule in Syria ensured it had little influence with Mehemet Ali. In these months the main hope for the prisoners rested on the idea that the French government should intervene and investigate the charges. It was France that held an unofficial alliance with Mehemet Ali and it was the French consul in Damascus, Ratti-Menton, who had pursued and helped convict the Jewish prisoners. The Prime Minister, Adolphe Thiers, however, did not come to the Jews' aid. His primary concern was to advance French interests in the region and to uphold the consul's reputation in the face of accusations that he was complicit in persecution and torture. On June 2, in his speech to the French Chamber of Deputies, Thiers demonstrated his reluctance to take up the cause of the condemned Jews. His goal, he averred, was to protect an agent of France in the face of attack from Jews "all over Europe" (Frankel 1997, 187–194).

This was the immediate context in which plans were drawn up in Paris and London for two leading figures from each community, Cremieux and Montefiore, to embark on a mission to Mehemet Ali and then to proceed to Damascus where they would conduct their own investigation into the case (Frankel 1997, 214–219). Cremieux's and Montefiore's enterprise, therefore, was conceived not only as a diplomatic mission but also as an investigative undertaking. The mission was publicly announced on June 23. From that moment until Cremieux and Montefiore's departed from Paris on July 13, the leaders of British Jewry and their allies organized a series of public meetings whose aim was to rally public opinion behind their cause as well as to gather financial support.

The two most significant meetings were held at the Great Synagogue on June 23 and at the Mansion House, in the City of London, on July 3. Both gatherings were

---

9. *Belfast Newsletter*, May 15, 1840, 1; *The Hull Packet*, April 15, 1840, 6; *Caledonian Mercury*, May 16, 1840, 4; *Times*, May 18, 1840, 5.

notable for the way in which the cause of the Jews in Damascus was aligned with progress and civilization, as well as with practices and values vested in Britain and its institutions. At the Great Synagogue these themes were expressed most forcibly by Salomons. He placed the ritual murder accusation in a narrative that congratulated British society on its modernity. "The gross calumnies circulated concerning the Jew," Salomons said, "afforded a striking contrast between the present age and the dark periods of history." The fact that England in the twelfth century had been the fount of the ritual murder narrative was thus transformed into a positive characteristic of the present. The nation's laws and constitutional traditions, moreover, were presented as superior to those of France. Thiers's indifference to the suffering of the Jewish prisoners, Salomons suggested, did not reflect the sentiments of the French nation. He pointed out, however, "there were greater facilities in this country for appealing to public opinion, as any individual might convene a public meeting on any subject." Finally, Salomons presented the issue as a humanitarian crusade and invoked the same liberal, imperial, and moral sentiments that infused Victorian opposition to the slave trade: "he felt they would have the support of the British public and their Christian brethren in improving the condition of mankind all over the world."[10] Implicit in Salomons's encomium to the British constitution and its imperial mission was the idea that these were expressions of the Protestant Reformation and its particular influence on "the British people, [who] with true religious feeling, have . . . nobly identified themselves with the sufferings of God's ancient people." It was the influence of Roman Catholicism which united the "dark ages" in England with early nineteenth-century France. He developed this theme in a pamphlet published the same year:

> Whatever religious sentiments may be professed by individuals, to whatever community they may belong, no reading or thinking man can deny the benefits which the Reformation has afforded to the civilized world. That great religious movement emancipated the human mind from the trammels of bigotry, and introduced those higher principles of individual responsibility so necessary to the good conduct of each member of society . . . The principle of civil and religious liberty acknowledged at the Reformation, must for ever prevent the recurrence of a period similar to that in which Europe was involved during the middle ages. (Salomons 1840, 61, 75–76)

British Jews did not stand alone. They were joined in denying the blood libel by significant elements in British society. The Lord Mayor of London provided his official residence, the Mansion House, for the "grand public meeting" held to publicize and

---

10. *Morning Chronicle*, June 25, 1840, 6. On this theme see Green 2012, 140–141; Green 2008. See also Huzzey 2012. It is significant that while in London Cremieux found to time to address the British and Foreign Anti-Slavery Society. Formed in 1839 with the aim of attacking foreign slavery it included the Ottoman Empire among its targets (Frankel 1997, 219).

denounce the persecutions in Damascus. The occasion brought together Evangelicals, Quakers, Radicals and anti-slavery activists in support of the persecuted Jews (Green 2012, 140). Whereas the speakers and listeners at the Great Synagogue were Jewish, those at the Mansion House were not. Here too the cause of the Damascus Jews was aligned with English love of liberty. J. Masterman spoke "with those feelings which must be common to all of England, who at all times were ready to assist in putting down any system distinguished by tyranny." The national and religious origins of the particular tyranny were underscored by the Reverend Noel. He condemned the persecution Jews suffered in Damascus at the hands of "a populace ignorant, more ignorant and degraded than the lowest of the European states." His audience knew, he said, "how exceedingly light human life was reckoned by the Turks" and, to make matters worse, the conduct of the Roman Catholics had brought shame on Christianity.[11] The meeting at the Mansion House was followed by others at Dublin, Falmouth, Liverpool, Manchester, and Portsea. Here too the assemblies passed resolutions, raised funds and identified the nation with the cause of the suffering Jews in Damascus.[12]

In these speeches, pamphlets and newspaper reports Jews drew support from a widespread and powerful vision of Britain as a kingdom whose liberties had been nurtured by Protestantism and had been forged in struggle with Roman Catholicism. Anti-Catholicism was an integral part of this national imaginary which traced the political evils of popery from Bloody Mary, to the Armada, the Gunpowder Plot, and finally the Glorious Revolution of 1688. It was a vigorous strand in political, literary and popular culture in the early nineteenth century, present, as Dennis Paz has demonstrated, in "a torrent of tracts, books, magazines and newspaper stories" (Paz 1992, 1–2, 299). It had been nurtured by a hundred years of war with France and it was legitimized in law. Not only were Catholics excluded from Parliament before 1829, their churches could not have steeples, their priests were banned from wearing clerical garb in public, they were barred from leaving charitable bequests for "superstitious" purposes, and their schools did not receive parliamentary grants. Far from waning in the face of Victorian modernity, in the 1830s anti-Catholicism was given fresh impetus by the combined threat carried by Catholic Emancipation in 1829, the rising pace of immigration from Ireland and the Romanish sympathies of Tractarians within the Church of England (Paz 1992).

The Damascus affair and the role of France and its representatives appeared to demonstrate the connections between Popery and persecution and Protestantism and freedom. Evangelicals, in particular, leapt to the Jews' defense in pamphlets and the press. On May 28, a distinguished delegation representing the London Society for Promoting Christianity Amongst the Jews waited on Lord Palmerston bearing a

---

11. *Times*, July 4, 1840, 6.
12. See for example, *Manchester Times*, July 4, 1840.

statement from the Society's thirty-second annual conference that expressed "deep sympathy with the Jewish nation" and asked for the Foreign Secretary to use his influence to help the victims and prevent further "atrocities" (Frankel 1997, 131). The belief that the Jews would one day turn to Christianity had been an abiding theme in Protestant thought, though its credit was far from constant. In the 1820s and 1830s, however, Evangelicals evinced a new emphasis on their connectedness to the Jews and this was connected to militant Protestantism. By championing the Jews, evangelicals made a statement that could outbid the historical claims of Roman Catholics and Tractarians. As Donald Lewis argues:

> In the Jews of Europe they found their link to their historical past: by championing the Jews, they were celebrating their age-old links with Scripture and the apostolic tradition, which in their minds superseded claims to rootedness in any particular time period of Christian history. (Lewis 2010, 103)

Alexander McCaul, the leading cleric in the London Society, published a lengthy pamphlet setting out *Reasons for Believing that the Charge Lately Revived Against the Jewish People is a Baseless Falsehood*. "Had the calumny and the persecution been confined to the ignorant followers of Mahomet, it would have been hardly worth notice," he explained. It was its currency among European (by which he meant Catholic) countries which stimulated him to publish his pamphlet (McCaul 1840). McCaul aimed to discredit rather than disprove the allegation of ritual murder. His emphasis fell on the history of the accusation, which, in the past, had been "brought forward amongst others, now universally acknowledged to be gross and ridiculous falsehoods." Characteristically, McCaul used his defense of Jews to highlight superstitions imposed on Christianity by Roman Catholicism:

> Does the reader . . . believe that they [Jews] used to crucify images, and shed their blood, or they could raise storms at will to destroy thousands of Christians, or produce a six years' pestilence, or that they could kill a Christian bishop by burning a wax image, or deprive a king of reason, or that they drew blood from consecrated wafers, and that miracles were wrought to discover their wickedness? Why then should he receive the charges concerning the use of Christian blood in the Passover? The testimony for the latter is not in the least degree stronger than that for the former. (McCaul 1840, 6)

More emphatically, Charlotte Elizabeth Tonna, a Tory evangelical and a friend of Moses Montefiore, asked "Do we ask for illustrations of unchanged Popery?" Her answer: "Look at Damascus" (Lewis 2010, 194).

As David Salomons's speech and pamphlet illustrate, the influence of anti-Catholicism extended beyond the ranks of conservative Anglican conversionists. Anti-Catholicism was implicit in every reference to the blood libel as a legacy from the "dark ages."[13] *The Standard* and the *Morning Herald* identified "the monks of the Latin convent" as the "principal actors" in "the horrible tragedy of Damascus."[14] Ratti-Menton was denounced as a "legitimist of the oldest and worst school—an advocate of the imbecile and fanatical party who by their folly brought about the revolution."[15] Despite the advent of the Orleanist regime, France remained indelibly marked by Roman Catholicism.

> This is the "France of July" under the revolutionary dynasty of the barricades—France at Algiers outvies the Arabs of the desert in barbarism—France at Damascus takes a part in re-enacting the savage atrocities against the Jews which begrimed Europe with blood and crime five centuries ago.[16]

Defense of the Jews against the blood libel was thus assimilated within a Protestant national imaginary that had the capacity to corral Tory and Whig, Christian and Jew, radical and Anglican, alike. The issue was presented as a matter of belief based on cherished doctrines, not empirical knowledge.

Blood and the Jews

The images of Britain that the Jews and their supporters showed to the British public should not be accepted at face value. These were not disinterested appraisals of public attitudes, but, rather, attempts to consolidate opinion in the Jews' favor, to deepen and extend this sentiment, and to marginalize more negative attitudes to Jews and contrary assessments of what had happened in Damascus. This much was acknowledged by one of the speakers at the Great Synagogue, Barnard van Oven:

> It was true that persecution now raged in only one town in Asia, but who dare assert that it would stop there, unless by the exertion of this and similar meetings, the facts alleged against them be clearly disposed, the malice of our enemies made manifest and their base motive exhibited to the world. [17]

One reason this effort was necessary was that "some of the English press were more disposed to open their columns to reports against the Jews than to defend their cause."[18] As this suggests, the opinion that Jews (or some Jews) murdered Christians to use their blood for rabbinically sanctioned rituals remained alive and well among many Britons in the early nineteenth century.

---

13. *John Bull*, April 26, 1840, 204.
14. *The Standard*, June 9, 1840, 3; reprinted the *Morning Herald*.
15. *Times*, April 18, 1840, 5.
16. *The Standard*, June 9, 1840, 3.
17. *Morning Chronicle*, June 25, 1840, 6.
18. *Morning Chronicle*, June 25, 1840, 6; see also *Manchester Times*, July 4, 1840.

The first Briton to learn that Jews were accused of the murder of Padre Tommaso and his servant, the British Consul at Damascus, Nathaniel Werry, was convinced of their guilt. On the basis of a confession extorted under torture, on February 28, Werry wrote to the British Ambassador at Constantinople setting out "the most cruel and revolting circumstances" of the assassination, including the saving of the priests' blood (Hyamson 1945–51, 50–51). He wrote again a month later giving reasons for his certain view on the matter and their basis in fact. First, he referred to the knowledge of the local Christian population and Turkish officialdom:

> It has been immemorially the received opinion and belief of the Christian population throughout Turkey, and several instances have been brought to light, by the local Governments in different parts that, the Jews scattered throughout the Country, immolated clandestinely Christians to obtain their blood, to celebrate their feasts therewith in their religious ceremonies. This fact has been proved. (Hyamson 1945–51, 51–2e)

Second, Werry noted that there had been "full and detailed confessions" and, further, that bones and other evidence had been found which corroborated these disclosures: "the facts have been so minutely proved on the spots that they were committed and of the remains disposed of and partly found that no doubt can exist thereof." Third, Werry claimed, the Talmudic and rabbinical sanction for the crimes had been revealed: "The extracts from the Talmud taken from the Rabin prisoners have been translated, which warrant these enormities and the Secret, which has hitherto been traditional and only imparted to the initiated, has now been imparted to the public." Werry presented his view, therefore, as based on empirical evidence in the present and supported by knowledge of the Jewish religion and Jewish practices. The argument operated in a circuit in which each component—the confessions, the circumstantial evidence, the historical precedents and the translations from the Talmud—reinforced the others (Hyamson 1945–51, 51–52).

Werry's opinions were not idiosyncratic. At Rhodes another British vice-consul, J. G. Wilkinson, took a leading role in the interrogation and torture of Jews (Frankel 1997, 70–72). The balance of press coverage was on the side of the Jews, but, as Barnard van Oven indicated, newspapers were far from unanimous. In the course of 1840 a wide range of newspapers and periodicals were prepared to consider the possibility that Jews were guilty of the charge of ritual murder or even expressed the firm conviction that they were. Frankel suggests that Tory political interests were at work in the case of the *Times*, and the same thing might be said of the *Morning Post*, which also opened its columns to the Jews' accusers. Both newspapers opposed the Whig government in general, Palmerston's preparedness to risk war in the Middle East in particular, and they also opposed Jewish emancipation (Frankel 1997, 207). However, the political affiliations of the publications prepared to indict the Jews were much broader than this. The Jews' innocence was questioned by the Chartist newspaper the *Northern Liberator* and by the scandal-mongering radical newspaper *The Satirist, or The Censor of the Times,* and in as early as mid-April, the influential and politically neutral *Literary Gazette and Journal of the Belles Lettres, Arts, Sciences &c,* had condemned them.[19]

The elements we have noted in Werry's account were also present in this press coverage. Here too writers placed weight on the confessions, the circumstantial evidence and on "expert" knowledge of Judaism and Jewish religious practices. The Jews' accusers did not deny confessions were extorted by the bastinado but they were impressed that "the criminals were kept separate, and the confessions of the three principals, being compared, are found exactly to tally."[20] They were also able to reinforce their case with other findings. Notably the bones that had been found in a sewer, and declared by experts to be human remains, and alongside them the remnant of a black cap which "clearly" came from one that Father Thomas wore habitually.[21] Taken together, *The Satirist* found these were "very stiff facts."[22] A correspondent to the *Morning Post,* writing from Smyrna, surveyed all the evidence of the confessions and concluded "no rational doubt could exist of the crime having been committed" by the accused. So convinced was he that the only way he could account for the contrary view taken by the Austrian consul was to attribute it to bribery.[23]

The evidence of the Jews' guilt in this particular case appeared all the more plausible in view of a commonplace understanding of Jewish law and practice. Sometimes this aspect of the case was presented in ways that highlighted the particular beliefs and practices of Syrian Jews. *The Penny Satirist* observed, "The Jews of England are Englishmen, and the Jews and Christians of Syria are only Syrians." The Jews there were "a rather barbarous race" whose religious practices sometimes involved the sprinkling of blood.[24] In late August, the *Times* carried a lengthy communication from a correspondent in Syria who, having arrived there convinced of the Jews innocence had now changed his mind. He had seen the *process verbal* in Arabic and French, "had communicated with disinterested persons *au fait* with the real state of the case," and had been impressed by the confessions which tallied in every particular. Europe's Jews, he proposed, had been hasty in identifying with the accused who belonged to a "fanatic sect" and followed not only the law of Moses and the Talmud

---

19. *Northern Liberator,* July 4, 1840, 7. The *Literary Gazette and Journal of the Belles Lettres, Arts, Sciences, &c,* sold for just 8d a copy, has been credited with being influential and reached a circulation of 4,000. See Thompson 1935. The magazine's reach was wider than this number suggests for the artists could be syndicated or pirated elsewhere. For example, "sketch" of "the late strange occurrences at Damascus" was reproduced in the *North Wales Chronicle* on May 5.

20. *Morning Post,* July 1, 1840, 6; see also August 24, 1840, 2.

21. *Morning Post,* July 11, 1840, 6.

22. *The Satirist, or The Censor of the Times,* June 28, 1840, 201; *Morning Post,* August 24, 1840, 2.

23. *Morning Post,* August 24, 1840, 2.

24. *The Penny Satirist,* July 17, 1840, 2; see also *The Literary Gazette and Journal of the Belles Lettres, Arts, Science, &c,* April 18, 1840, 252.

but also "certain oral traditions" which call for human sacrifice. Indeed, having been made acquainted with some "atrocious passages" in the Talmud, he could well believe that such fanaticism existed among Jews.[25]

However, in view of the authority given to the Talmud by the overwhelming majority of observant Jews in the early nineteenth century, it was impossible to draw a clear line separating the beliefs and practices of Syrian Jews from those of their European coreligionists.[26] Indeed, the charge of ritual murder was often presented as a genuine expression of Judaism, rather than as a rogue, Levantine development. These opinions invoked the Old Testament, the Talmud and rabbinical authority to demonstrate that the Jews really were capable of ritual murder, however vicious and incredible the crime. This line of thought followed the path taken by the investigation in Damascus. On May 9, the *Times* reproduced a letter sent from the city by Father Francois de Sardaigne, originally written in early March, which related that the Pasha had ordered "frequent and extreme bastinadoes" so as "to satisfy himself whether it is true that that the Jewish or Talismund [sic] worship defiles her religious ceremonies with human blood."[27] However, the newspaper's great coup, in this regard, came on June 25, when it published a translation of an 1803 document written, so it claimed, by a Moldavian rabbi who had converted to Christianity. The "mystery of blood" he explained is not known by all Jews, "but only by the rabbins, the haham (doctors) [sic], the Scribes and Pharisees, who are called by the Jews Hasseidim." There were three underlying reasons, the author explained, why these rituals were carried out: the great hatred Jews feel for Christians and the belief that in killing them they are doing God's work, the requirement for Christian blood in many of the rites the Jews perform, and, finally, the Jews' secret suspicion that Jesus may be the true Messiah and that by sprinkling themselves with the blood of Christians they may be saved.[28]

What is significant for us is less the question whether or not the article was accurate—it was not—but the degree of authority and plausibility it carried. The author presented himself as a former rabbi and so claimed authority. He appeared to be familiar with rabbinical texts, with the Jews' feelings about Christians, and with a number of rituals which involved the use of Christian blood. Moreover, the fact that the document appeared in the *Times* gave it additional weight. It is, perhaps, not a coincidence that only three days after it appeared, *The Satirist* observed that the Jews were endogamous and secretive and "cordially hate the Christians." It was not improbable, the author reasoned, that "the worst of a race that consists of thieves, rogues and cheats" might think it right to substitute the blood of Christian for the

---

25. *Times*, August 29, 1840, 5; see also *Times*, August 26, 1840, 5.
26. For example see *Morning Post*, August 24, 1840, 2.
27. *Times*, May 9, 1840, 6.
28. *Times*, June 25, 1840, 12.

blood of a lamb, "wherever the blood of a lamb is enjoined to be used." With ecumenical chauvinism, the writer concluded that, "this is no more impossible than that Catholics should take to worship saints."[29]

Although the *Times* stopped short of endorsing the charges against the Jews, it continued to encourage debate. In August, with parliament in recess, the newspaper found "nothing more important in its present bearings and future consequences" than "the subject of the Damascus Jews."[30] This was no mundane killing but one that raised the question of what sort of religion Judaism is and what sort of people the Jews are. A flurry of correspondence suggested some answers. On August 17, a letter from Sigma drew on the growing influence of stadial theory, conjectural history and the new biblical criticism to point out that since the enlightened nations of the epoch—the Egyptians, Chaldeans, and Greeks—had their human sacrifices, "how could the Jews, an ignorant, a stiff-necked and idolatrous people, as their whole history attests, escape the history of so bright an example." He argued that "the religion of the Jews" was "essentially a bloody one . . . the altars were not only reeking with the blood of sheep and goats and oxen, but that the sanguine streams of human victims also crimsoned the astounded earth and flowed in propitiation to Jehovah." He conceded that there were different sorts of Jews in Damascus and London yet maintained, "If a Jew really and implicitly believes every word of the Old Testament, how could he in his secret mind believe human sacrifice a crime?"[31]

These associations of the religion of the Old Testament and the Talmud with a state of civilization that had now been superseded in Christian Europe illustrate how a self-congratulatory appreciation of modernity was as compatible with belief in the Jews' guilt as it was with their innocence. Earlier in the year, *The Literary Gazette* observed that the narrative from Damascus was "reminiscent of the dark ages in Europe and the charges which in those days, led to Jewish massacres." But whereas for the Jews and their supporters this allusion to the medieval past was a cause for disbelief, for their accusers it was the occasion for dismay: "Is it not dreadful? What horrors superstition will lead men to perpetrate."[32] Contrary to the Jews' protestations, in early Victorian Britain the blood libel was not a mere archaism, a relic of a bygone age, but was easily integrated within modern paradigms and theories of social development.

With good reason, Jews and their supporters were perturbed by these currents of opinion which entertained the validity of the charge of ritual murder. Negative newspaper coverage and letters in support of the ritual murder accusation were met with replies from defiant Jewish correspondents; David Salomons published a one hundred page pamphlet on the subject and Morris Raphall, a rabbi in Birmingham,

---

29. *The Satirist, or The Censor of the Times*, June 28, 1840, 201.
30. *Times*, August 13, 1840, 4.
31. *Times*, August 17, 1840, 3.
32. *Literary Gazette and Journal of the Belles Lettres, Arts, Sciences, &c*, April 18, 1840, 252.

also responded with a pamphlet in reply to charges laid against Judaism.[33] As we have seen, one rejoinder made by Jews was that the charges were not worthy of serious consideration. They were a legacy of the "dark ages" and out of place in more civilized and tolerant times; they were based on torture and an absence of those constitutional traditions that were the hallmark of British history and of Protestantism. But this line of attack, though it affirmed a set of beliefs to which both Jews and their Christian supporters could subscribe, rapidly appeared insufficient as significant sections of the press continued to give the charges serious consideration and also critically scrutinized Jewish beliefs and practices. These allegations—both the particular in Damascus and those against Judaism more broadly—had to be confronted.

Montefiore and Cremieux had departed with the aim of conducting the necessary investigation in Damascus. In the meantime, the Jews' most effective weapon in the debate over what had and had not occurred in the city was the report written by the Protestant missionary and former rabbi, George Wildon Pieritz. Pieritz had settled in Jerusalem where he worked for the London Society for Promoting Christianity among the Jews. He travelled to Damascus at the request of Jews in Jerusalem, "to rid them of this calumny" (Frankel 1997, 82). Extracts of his report were published in the *Times* and the entire text was reproduced in David Salomons's pamphlet. Pieritz "found the whole charge against the Jews there [in Damascus] a vile fabrication, and that all means and right of legal defence was denied them; while the most cruel tortures were employed to extort from them false confessions of guilt."[34] Salomons's pamphlet provided a detailed examination. He found, "the more the story is scrutinized, the more impossible do its details appear." The accusation, as one non-Jewish speaker proposed at the Mansion House meeting, was "too bad to be true" (Salomons 1840, 53). For example, Salomons scoffed at the idea that the leading Jewish merchants of Damascus could have been involved in the murderous enterprise. Merchants, he pointed out, are "a class of men who seldom involve themselves in hazardous enterprises unconnected with commercial pursuits" (Salomons 1840, 53). However, this claim, like Salomons's dissection of the case more broadly, rested on the assumption that Jews—the merchants among them—were governed by the same sentiments and constraints as Christians. But it was precisely this assumption that the Jews' opponents brought into question in their criticisms of the Bible and the Talmud.

Because narratives of events in Damascus frequently led to discussion of the character of Judaism, the Old Testament, and the Talmud, Jews were obliged to claim not only that their coreligionists in Damascus were innocent of murdering the priest and his servant for ritual purposes, but also that Jews could never perform

33. For example, *The Literary Gazette and Journal of the Belles Lettres, Arts, Science, &c*, May 9, 1840, 295–296; *The Southern Star and London and Brighton Patriot*, July 12,1840, 2; The *Times*, May 14, 1840, 3; July 6, 1840, 6; November 5, 1840, 6; Salomons 1840; Raphall 1840.
34. *Times*, July 6, 1840, 9; August 13, 1840, 3; Salomons 1840, 48.

such an action. Just over a week after the *Times* published its Moldavian fabrication, British Jews broadcast a letter written to Moses Montefiore by Solomon Herschel, the Chief Rabbi of England, and the Sephardi *Haham*, David Meldola. Ostensibly offering Montefiore advice as he set forth on his mission, the real audience for the letters was the British public. Addressing a precise claim made in the *Times*, Herschel predicted that Montefiore will be told that "'this mystery of blood' is not known by all Jews but only by Rabbins and that therefore, it will be said, his denial may be true so far as his personal knowledge is concerned but yet be false 'as to the crime of which our nation is accused.'" Herschel tried to meet this problem: he had been a rabbi for the last forty years, he wrote, his father and grandfather had both been rabbis before him, he would swear an oath that he had never seen human blood used in a Jewish rite and, moreover, that there is neither divine precept nor an ordinance laid down by the Jews' wise men that tells them to do such a thing. He then swore:

> If I lie in this matter then let all the curses mentioned in Leviticus and Deuteronomy come upon me, let me never see the blessing and consolation of Zion, nor attain to the resurrection of the dead.[35]

As Herschel acknowledged, the charge against Judaism required him to make a general negative claim: that Jews had not and would not murder Christians for ritual purposes. This was an impossible task and not something anyone could prove empirically. The oath must have appeared to Herschel as the best he could do in the circumstances. Nevertheless, his course provides a vivid illustration of the cultural distance between orthodox Jews and their Victorian fellow subjects. For many readers, it would have confirmed their view that Judaism was a superstitious and morally under-developed religion—two commonplace charges that were used to render the ritual murder charge more credible.[36]

The Jews struggled hard in these debates, but even Pieritz's report did not effect a knock-out blow. Pieritz had been born a Jew, educated as a rabbi, and had renounced the religion of his fathers to become a Christian missionary. As David Salomons pointed out, he was well acquainted with Hebrew literature, the duties of the Jewish clergy, and the laws of religious conduct, but, at the same time, "he had no motive to palliate crime, nor desire to conceal abominations which ought to be exposed to public view" (Salomons 1840, iii–iv). In other words, what was important was not merely the content of his report, but the authority of the man. The *Times* agreed. Not only was the report "cogent," but the writer was unlikely "to strain either the facts or the argument in their [the Jews] favour."[37] Yet despite these friendly words, the newspaper continued to publish letters taking a contrary view and it continued to report

---

35. *Morning Post*, July 3, 1840, 2.
36. *The Satirist, or The Censor of the Times*, June 28, 1840, 201; see also *Times*, October 20, 1840, 3.
37. *Times*, August 17, 1840, 3.

new blood libel accusations.[38] Pieiritz's testimony competed with the confessions made in Damascus and the supporting evidence found there in a sewer. Moreover, as we have seen, each side had its convert to pronounce with authority. Similarly, both sides were able to place their arguments within a narrative of progress. For the Jews and their supporters this was the journey from the "dark ages," via the Reformation and the Glorious Revolution to the Victorian present. Their opponents operated on a larger time scale and presented Judaism as an archaic—and bloody—remnant of a stage in human history which had been surpassed with the appearance of Christ. Ultimately, the Jews' vindication would not rest on empirical evidence or the unassailable authority of converts and scholars but on events beyond their control and on the larger set of beliefs within which their cause was positioned.

The Jews Vindicated

Montefiore and Cremieux reached Alexandria on August 4 as the conflict between Turkey and Egypt threatened to lead to war. Mehemet Ali depended on his alliance with France and the French consul at Alexandria, Adrien-Louis Cochelet, firmly believed in the Jews' guilt. He supported Ratti-Menton and in turn, received backing from Thiers. Inevitably, in these circumstances the meetings Montefiore and Cremiuex engineered with the Pasha were fruitless. The situation changed dramatically, however, after August 16 when the Turkish foreign minister presented Mehemet Ali with the text of an ultimatum agreed a month earlier by Britain, Russia, Austria, Prussia and Turkey. The ultimatum required Mehemet Ali to submit to the Sultan. If he failed to do so within ten days he would lose all his territories except Egypt, if he persisted for a further ten days he would lose Egypt as well. It was after the first ten-day period had passed that Mehemet Ali crumbled. It was only now that he also agreed not merely to pardon, but to set at liberty the Jewish prisoners in Damascus. It had been important that Montefiore and Cremiueux had persisted in pressing the cause of the Jewish prisoners but it was Palmerston's strategy that had enabled them to secure their release from jail (Frankel 1997, 345–354).

The allies relied on armed force to remove Mehemet Ali's troops from Syria and not the Pasha's word alone. With the region in turmoil it was too dangerous for Cremieux and Montefiore to proceed to Damascus and carry out their investigation as they had planned. Instead, Montefiore left for Constantinople with the intention of persuading the Sultan to issue a *firman* denying the truth of the blood libel. Here too his success owed much to the support he received from Palmerston, indirectly, and, on the spot, from John Ponsonby, the British ambassador. Palmerston wanted to promote Jewish interests in the Ottoman Empire. The Jews, he hoped, would provide Britain with a client population and a source of influence within the Empire. He also hoped that as

---

38. *Times*, August 13, 1840, 5; September 8, 1840, 56.

financiers and traders, they would strengthen efforts to modernize and reform the Porte. The Sultan was well disposed, advised by the architect of the British alliance, Reshid Pasha, and mindful that pleasing Montefiore, as a relative of the Rothschilds, might rebound to the benefit of the Ottoman finances. Montefiore was pushing at an open door and was rewarded with a *firman* that not only denied the blood libel but also promised the same protection as other subjects. It was Montefiore declared, as he alluded to a specifically British tradition of constitutional liberty, a "Magna Charta for the Jews in the Turkish Dominions" (Frankel 1997, 375–377).

Both in Alexandria and Constantinople, the diplomatic component of Montefiore's mission was a success. The investigative aspect, however, had been abandoned. Writing to the *Times* under the moniker "T. J. C.," one correspondent declared himself disappointed that Montefiore and Cremieux left the issue unresolved. Even "Cantab," who wrote to contest much that T. J. C. had written about the Jewish liturgy and practice, conceded that the matter remained "open to question."[39] However, these doubts were not characteristic of the debate or, rather, of the silence that soon descended. On November 5, the *Times* published a lengthy rebuttal of the points raised by T. J. C. and declared itself "quite satisfied" at the explanation given for the "postponement" of the inquiry at Damascus. The newspaper, adopting a stadial perspective, was still inclined to take a negative view of "dogmas laid down many centuries ago," but was certain that they had never been put into practice "in any European society." Western Jewry was given a clean bill of health. And there, imperiously, the newspaper announced it would "take leave of the question." [40]

Although the balance of British newspaper opinion throughout the Damascus affair favored the Jews' innocence, as we have seen there was a significant current which took the accusation seriously, as well as a stream of opinion that was convinced of the Jews' guilt. It is these voices that were silenced by the conclusion to the Damascus affair. However, they were not stilled by the remorseless march of reason and enlightenment. As we have seen, the voices raised to prosecute the blood accusation, or that were prepared to give it serious consideration, were able to assemble both evidence and erudition to support their case. Jews and their supporters were not out done here. However, the change in opinion took place without either a definitive verdict from Damascus or a settled and positive assessment of the character of Judaism.[41] So what did change? Chronology is revealing. For it was the release of the prisoners and the Sultan's *firman* that led the *Times* to declare closed the controversy it had done so much to keep alive. It was not the march of knowledge that led to a positive political outcome for the Jews but, rather, it was a political outcome that

39. *Times*, October 20, 1840, 3; October 31, 1840, 5.
40. *Times*, November 5, 1840, 4.
41. See *Times*, October 26, 1858.

generated a new consensus, a new state of belief in Britain, regarding Jews and the blood libel.

The year 1840 did not mark an end to ritual murder cases. There was an efflorescence of allegations in the decades that followed, culminating in the notorious Beilis case in 1913. What is notable, however, is that none was treated in Britain as a point for serious examination and inquiry in the same way that the Damascus affair had been by significant sections of the press, pulpit and public. The "flood" of books, pamphlets, and articles that characterized the response in Europe to these did not receive even a faint echo (Frankel 1997, 411–424, 442). One telling indication of the disrepute into which the blood accusation had fallen is that the manuscript, titled "Human sacrifice among the Sephardine or Eastern Jews, or the Murder of Padre Tomasso," written in the 1870s by the orientalist, adventurer, and diplomat Richard Burton, was never published in his lifetime. This is all the more notable since Burton completed his manuscript just as Benjamin Disraeli, the prime minister, became the butt of a popular campaign that highlighted his Jewish ancestry as the fount of his amoral and "unBritish" statecraft. Even in these propitious circumstances, Burton did not feel safe to publish. When a part of the work was published posthumously it received a hostile reception (Holmes 1979, 52).

We are left, then, with the contrast in attitudes to the ritual murder accusation in Britain and Europe. This chapter has argued that in 1840 attitudes the response in Britain to the Damascus affair was more diverse and more negative toward the Jews than previous accounts have allowed. It is, nevertheless, the case that belief in the veracity of the charge never achieved the currency or resonance in Britain that it had in France, for example (Kalman 2005). Moreover, Britain was unusual in its widespread and longstanding resistance to the blood libel in the decades after 1840. In explaining this difference, we must reckon with the pervasive influence of an image of Britain as a kingdom whose constitutional freedoms had sprung from Protestantism. This was the prevailing national imaginary (Wolffe 1991; Colley 1992). The cause of the Jews in the Damascus affair and the cause of the nation were one. The Damascus affair has conventionally been presented, in part, as a confrontation between East and West, sometimes as in the grand historical narrative pioneered by Graetz and, more recently, as an exploration of orientalist tropes (Kalman 2005). In Britain too there was an orientalist current. We find it in the words of those who defended the prisoners from torture and popular fury, as well as from those prepared to accept the truth of the blood accusation as something characteristic of a land still permeated by barbarism. However, it is the Protestant and anti-Catholic dimension to support for the Jews that was distinctive in the British context and also deeply influential. It was the alignment of the Jewish cause with the Protestant nation, as well as the vindication that came in late autumn 1840, which drained the remaining credibility from the blood libel.

The support the Jews received from militant Protestantism, however, was complex and double-edged. The Jews' most ardent allies in the Damascus affair were conversionists who, though they venerated Jews, scorned normative Judaism. For the members of the London Society for the Promotion of Christianity Amongst the Jews, the Jews' held a particular spiritual role in the fulfillment of prophecy: they were to be protected from their persecutors but also won to Christianity. The Jews' purpose lay only in the fulfillment of the Divine plan. They had no temporal role. Lord Ashley and other members of the London Society ranked among those most eager to continue to exclude Jews from Parliament and so keep it a Christian assembly (Feldman 1994, 55–56).

Conversionist thinking on Judaism reached its fullest expression in the writing of Alexander McCaul. In the 1830s, McCaul regularly preached to Jews on Saturday evenings and published weekly pamphlets, *Old Paths*, which in 1837, were gathered and published as a single volume. He also wrote a series of essay for the *British Magazine* which formed the content for another book, *Sketches of Judaism and the Jews*, published in 1838. He went on, in 1841, to become Professor of Hebrew and Rabbinical Literature at King's College in London. His understanding of Judaism was influential and set the template for leaders and members of the London Society (Feldman 1994, 54–55). McCaul aimed to demonstrate that Christianity was a faithful continuation of the divinely inspired writings of the Old Testament. Judaism, by contrast, was "a new and totally different system, devised by designing men and unworthy of the Jewish people." The term McCaul used for this system was "rabbinism" and it held the same evils that the evangelical habitually found in Roman Catholicism.

> If asked to give a concise yet adequate idea of this system, I should say it is Jewish Popery: just as Popery may be defined to by Gentile Rabbinism. Its distinguishing feature is that it asserts the transmission of an oral law or traditional law of equal authority with the written law of God, at the same time, that, like Popery, it resolves traditions into the present opinions of the existing Church. (McCaul 1838, 2)

It is testimony to the double-edged quality of the Evangelical understanding of Jews and Judaism that we find McCaul's account of the Talmud cited with approval by a correspondent to the *Times* who was convinced of the Jews' guilt.[42]

This critique, emanating from powerful friends, unsettled Jewish leaders in Britain. We can trace its impact in debates on religious reform that raged over the next two decades. The Damascus affair was followed two years later by the creation of the West London Synagogue of British Jews. In abolishing customs without a scriptural basis, such as the second day of religious holidays, these British reformers appeared to address Evangelical criticisms. McCaul, for one, welcomed the new synagogue as

---

42. *Times*, August 26, 1840, 5.

testimony to the influence of his writings (Feldman 1994, 57–58). A decade later, the minister of the new synagogue, David Marks, gave a series of lectures on *The Sufficiency of the Law of Moses as a Guide for Israel*; the title and content loudly echoed McCaul's critique. The orthodox insistence on rabbinical interpretation brought to mind, Marks suggested, "the substance . . . of the theology of Rome." Reform attracted only a minority of British Jews but the same features of the Evangelical critique were echoed elsewhere. The communal newspaper the *Jewish Chronicle* in 1847 decried "the numberless and thickly twined fences with which modern rabbinism has hedged in the true law of God." A year later, it thundered, "Rabbinism in our age is an incongruity" (Feldman 1994, 57–62). The critique of Catholicism carried with it a challenge to the Jews. The Jews' vindication did not reflect a new and positive consensus on the character of Jews and the nature of Judaism.

At the outset of this chapter, I noted that the British response to the Damascus affair has been exempted from recent revisionist historiography. This reticence is unnecessary. Belief in the veracity of the blood accusation was more widespread than historians have allowed hitherto. More important than this, the Jews' victory does not provide a last vestige of support for an interpretation of the affair as a victory for the progress of reason and toleration in the face of barbarism and prejudice. The Jews' exculpation in Britain was not achieved by a new appreciation of the facts of the case in Damascus—these were abandoned—but by the political and military outcome in the near East. Moreover, the political culture which protected the Jews in Britain was steeped in an anti-Catholic current that ranged from sober assessments of papal intolerance to partisan national history to lurid imaginings of priestly lust for money, sex, and power. The Jews' victory, we might say, signified defeat for one form of prejudice and victory for another.

References

Colley, Linda. *Britons: Forging the Nation, 1707–1837*. New Haven: Yale University Press, 1992.
Endelman, Todd M. *The Jews of Georgian England, 1714–1830*. Michigan: University of Michigan Press, 1979).
Feldman, David. *Englishmen and Jews: Social Relations and Political Culture, 1840–1914*. London: Yale University Press, 1994.
Frankel, Jonathan. *The Damascus Affair: "Ritual Murder", Politics and the Jews in 1840*. Cambridge: Cambridge University Press, 1997.
Green, Abigail. "The British Empire and the Jews," *Past and Present* (May 2008): 175–205.
———. *Moses Montefiore: Jewish Liberator, Imperial Hero*. Cambridge, MA: Belknap Press, 2012.
Hansard's Parliamentary Debates, 54. London: Baldwin and Craddock, 1840.
Holmes, Colin. *Anti-Semitism in British Society 1876–1939*. London: Edward Arnold, 1979.
Huzzey, R. *Freedom Burning: Anti-Slavery and Empire in Victorian Britain*. Ithaca: Cornell University Press, 2012.

Hyamson, A. "The Damascus Affair—1840," *Transactions of the Jewish Historical Society of England* 16 (1945–51): 47–72.

Kalman, Julie. "Sensuality, Depravity and Ritual Murder: The Damascus Blood Libel and Jews in France." *Jewish Social Studies* 13.3 (2005): 35–58.

Lewis, Donald M. *The Origins of Christian Zionism: Lord Shaftesbury and Evangelical Support for a Jewish Homeland.* Cambridge: Cambridge University Press, 2010.

McCaul, Alexander. *Reasons for Believing that the Charge Lately Revived Against the Jews Is a Baseless Falsehood.* London: Macintosh, 1840.

———. *Sketches of Judaism and Jews.* London: Macintosh, 1838.

Paz, Denis G. *Popular Anti-Catholicism in Mid-Victorian England.* Stanford, CA: Stanford University Press, 1992.

Raphall, M. *Judaism Defended Against Attacks of T. J. C.: A Reply to Two Letters on the Damascus Question in "The Times" Newspaper of the 20th and 27th October.* London: n.p., 1840.

Salomons, David. *An Account of the Recent Persecutions of the Jews at Damascus.* London: Longman, 1840.

Thompson, D. "The Higher Journalism in the Nineteenth Century," *Scrutiny* iv (1935): 25–34.

Wolffe, John. *The Protestant Crusade in Great Britain, 1829–1860.* Oxford: Clarendon Press, 1991.

8

Interreligious Love in Contemporary German Film and Literature

Katja Garloff

Introduction

One of the most influential analyses of German Jewish relations before the Holocaust is Gershom Scholem's 1966 essay "Jews and Germans." Scholem, who had been born into an assimilated German Jewish family but became a Zionist and in 1923 immigrated to Palestine, delivers there a trenchant critique of what he calls the "false start" of German Jewish relations in the modern age. He argues against the idea that the process of Jewish emancipation and acculturation, which began in the late eighteenth century, had created something like a "dialogue" between Jews and non-Jews. In his view this dialogue had always been chimerical, a delusion on the part of Jews who failed to realize that their desire for social integration lacked a German counterpart. Jews simply did not see that assimilation dissolved the communal bonds among them without truly granting them access to German society. In rather broad strokes, Scholem sketches the history of German Jewish relations, from sporadic economic interactions before the eighteenth century to the struggle of the Jews for equal political rights and, finally, to their passionate identification with German culture in the nineteenth and early twentieth centuries. One implication of Scholem's essay is that the social exclusion of the Jews persisted despite this identification and ultimately culminated in the Holocaust.

Beneath the veneer of this historical narrative, however, Scholem tells a love story. More precisely, he tells an unhappy love story in which one partner is repulsed by the intensity of the other's desire. He describes how Jews after the dissolution of their own communities and traditions tried to enter German culture too quickly and therefore met with resistance, just as an overly stormy lover would. At one point he sums up: "By and large, then, the love affair of the Jews and the Germans remained one-sided and unreciprocated" (Scholem 1976, 86). At the time of Scholem's writing, this trope of a "German Jewish love affair" had already been in existence, but it acquired new valences after the Holocaust. I could cite any number of books on German Jewish history and culture—books from 1950 and from 2010, popular histories and specialized academic works—that use this trope, often for opposing interpretations of the historical process. While some claim that "the unrequited love affair of Germany's Jews with their native country *led* to the unspeakable horrors of the Holocaust," (Blumenthal as quoted in Hertz 2007, 15) others evoke love in order to counter such historical determinism. Thus Steven Aschheim calls for an analysis of real-life German Jewish love affairs and marriages as "a necessary corrective to the view of all German-Jewish history, in the light of its terrible conclusion, as a history of unremitting hostility and estrangement" (Aschheim 2001, 41).

Why has love—and especially unhappy or one-sided love—become such a popular metaphor for German Jewish relations? Among the terms that have been used to describe German Jewish relations before the Holocaust—terms such as dialogue, symbiosis, and subculture—love intuitively seems to be the most problematic. The use of love as a model for group relations can personalize the political, individualize the social, and romanticize power relations; it can gloss over or even legitimize the hegemonic forces of a dominant culture. We therefore need to rephrase the question: If love is such a popular metaphor for German Jewish relations, is it also a culturally and politically productive one? What models of interaction, communication, and collaboration between social groups does love generate?

This essay focuses on a period in which the trope of the German Jewish love affair enjoyed particular popularity, namely in the decade after the reunification of Germany. When in 1989/90, the Federal Republic of Germany and the German Democratic Republic were reunited after more than four decades of separation—ironically at a time when, thanks to globalization, the nation state seemed to become increasingly obsolete—the question of what it means to be German acquired new urgency. One of the key issues in the public debates was the quest for a "normalization" of German identity, especially in its relation to the German past.[1] Architectural projects such as the restoration of the parliament (*Reichstag*) of the former German Empire, which highlights the openness and transparency of the building, strove to embed Germany firmly in Western traditions of liberal democracy. But the question of how to publicly acknowledge German responsibility for the Second World War and the Holocaust remained a thorny one, as evinced by the controversies surrounding the Holocaust memorial in Berlin. Filmic and literary representations of the Third Reich abounded, often with a new focus on German victimhood, such as the bombings of German cities or the mass rapes of German women at the end of the war. These works at times introduced new and interesting gradations of perpetration and victimhood; at other times they were quite transparent attempts at exculpation. They also raised new questions of how to commemorate the "symbiosis" or "dialogue" between Germans and Jews before the Holocaust.

In what follows, I will discuss two divergent ways in which stories of Jewish Gentile love were deployed at this moment of re-remembrance. On the one hand, a number

1. On the concept of "normalization," see especially Taberner 2005, xiii–xxvii, 106–198.

of German feature films dramatize interreligious love to highlight moments of solidarity and collaboration between Jews and non-Jews during the Third Reich. On the other hand, the German Jewish writer Barbara Honigmann depicts the memory of the National Socialist past as a lasting obstacle to Jewish Gentile love relationships. Whereas the films use love stories to project the possibility of interreligious collaboration into the past, Honigmann uses such stories for the opposite end, to show how conflicts of the past continue into the present. But as I will argue, this is not a simple negation of love as a trope of interreligious or intercultural mediation. Love remains an important trope in Honigmann, one that allows her to imagine a new kind of German Jewish diaspora.

German Heritage Films

The film critic Lutz Koepnick has aptly spoken of a wave of "heritage films" that hit the German movie theaters starting in the late 1990s (Koepnick 2002). The term "heritage film" was originally coined for late twentieth-century British films that cast the English past in a nostalgic light. While the new German films on the Third Reich can hardly be called nostalgic, they send a positive message in the sense that they "reclaim sites of multicultural consensus from a history of intolerance and persecution" (Koepnick 2002, 57). These films construct a useable past that can be easily consumed and enjoyed by contemporary viewers, without remainders of trauma and irredeemable dispersion. Interreligious love stories play a crucial role in this representation. Thus Max Färberbock's *Aimée & Jaguar* evolves around a lesbian love affair between a Jewish woman and the "Aryan" wife of a German soldier, and Joseph Vilsmaier's *Comedian Harmonists*, which recounts the rise and fall of a popular German musical band during the 1930s, features three Jewish Gentile couples. Both films depict the increasing oppression and persecution of Jews under the Nazi regime but shy away from a direct discussion of the Holocaust. Instead they focus on private dramas of love, jealousy, and reconciliation. The depiction of love affairs in which non-Jews steadfastly hold on to their Jewish partners, despite insults, threats, and dangers to their own life and liberty, adds to the feel-good quality of the films.

This is true even for the most somber among the German heritage films, Didi Danquart's *Jew-boy Levi*. *Jew-boy Levi* tells the story of a Jewish peddler who has long been an integral part of the rural economy and sociability but finds himself increasingly ostracized after the rise of Nazism. In the end, only the Christian girl whom he has hoped to marry and who harbors for him a strong, if rather non-erotic, affection stands by him. The girl saves Levi from mob violence by holding a pistol at the crowd while begging him to leave the town: "Go! Go!" she exclaims, and the very last scene shows the backlights of Levi's truck fading into the night. Though darker and more pessimistic than *Aimée & Jaguar* and *Comedian Harmonists*, *Jew-boy Levi* still conveys the message central to the German heritage films of the 1990s: that love may inspire acts of solidarity and resistance that could have forestalled genocidal terror had they only occurred with greater frequency and on a larger scale. By high-lighting moments of collaboration and consensus between Jews and non-Jews, the German heritage films imaginatively undo the traumas wrought by Nazism in a way that verges on historical revisionism.

The hopeful and conciliatory message of these films derives at least in part from their conflation of different subject positions. As viewers, we easily forget that the two partners in the Jewish Gentile love affairs fall into different places on the spectrum of victims and perpetrators and as such face radically different problems and choices. Instead, everybody alike seems to experience the pleasures and pangs of love. One effect of this conflation of subject positions is that attention is deflected away from Jewish to German suffering. *Aimée & Jaguar* focuses not on the plight of the Jewish Felice, who in the end is deported and murdered, but on the sadness of the Gentile Lily, who even decades after the end of the war is still mourning the loss of the love of her life. And one of the most gripping moments in *Comedian Harmonists* is the one in which the group, which has just been barred from public performance because three of its members are Jewish, bids farewell to its German audience with a song that fuses love, loss, and longing. The camera focus is mostly on Erna, the some-time Gentile girlfriend of the band's founder Harry, who realizes the depth of her love for Harry while listening to the song. Her sadness and regrets seem to radiate to the audience in the concert hall. According to Koepnick, this also applies to the audiences of contemporary German heritage films: "What makes audiences weep is not that Hitler's Germany exterminated the Jews of Europe in the name of the German nation, but rather that the Nazis betrayed the nation by prohibiting Germans to love their Jewish compatriots" (Koepnick 2002, 72).

This kind of false reconciliation culminates in Margarethe von Trotta's 2003 film *Rosenstrasse*, which turns love into a political program. The film dramatizes a real historical event, one of the very few instances of public protest against the anti-Jewish policies of Nazi Germany. When, in March of 1943, Jewish men living in mixed mar-riage—a status that had thus far protected them from deportation—were arrested, their non-Jewish wives and relatives gathered and protested until the men were released. The film *Rosenstrasse* focuses on the story of Ruth, a Jewish woman living in New York City, who as a child in Nazi Germany had been rescued by one of the women participating in the protest. She has never talked about this until her daughter Hannah flies to Germany and, in a series of interviews with the woman who saved her mother, reconstructs her mother's story as well as the history of the protest. The film casts this protest as a *Resistance of the Heart*—which is the title of a book on the events by the historian Nathan Stoltzfus—and intimates that if such behavior had occurred on a broader scale, it could have curbed or even prevented the Nazi persecution of the Jews. Historians are actually still debating the effectiveness of the protest: it is unclear, for instance, whether the Jewish men were actually facing deportation, and, if yes, whether it was the protest that prevented it.[2] But the film quite unambiguously suggests that the wives' love, devotion, and courage saved the husbands. According to its logic, intermarriage is a good thing because it creates kinship networks that protect minorities against persecution.

Even more problematic than the film's rather facile celebration of love as political resistance is its implication that Jews objecting to intermarriage might be to blame for their own persecution. This message is conveyed by the frame narrative, which shows how Ruth, after her husband's death, suffers from psychical symptoms including anxiety, flashbacks, and overly ritualistic behavior. During the *shiva*, the weeklong Jewish mourning ritual, she insists on observing the traditional religious customs in a way that her children find strained and inauthentic. One of the manifestations of this new religious zeal is her sudden and vehement rejection of Hannah's Nicaraguan fiancé, Luis, who is not Jewish. After a flashback shows the eight-year-old Ruth barely escaping incarceration and deportation, we see the grown-up Ruth staring first into the camera and then to Hannah and Luis. Turning to her son, she demands that Luis leave the mourning room: "He just doesn't belong . . . Tell [Hannah] that if she marries him, she's not my daughter anymore." During her trip to Germany, Hannah learns what must be the reason for this behavior: Ruth herself had a non-Jewish father, who during the Third Reich abandoned her and her mother, thereby indirectly causing the deportation of her mother. Upon her return to the United States, Hannah apparently persuades Ruth to recognize the story of her life and remember the bond with her adoptive Gentile mother.[3] This restoration of trust—made possible by the memory of the Gentile women who courageously stood by their Jewish husbands—seems to have a curative effect on Ruth, who in the final scene can be seen happily attending Hannah's wedding and blessing her son-in-law. As Sara Horowitz has pointed out, the wedding is only ambiguously coded as Jewish. It contains some elements of a Jewish ceremony, especially the breaking of a glass, but not others, notably the canopy (Horowitz 2010, 211). The film leaves open the question of whether Luis converted to Judaism or whether the couple is having an interfaith ceremony, thus continuing the themes of intermarriage and hybridity through the end.

By framing the history of the public protest by the story of a Jewish woman who learns to overcome her objections to intermarriage, *Rosenstrasse* at best pathologizes the victims and at worst blames them for their own persecution. The film suggests that Ruth's opposition to intermarriage is a pathological condition, a symptom of

---

2. The film begins by announcing "the events that unfolded on Rosenstrasse in Berlin from February 27 till March 6, 1943 are a historical fact," yet it distorts historical reality in several ways. See Meyer 2004, 23–36.

3. On the importance of mother-daughter relationships in the film, see Parkinson 2010, 109–135.

post-traumatic stress disorder rather than, for instance, a theologically justifiable position. *Rosenstrasse* leaves no room for expressions of particularity such as the commandment to marry within the faith, which is important in traditional Judaism. In its portrayal of Ruth, a Jewish woman who rejects the claims of love in favor of a compulsive adherence to rules and customs, the film revives one of the oldest religious stereotypes: the opposition between "Jewish law" and "Christian love."

Barbara Honigmann

The contemporary writer Barbara Honigmann was born in 1949 to Jewish parents who had returned to East Germany in 1947 after years of exile in Paris and London. While Judaism in a religious or cultural sense played no role in her parents' home, Honigmann herself began in the 1970s what she describes as a "search for a minimum of Jewish identity in my life" (Honigmann 1999, 15). She started learning Hebrew, got married in a Jewish ceremony, and in 1984 left the GDR for Strasbourg, a French city close to the German border that is home to a sizable and vibrant Jewish community, with members of various geographical origins and religious orientations.[4] It is here that she wrote her first collection of short stories, which upon its publication in 1986 became an instant success on the German book market. Honigmann would stage and restage this central fact of her life—that she became a German-language writer at the very moment she left Germany—in a series of autofictional texts. One of the main motives of her literary oeuvre, one may say, is the birth of writing out of the spirit of exile.

In Honigmann's 1991 *A Love Made Out of Nothing*, the narrator, a young Jewish woman working at a theater, leaves the German Democratic Republic for Paris in the hope of gaining new experiences and perspectives. But she soon finds that by going to Paris she involuntarily repeats the journey of her parents, who during the Third Reich were persecuted both as Jews and as socialists and forced into Parisian exile. The book never fully resolves the tension between these two different conceptions of exile—of exile as a grand awakening to new possibilities and of exile as the result of persecution and expulsion—leaving us with a peculiar sense of circularity and "stuckness." As the narrator states at one point: "Perhaps more than anything else, I've been running away from my parents and yet still go on trotting along behind them" (Honigmann 2003, 22). Only at the very end the narrator stands a certain chance of breaking the cycle of repetitions. After attending her father's funeral in Berlin, she departs a second time for Paris, and while sitting in the train, she closes the window curtains because she cannot endure seeing the scenery "again" (Honigmann 2003, 76). Significantly, the narrator's refusal to reenact her parents' past coincides with the beginning of

---

4. On the heterogeneous character of Strasbourg's Jewish community and Honigmann's conception of diasporic writing, see also Günther 2003, 215–231.

her own writing. Among her deceased father's belongings she found a notebook her father had kept after the end of the war and now, while leaving Germany for good, she decides to fill the remaining empty pages with her own entries.

One of the ways in which *A Love Made Out of Nothing* figures the necessity of a distance from Germany is through an impossible love story. While still in Berlin the narrator has a relationship with a theater colleague named Alfried. That relationship is secretive and distanced throughout—even while they are both in Berlin, they cannot look into each other's eyes, and they communicate mostly through brief written notes—and it is only after Alfried has left the GDR that the narrator writes to him of her love in long letters she composes but never puts into the mail. She makes it quite clear why the two of them can never truly come together: "From the very beginning I hated Alfried's name; I could hardly bring myself to say it because it sounded so Germanic and because I didn't want to love a German, because I couldn't and wouldn't forgive the Germans for what they had done to the Jews" (Honigmann 2003, 33). The narrator's insistence on the incompatibility of Germans and Jews culminates in a nightmarish vision of a monstrously divided child that would be born to her and Alfried: "I saw the child in nightmares, the way it was put together loosely from individual pieces and then came undone and fell apart and couldn't stand upright" (Honigmann 2003, 33).

The involuntary bond between Alfried and the narrator in *A Love Made Out of Nothing*—she also speaks of a "connection or even an adhesion that we couldn't pull away from" (Honigmann 2003, 33)—epitomizes the "negative symbiosis" between Germans and Jews after Auschwitz. This term has been coined by the historian Dan Diner, who argues that the Holocaust created a new, negative interdependency of German and Jewish cultures. According to Diner, since the end of the Second World War, German and Jewish identities have largely been constituted in relation to the Holocaust and the, naturally opposed, traumas it inflicted on the collective of the perpetrators and that of the victims. This situation has created a mutual dependence of postwar Germans and Jews, who need each other to work through the screen memories that cover up the core of each collective's trauma (Diner 2003). But what happens if we convey this idea through an impossible love story rather than a theoretical concept such as "negative symbiosis" or "distanced dialogue"? In other words, what is the theoretical, artistic, or political purchase of love?

One of the things the rhetoric of love does for Honigmann is help carve out a space for diasporic writing. In an essay titled "On My Great-Grandfather, My Grandfather, My Father, and Me," she recalls her family's commitment to German culture in terms quite similar to Gershom Scholem. Her ancestors' models of acculturation—including her great grandfather's struggle for political rights, her grandfather's commitment to academia, and her father's membership in the East German Communist party—all turn out to be fueled by love for German culture. All of them were, in addition to their professional occupations, authors of literary texts. Like Scholem, Honigmann believes that the devotion of Jews to German culture did not help them but only blinded them to the precariousness of their situation. Her ancestors "desired [the German culture], reached out for it, and stretched and contorted themselves unbelievably in order to unite themselves with it. Instead of unification, they mostly experienced denial and repulsion, and my father was given the privilege of witnessing the final destruction of German-Jewish history with his own eyes" (Honigmann 1995, 513). Honigmann decides to distance herself from this model of acculturation, conceptually by giving up the idea of a social avant-garde and geographically by moving from Germany to France.

However, she finds that she remains connected to Germany through her writing in two ways. First, all of her writing circles around the failed hopes and the unrequited love experienced by her ancestors. She may no longer try to spearhead ideas as they did, instead recycling and recharging the words of everyday life, but she nevertheless remains thematically focused, even fixated, on her family's failed love affair with German culture. Secondly, and more importantly, she uses the rhetoric of love to depict her own development as a writer. The primary scene of her literary work—how she became a German writer by going into exile—is now recast as a romantic break-up. Her writing is a form of farewell from Germany, comparable to the letters composed by lovers after a separation. This separation, she conjectures, guarantees an abiding attachment. Her writing is still a form of love, now understood as a desperate appeal to another who may or may not be listening. Here is this passage, cited at some length:

> But perhaps writing was also something like homesickness and an assurance that we really did belong together, Germany and I, that we, as they say, could not get away from each other, especially not now, after everything that had happened . . . My writing had in effect come from a more or less fortuitous separation, just as couples write each other love letters at the very beginning of their infatuation and then not again until their breakup . . . (Honigmann 1995, 513)
>
> I wanted to present myself completely differently than my great-grandfather, my grandfather, and my father, and now I saw myself, just like them, speaking again to the Other, hoping to be heard, perhaps even to be understood, calling to him, "Look at me! Listen to me, at least for five minutes." . . . I understood that writing means being separated and is very similar to exile, and that it is in this sense perhaps true that being a writer and being a Jew are similar as well, in the way they are dependent upon the Other when they speak to him, more or less despairingly. It is true of both that approaching the Other too closely is dangerous for them and that agreeing with him too completely will bring about their downfall. (Honigmann 1995, 514)

While the connection Honigmann establishes here between writing, exile, and Jewishness is not an entirely new idea, the rhetoric of love adds an interesting twist, as it creates a sense of continuity with the earlier tradition of German Jewish literature. Even if Honigmann's German-language texts are farewell letters to a lover rather than the wooing calls uttered by her ancestors, they are still driven by the same impulse. In fact, they for the first time render this impulse fully tangible. According to Honigmann, writing means to sustain a tension between distance and proximity, to endure the dependence on another whom one addresses but from whom one remains separated. All writing is a desperate call across a necessary distance, a one-directional communication with someone who potentially misunderstands everything. As a self-professed diasporic writer, Honigmann does in a conscious and critical manner what her forefathers did unconsciously, desperately, and futilely.

Here we find one reason as to why interreligious love is so important in Honigmann, although she mostly stages its failure. Love is central to Honigmann's conception of the relationship between self and other in the diaspora. Love stories capture the constant negotiation between proximity and distance, recognition and rejection, collaboration and conflict in the diaspora. In that process, love itself becomes redefined as a force of disruption rather than of fusion. In her 2000 *With All My Love* (*Alles, alles Liebe!*), an epistolary novel that plays in 1970s East Berlin and features a failing love story between a Jewish woman and a Gentile man, Honigmann depicts the gradual surfacing of ever more differences between the lovers. The aspiring theater director Anna Herzfeld moves from Berlin to the provincial town of Prenzlau, leaving behind her new lover Leon. Their initially passionate love letters grow increasingly disappointed as all sorts of misgivings and misunderstanding arise. The relationship finally ends when Leon expresses his aversion to Anna's Jewish circle, which he considers very German and partly responsible for the political oppression in the GDR. He also points to the differences between their respective family's stories: unlike Anna's parents, his mother had not been able to emigrate during the Third Reich. She, too, suffered hardships on account of having a child with Down Syndrome (Honigmann 2000, 159).

This failure of love, however, appears necessary as well as productive. Already the novel's title, *Alles, alles Liebe!*, hints at a constitutive distance built into affectionate relationships. A standard letter ending, *Alles, alles Liebe* serves simultaneously to express affection and to bid farewell. The title may also be an elliptical clause— "(Es ist) alles, alles Liebe"—an allusion to the constantly changing love constellations in the circle of friends described in the novel. One of the characters claims that the mobility of love is a form of political resistance, part of a life style that will transform society gradually and without the violence of a revolution (Honigmann 2000, 115). The novel seems to call for what Zygmunt Bauman calls "liquid love," or the ability to quickly tie and untie bonds to others in order to adapt to ever changing circumstances (Bauman 2003). Furthermore, one of its central lines—"where there is love there is also betrayal" (Honigmann 2000, 103, 160)—posits an inherent negativity of love.

I would argue that the repeated failures of Jewish Gentile love affairs in Honigmann are a sign of this structural negativity rather than the result of biological incompatibility, irresolvable historical conflict, or anything along these lines. I would further argue that this essential negativity of love is part of its appeal as a trope for inter-religious relations—for Honigmann as well as for contemporary critics in search of new models of particularity and universality. When we understand love as a force that proliferates differences rather than creates a union, it makes for not quite so cheesy a metaphor, not quite so conciliatory a story.

This new conception of love can also change our understanding of what the collaboration between ethnic or religious groups might look like. Rather than a union or dialogue, such collaboration may take the form of a disjointed, non-contemporaneous exchange between multiple parties. Honigmann's essay "On My Great-Grandfather" itself provides an example of such a disjointed exchange. This essay has a frame narrative I have thus far neglected. Honigmann's meditation on her family's past is triggered by her encounter with a German Turkish (i.e., Muslim) family that now lives in Strasbourg and that confronts her with some well-worn stereotypes about Jews. When the family wonders why Honigmann and her husband do not have a shop like all the other Jews, they are sending her mind off to her ancestors' decidedly intellectual pursuits. After telling the story of her ancestors, she reminds the reader that she did this only in her mind and avoided responding to the question of the Turkish family in reality. Instead of attempting to overcome the barriers between them, she decides to play ball with one of the children:

> I walk a ways and play with [the Turkish child] . . . because I find doing so less stressful than explaining to his parents why we have no shop, less stressful than setting straight their picture of Jews—a picture which is apparently just as distorted as ours is of them—less stressful than clearing away all the misunderstandings that emerge between us in just this one afternoon and telling them the whole story of my great-grandfather, my grandfather, my father, and me. (Honigmann 1995, 516)

Ironically, what the narrator refuses to do for her Turkish neighbors—to explain her family's background—she has just done for her German readers, from whom she presumably feels no less separate. This is an example of how one failed dialogue generates another form of exchange, one that is written rather than spoken, distanced rather than immediate, unidirectional rather than reciprocal. We can see the potential of this model by looking at the actual effect of Honigmann's essay. While the essay itself describes her unwillingness to engage with her Turkish neighbors, to dispel their prejudices and establish a common ground, it subsequently became an inspiration for the contemporary German Turkish writer Zafer Şenocak. Şenocak cites Honigmann's text in one of his own essays, which traces points of contact between Turkish Islam and the secularized Christianity of the German Enlightenment. Among other things, he recounts how his Turkish ancestors, who were pious Muslims, eagerly read the German classics, which one of them adorned with jottings in Arabic script. Şenocak also writes that life stories and family genealogies such as Honigmann's inspired him to reconstruct this history of transreligious and transcultural exchange. According to him, cultures open up to each other in the singularity of personal experience, which registers but also exceeds different cultural influences. For Şenocak, the German Jewish experience described in Honigmann and others becomes a model of Turkish German transculturation (Şenocak 2011). Of course, the history of German Turkish relations is long and complex and their character not uncontroversial. The political alliance between the Wilhelminian and Ottoman Empires, the flight of German Jewish academics to Turkish universities in the 1930s, and the influx of Turkish *Gastarbeiter* (guest workers) into postwar German society provided much intercultural contact yet were far from being equal exchanges. A firm believer in Enlightenment principles, Şenocak tends to idealize German Turkish relations and to downplay the anti-Muslim biases of many German intellectuals. One may even speak here of another "one-sided love affair" between twentieth-century Turkish and German thinkers. However, this takes nothing away from Şenocak's point that German Turkish writers in search for new models of transculturation may draw inspiration from German Jewish writers.[5]

In other words, the failed Turkish Jewish encounter *described* in Honigmann's essay generates the indirect Jewish German exchange that *is* Honigmann's essay, which in turn generates the complex Turkish German Jewish exchange that is Şenocak's essay. I would venture to say that here we have one explanation as to why love supplants dialogue as a privileged trope of mediation in Scholem, Honigmann, and others: Love—and especially unrequited love—can inaugurate potentially infinite chains of encounters.

References

Aschheim, Steven E. *Scholem, Arendt, Klemperer: Intimate Chronicles in Turbulent Times.* Bloomington: Indiana University Press, 2001.
Bauman, Zygmunt. *Liquid Love: On the Frailty of Human Bonds.* Malden, MA: Polity Press, 2003.
Diner, Dan. "Negative Symbiosis: Germans and Jews after Auschwitz." In *The Holocaust: Theoretical Readings*, edited by Neil Levi and Michael Rothberg, 423–430. New Brunswick, NJ: Rutgers University Press, 2003.
Guenther, Christina. "Exile and the Construction of Identity in Barbara Honigmann's Trilogy of the Diaspora." *Comparative Literature Studies* 40.2 (2003): 215–231.

---

5. I would like to thank my colleague Ülker Gökberk for sharing her knowledge of the history of Turkish German relations with me. I would also like to thank her for her incisive comments on an earlier draft of this essay and for the inspiring conversations she and I and our students had on the subject while we were co-teaching a seminar on contemporary German literature at Reed College in the spring of 2012.

Hertz, Deborah. *How Jews Became Germans: The History of Conversion and Assimilation in Berlin.* New Haven: Yale University Press, 2007.

Honigmann, Barbara. *A Love Made Out of Nothing.* John Barrett, trans. Jaffrey, NH: Godine, 2003. [German edition: *Eine Liebe aus nichts.* Reinbek: Rowohlt, 1991.]

———. *Alles, alles Liebe.* Munich: Carl Hanser, 2000.

———. *Damals, dann, danach.* Munich: Carl Hanser, 1999.

———. "On My Great-Grandfather, My Grandfather, My Father, and Me." Meghan W. Barnes, trans. *World Literature Today* 69.3 (1995): 512–516.

Horowitz, Sara R. "Lovin' Me, Lovin' Jew: Gender, Intermarriage, and Metaphor." In *Antisemitisim and Philosemitism in the Twentieth and Twenty-First Centuries: Representing Jews, Jewishness, and Modern Culture,* edited by Phyllis Lassner and Lara Trubowitz, 196–216. Newark: University of Delaware Press, 2010.

Koepnick, Lutz. "Reframing the Past: Heritage Cinema and Holocaust in the 1990s." *New German Critique* 87 (2002): 47–82.

Meyer, Beate. "Geschichte im Film: Judenverfolgung, Mischehen und der Protest in der Rosenstraße 1943." *Zeitschrift für Geschichtswissenschaft* 1 (2004): 23–36.

Parkinson, Anna M. "Neo-feminist *Mütterfilm*? The Emotional Politics of Margarethe von Trotta's *Rosenstrasse.*" In *The Collapse of Conventional: German Film and Its Politics at the Turn of the Twenty-First Century,* edited by Jaimey Fisher and Brad Prager, 109–135. Detroit: Wayne State University Press, 2010.

Scholem, Gershom. "Jews and Germans." In *On Jews and Judaism in Crisis,* edited by Werner J. Dannhauser, 71–92. New York: Schocken, 1976.

Şenocak, Zafer. "Mein Erbe spricht auch Deutsch: Vergessene deutsch-türkische Verwandtschaften." In *Deutschsein: Eine Aufklärungsschrift,* 172–190. Hamburg: Edition Körber-Stiftung, 2011.

Taberner, Stuart. *German Literature of the 1990s and Beyond: Normalization and the Berlin Republic.* Rochester, NY: Camden House, 2005.

9
Interrogating Diaspora

*Beyond the Ethnic Mosaic—Faith, Space, and Time in
London's East End*

Jane Garnett and Michael Keith

> Whoever has walked slowly down Brick Lane
> . . .
> would know rich history is the present before us,
> laid out like a cloth—a cloth for the wearing,
> with bits of mirror and coloured stuff . . .
> —"Brick Lane" by Stephen Watts (Leech 2001, 7)

This is an essay about religion, diaspora, place, and history. Its vantage-point is the East End of London, a place in which long-standing self-conscious reflection on its history as a zone of transition has the potential to illuminate many broader theoretical questions about diaspora, religion, and religion-in-diaspora. Recent works on diaspora and on the interrelated fields of religion and diaspora have cautioned against too dispersed or essentialized a usage of either concept. There has been a call for a refocusing of attention both on the local and on the subjective nature of experience and formation of casts of mind. It is recognized that in order to be analytically useful, the conceptual relationship between the local, the global, and the transcendental needs to be firmed up (Brubaker 2005; Johnson 2012). Much more rarely has there been a demand for a historical sensibility—either in understanding the particular, or in interrogating the very development of the theoretical positions themselves, and their wider political and cognitive significance. Local situations are inflected with the language of contemporary social theory, which can easily become reified, pretending to a universalism which occludes on the one hand the historical contingency of its formation and on the other the messiness and overlapping nature of its use on the ground. In this way the historical ordering of things and the geographical mapping of peoples are rarely innocent or free from their own chains of metonymic association. Immigration, migration, diaspora, transnational, multi-cultural, ethnic/religious community: all these terms carry baggage with them—the residue of accumulated strata of use and of diversity of understandings. A sharper sense of historical specificity does not imply the abandonment of theory, but the thickening of its texture. History here means "the present before us"—a dynamic in a series of "present moments" rather than simply a backdrop of the past.

Likewise geography is relational, a geometry implicit in a cartography. Here we consider two examples that confuse and complicate dominant narratives of diasporic association and conventional readings of diasporic transnationalism. We argue that a nuanced sense of diaspora formation and development demands an understanding of how the analytical vocabulary of diaspora could cross borders between the humanities and the social sciences more productively. The concept generates not only a sense of social formation at a distance. It involves an iterative sense of reinscription, rewriting, and remembering. Both the historical narratives through which diaspora becomes visible and the active mapping of the transnational occur at a given contemporary moment or series of such moments but draw upon remembered pasts, futures present, and imagined geographies that make the term more tentative and its power more contingent than conventional social scientific language would at times suggest. In exploring the ways in which diaspora and religion interrelate, we here present two examples of the complexities we are interested in exploring.

Confusing Communion

The first concerns the Anglican Church—still the established Church of England, but also a transnational religious communion with well-rooted diasporic attributes. Its extensive missionary activity from the early nineteenth century related discursively the mission project abroad and at home, particularly in inner-city contexts of considerable intranational (often highly localized) migration. Debates about diaspora should take account of the micro-geographies of such interactions, which often shared characteristics. Both on the ground and in contemporary theorization, different types of migratory movement were analogized productively. London's East End was one such context, which acquired particular resonance given London's status as the metropolitan imperial capital. Awareness, and in many cases experience, of the demands of variant forms of mobility and of a multiplicity of perspectives and aspirations gave clergy, missioners, and a wide range of other lay workers an impetus to creative activity: in conditions of heightened religious (and non-religious) pluralism, the nineteenth century was one of religious revival and theological radicalization (Garnett 2000). In the recent past (especially since the mid-1980s, when confrontation on the part of many Anglicans with Thatcherite politics moved them into a more countercultural position), the Anglican Church has carried the potential for reinventing itself—especially in inner-city contexts as a sacred space—a point of reference capable of transcending bonded, gathered, often mono-ethnic religious communities. No longer hegemonic, it still has cultural, political, and a certain level of financial confidence, as well as the functional tradition of responsibility for the whole territorial parish, not just formal adherents of a "gathered church." As a result, Anglican churches in some cases in East London have become the space within which inter-religious marriages can take place—an Orthodox Christian with a Hindu, say—to avoid cooption by one or other religious group. At the same time, its own history gives opportunities for migrants brought up in mission schools or singing Anglican hymns in churches in India or Africa to feel at home, while also drawing on other traditions to supplement and reconfigure their devotional lives (Garnett and Harris 2013). Just as in the nineteenth century, inhabitants of a given parish continue to interact with different religious organizations for different—often instrumental—spiritual, cultural, and socio-economic purposes.

In the spring of 2004, an installation of eighty-three thousand shimmer disks by the artist Rose Finn-Kelcey was set up on the façade of St Paul's Anglican Church, Bow Common in the London borough of Tower Hamlets. Called "Angel," it took the form of an "emoticon"—a halo, two eyes, a nose, and a smile—on an orange-gold-red field that caught every shift of light and weather. The Bollywood connotations were intentional, as was the contemporaneity of text language, designed to speak to young local people in this culturally extremely mixed part of London—Christians, Hindus, Muslims, Jews, of other faiths or none—without being any less a Christian symbol. Some Christian viewers saw in it Pentecostal, apocalyptic, or Marian significance. The vicar who had commissioned it commented on its position on the west wall facing the setting sun—the traditional place for a last judgment: "it carries all the magnificence and solemnity of that idea" (Wedderburn 2004). His conception of the role of the church was that it should have strong symbolic power, emphatically not in a missionary sense, but embodying a confidence in its own integrity.

The church itself, built between 1958 and 1960 to replace a mid-Victorian church destroyed in the Blitz, represented at the time a pioneering redefinition of the role of the Anglican Church as the focal point of the parish (Maguire 2002; Adler 2012, 16–29). Starting from the provocative proposition that the Church did not need buildings, the architects, Robert Maguire and Keith Murray, developed a conversation with the parish about what it really meant to design a "space apart," confronting the complex interweaving of the functional and the symbolic, liturgically and spiritually (Maguire and Murray 1962, 14; Banham 1960). Designed with no permanent structure internally beyond the tented canopy over the centrally positioned altar, and built of industrial materials, the church was intended to express in a new idiom both the people as the body of Christ and the church as embedded in the everyday and the provisional. It incorporated a processional path around its internal perimeter both to evoke the history of parochial processions and to signal mobility and flexibility. The architects commented that it grew out of the life of a particular community at a particular time, and that "on this very matter of particularity" they had been strongly criticized by the architectural profession, which in the late 1950s and early 1960s spoke the formal language of a crystallized high modernism, consonant with the confident generalizing of contemporary social science (Maguire 1962, 68; Maguire 1976, 70–72). They observed, however, that:

> We are still sure that a building which "lives" now for and because of the local community will continue to be "alive" for others who follow, precisely in the way that good churches built in the past still have this quality. (Maguire and Murray 1962, 16)

This was an approach to modernity grounded neither in fashionable stylistic orthodoxies nor in historicism, but in a profound and radical sense of history (cf. Jackson 1996).

The architects' vision was shaped through close engagement with the then vicar, Gresham Kirkby, a leading Christian communist/anarchist, who believed passionately in the revolutionary potential of the Church. As a recently ordained priest, on August 15, 1947—the independence of India and Pakistan—he had celebrated the feast of the Assumption of the Virgin in explicit interrelationship with heralding the beginning of the end of the British Empire. In the 1950s, when one of the first "Keep Britain White" slogans was daubed on a wall in the St Paul's parish, he led the congregation with a processional cross, candles and incense, and a pot of red paint, to replace "white" with "brotherly" (Leech 2009, 8). Pride in this act of "godly civil disobedience" was passed on in collective memory to the current priest, an Anglo-Indian whose family had left Calcutta for East London during Partition, when he was eight, and whose traumatic formative childhood memories were of interreligious conflict. His arrival in Bow in the late 1990s spearheaded a re-radicalization of the church at a historically low ebb for Anglican church attendance and within an area characterized by long established Asian and Black British settlement. One of his first initiatives was to organize in association with the Victoria and Albert Museum, or V&A, *Shamiana*, a large exhibition of over fifty embroidered tent panels created by British South Asian women of different religious and cultural backgrounds from across the country. This was a project arising out of the fiftieth anniversary of Indian/Pakistani independence, and intended symbolically to cut across the fault lines of contested memory, not least by its showcasing of the work of women as community builders. Encouraging mostly working-class and unemployed women who had never heard of the V&A to look at historic Mughal panels and reinvent them in modern terms was to facilitate a dialogue with historic South Asian artifacts brought to an imperial museum in the mid-nineteenth century, and to revalidate them in a new context. Dramatically opening up a church in the midst of a mostly non-Christian Asian population to non-church-goers, it also rejuvenated the congregation itself (Melhuish 1998). Like many other Anglican churches in East London, as well as its associated primary school, it supports a wide range of local and transnational associational culture and welfare bodies.

In a political context in which it is convenient for "faith" and interfaith organizations to be affirmed and relied upon, Anglicanism here can play at once on its residual centrality and its religious vulnerability. At the memorial service for Gresham Kirkby in Bow in 2006, the Bishop of London explicitly related his radical theology to the architecture of the church: "This is a tent for a pilgrim people who have no abiding city here. But at its very heart there is the seed of a new social/spiritual order" (Chartres 2009, 12). For all Christians, the metaphor and often the reality of life as pilgrimage, and the underlying force of eschatology, root their theological reflection in the creative tension between worlds and horizons—this-worldly and otherworldly. For the Anglican Church in East London, engagement with the diasporic has become increasingly urgent, both theologically and practically. But they have not started from a tabula rasa. The process is shot through with complex threads of history and of self-reflexivity.

The St Paul's / V&A collaboration was coordinated by British Bangladeshi curator Shireen Akbar. Akbar was born in Calcutta, then qualified and taught in the University of Dhaka after her family moved to Bangladesh. After studying English at Cambridge, she moved on to Tower Hamlets to work with the borough youth service, developing projects with young Sylheti women, routing cultural traffic between London and Bangladesh. She produced a set of banners on which were embroidered the Bengali alphabet, displayed in the Whitechapel Art Gallery in 1979, initiating the first of a number of collaborations. In the same year she worked closely again with the Whitechapel to curate an *Arts of Bengal* exhibition which gave a new perspective to the presence of the migrant community from Sylhet in the East End, and, in 1983, she mounted a linked exhibition of South Asian domestic artifacts at the Commonwealth Institute in west London. In 1988 she went on to create *Woven Air*, the exhibition at the Whitechapel of woven and embroidered textiles from Bangladesh. *Woven Air* both celebrated the ancient traditions of Jamdani muslin weaving and Naksha Kantha (traditional quilts) embroidery and brought them up to date with the presence in the gallery of working weavers from Bangladesh (Adams and Rae 1997). Powerfully, in all these projects she was working deliberately to reposition established traditions in Bangladesh as well as London. She worked within and complicated both the particular pedagogical tradition of the late nineteenth-century Christian settlement movement identified with the Whitechapel Gallery and the rhetorically inclusive idiom of the Commonwealth Institute. At the same time she personified the manner in which histories are contested as much abroad as at home.

Henrietta Barnett, who with her husband Samuel Barnett founded Toynbee Hall in 1884 as a means of creating connections between different social classes, developed art exhibitions as one way of engaging the east London of the late nineteenth century that so alarmed social reformers of the time (Koven 1994; Koven 2004). The exhibitions led to the foundation of the Whitechapel Art Gallery in 1901 and were part of a more general movement through which diasporic identities and domesticating interventions became central to settlement-led reforms in the early twentieth century (Bradley 2009). Anglican and other Christian denominational and non-denominational settlements were paralleled by Jewish organizations in attempting to mediate between different, often fragmented, elements of the local population. Akbar's work recognized its antecedents, however different her terms and strategies. Her diasporic retelling of the significance of the alphabet of Bengali spoke self-consciously to the East Pakistan language movement of the post-partition era. Its legacies play out in the streets and squares of Bangladesh today and in tandem in the park opposite the Whitechapel Art gallery where the shadow of the original White Chapel can still be traced in a public space that is now known as Altab Ali Park.

Contested Inscriptions—Between Bangladeshi and Islamic Diasporic Belonging

In the early months of 2013, a growing social movement in Dhaka, starting online but rapidly taking to the streets, put pressure on Sheikh Hasina's Awaami League–led government to follow through the trials of those who had been identified with the killings of secular activists in the 1971 War of Independence. In 1971, a large if contested number were killed supporting West Pakistani military suppression of Sheikh Mujib's first national government of East Pakistan/Bangladesh. Both the mass mobilizations of 100,000 to 500,000 that occupied large parts of the Shahbag neighborhood of Dhaka in February and March of 2013 and the Jamaat linked Hefazat-e-Islam long march from Chittagong to occupy a different part of Dhaka in May this year occupied the space of the city to make visible a contest over Bangladeshi identity. Both movements generated a violent reaction: one of the lead Shahbag protesters was killed in a machete attack and the leaders of the Hefazat-e-Islam initially claimed that three thousand of their activists and supporters died when confronted by government forces on May 6, 2013, when they were peacefully gathering at Motijheel Shapla Square in front of Bangladesh Bank (Central Bank of Bangladesh) in downtown Dhaka city, although human rights organizations subsequently estimated significant deaths at a lower number (normally in tens rather than thousands). The Shahbag protesters demanded the protection of secular identities and the death penalties for those such as Delwar Hossain Sayeedi, convicted of war crimes from 1971. Sayeedi was found guilty in February 2013 of charges of mass killing, rape, arson, looting, and religious persecution during the liberation war twenty-two years earlier. Hefazat claimed that the integrity of religious faith in the country was under threat and their eponymous aim was to "safeguard Islam." The violent suppression of the Hefazat mobilization and the numbers of casualties in Dhaka prompted international concern from transnational NGOs, with Human Rights Watch demanding an independent tribunal to inquire into the confrontation.

In East London each Friday for much of the time between February and May demonstrations played out a London vernacular version of the same controversy in Altab Ali Park. Prompting major police interventions to preempt any direct confrontation on a regular basis, an iterative set of protests have made claims on both the space of the city and the future of both British Bangladeshi and Islamic diasporic identities as demonstrations alternate the weeks in which they make their presence felt. The choice of this particular space of inscription is significant (Keith 2003).

In 1978 Altab Ali, a young Bangladeshi clothing factory worker was murdered in one of the more extreme of the grim catalogue of racist assaults that characterized East London at the time (BGTC 1979). He was attacked in St Mary's Gardens, the site of the church of St Mary Matfelon, known locally at the time as one of the "Itchy Parks" after the tramps and vagrants that so often slept there, a coinage allegedly celebrated in the Small Faces 1960s record "Itchacoo Park." The murder provoked a mass mobilization of the Bengali community locally. It came to represent a watershed in the self-organization of the community, as the protests against the murder, initially fronted by antiracist activists and worthies from outside the area, politicized a generation of young Bengali activists (Eade 1989). Demonstrations and sit-ins on Brick Lane, just a few hundred yards from the site of the murder were aimed to drive out and purify the area of far right National Front activists who at that time used Brick Lane as both a point of congregation and a focus of fascist activity, not least against the stallholders and restaurant owners from ethnic minorities that were common in the street (Keith 1995).

The renaming of the park was contested by graffiti tags and through sustained debate about the future of the park over the following decades. The stories through which the landscapes of the city are rendered legible are commonly contested, and in Altab Ali Park this contest in 1998 coalesced around proposals to site a Bangladeshi martyrs' memorial in the park. The original Shahid Minar was a memorial erected by medical students in Dacca Medical College in 1952 to commemorate their peers who had died the preceding year in the effort to establish Bengali as a recognized language. In the years after independence in 1947 the Pakistani state attempted to impose Urdu universally across both West and East Pakistan, as part of the "nation-building" process, and was concerned at the perceived corruption of the Bengali language by Sanskrit words and phrases. The contest over the putative Arabization of the Bengali language contained within it the microcosm of confrontation between contrasting essences of identity, between a shared Islam that was the raison d'être for the state of Pakistan West and East in 1947 and the secular nationalism that emerged as a Bangladeshi independence movement. Replicas of the original Shahid Minar have been constructed globally as commemorative marks by the Bengali, including one built prior to 1998 in the northern British town of Oldham, and February 21 is observed in Bengali communities across the world as National Language Day.

The choice of Altab Ali Park for the East London copy of the Shahid Minar was a symbolically deliberate claiming. The martyrs' memorial in East London consciously linked Altab Ali to the nationalist struggle and reinforced one particular telling of this space (Alexander 2013). Consequently, opposition came from both those Bengali voices that rejected secular nationalism as opposed to Islamic universalism as the basis of British-based diasporic politics and also from expressions of white populism that resented this appropriation of the history of the park.

In the most recent articulation of this debate, Sayeedi was remembered as somebody who had visited the United Kingdom and whose talks at East London Mosque prompted demonstrations in the early 1990s in Altab Ali Park organized by the Nirmul Committee. The Nirmul Committee was founded to campaign for justice for those killed in the Bangladeshi Liberation War and organizes branches in both Bangladesh and the UK (Ahmed and Eversley 2010). Numerically it is much weaker in East London than the groups associated with Jamaat, such as the Young Muslim Organisation and Islamic Forum Europe, and so in spring 2013 the spectacle of the Shahbag protests brought about a momentary celebratory flourishing of support and numbers in the park.

Such disputes exist within a frame of reference that approximates to the notion of an alternative public sphere. It is unruly, contested, and disputatious. Through such arenas the uncertainties of diaspora appear and are then rendered invisible. The spaces are important because they disrupt the certainties of assimilatory success and stigmatized segregation. They link here and elsewhere, parts of East London and cartographies of both the Islamic ummah and the Bangladeshi national imaginary.

What is at stake in the park does not fit neatly into the conventional typologies of migrant settlement and transnationalism. The disputes are not between a Sylheti village past and an assimilatory future. Nor are they about either a politics of Bangladesh or a politics of the United Kingdom. The geographical coordinates run partly through Bangladesh and Britain, but also circumscribe a notion of theological debate that runs through Syria, Egypt, Saudi Arabia, and India. The histories present invoke 1971 but are also about the "present before us" that structures the kind of society that will emerge in both Bangladesh and east London in decades to come. Social drama takes place here and elsewhere simultaneously, in sites that are shared virtually and in a temporal rhythm that communicates an injustice, a protest case, or a killing instantaneously between Sylhet, Whitechapel, Dhaka, and London. The routes of diaspora, the development of diaspora formation, and the sensibility of the diasporic imagination are all challenged by this simultaneity of past and present, here and there. But the challenge is precisely a product of historical and geographical specificity that configures what is both extensively global and intensely local through the power of inscription.

Conclusion

Inscriptions are multilayered and build deliberatively on the historical archaeology of the particular place. When in 1990 Kenneth Leech, the Christian socialist Anglican priest, established a base for the practice of urban theology in the disused St Mary's clergy house and former post office in Altab Ali Park, he invoked an interlocking set of associations, and made a strong statement both about the significance of "local theology" and about the potential for an Anglican to enact the experiment (Leech 2006). He had been invited to take part in the dedication ceremony for the formal gates set up in memory of Altab Ali in 1989, a testimony to his deep local roots and respect for his long-standing work to combat racism. In 1988 he had moved the Runnymede Trust of which he was then Director to the East End, one of its predecessors—the Campaign against Racial Discrimination—having been based at Toynbee Hall. The clergy house, positioned at the intersection of a number of roads at the heart of Whitechapel on the one hand spoke to a historic Anglican presence and on the other to its present pastoral absence on the site. His project—itself self-consciously at an angle to the diocesan hierarchy—drew energy from an older East End Anglo-Catholic tradition as well as from a more recent transnational Catholic liberation theology working through the idiom of movement, exile and strangeness (Leech 2001, 9, 119–120, 229). While the specific experiment ended in 2004, its legacy lives on in different initiatives, not least the Contextual Theology Centre at the St Katharine's Foundation in the East End (which also houses the Leech archive). This center coordinates church-based community organizing and leadership training, by analogy with (and in close association with) broad-based community-mobilizing associations like London Citizens, itself rooted both in London interfaith and US urban activism.

The predominant political languages of appeal and assembly have changed over the last couple of decades—from race, through culture to faith—from multiculturalism to community and dialogue. The concept of diaspora takes its place on the one hand as part of a constructive process of recognizing complexity, but on the other as a means of distancing and of sanitizing language. In purporting to describe rather than implying a normative construction it conceals the imaginative tenacity of less acceptable languages of intolerance and the creation of new ones. Close attention to the historical existences of groups of people thinking diasporically over a much longer period than the modern currency of the term itself implies, opens up a more critically helpful understanding of its analytical traction. Race, faith, and place have intersected in competitive, conflicting, and consensual ways in the processes of negotiation of the local and global oscillations of mobility and settlement.

What is the autonomy of diaspora, what agency does it possess, how does it claim rights and a voice? Michel Foucault famously suggested that this problem of sovereignty was a major shibboleth of political theory, that "at bottom, despite the differences in epochs and objectives, the representation of power has remained under a spell. In political thought and analysis we have still not cut off the head of the king" (Foucault 1990, 88–89). In this essay we have argued that a sensibility that is historically and geographically nuanced might complicate diaspora's ontology. The confection of pasts and presents, here and elsewhere in its constitution make us think differently about the sovereign power of the diasporic as well as its contingency. Altab Ali Park shelters the tomb of the executioner of King Charles I. It also hosts contested and multiformed aggregations of people and material cultures that claim an agency that is geographically and historically specific. In all its complexities the inscriptions of the park, like those of St Paul's Bow Common, or Whitechapel Art Gallery, point beyond sovereign power to a sense of twenty first-century social formation.

References

Adams, C. and Rae, A. 1997 "Shireen Akbar: Obituary." *Independent*, April 1, 1997. Accessed August 13, 2013. http://www.independent.co.uk/news/people/obituary-shireen-akbar-1264610.html.

Adler, Gerald, Robert Maguire, and Keith Murray. *Twentieth Century Architects*. London: Royal Institute of British Architects, 2012.

Ahmed, A. and Eversley, J. *Bengalis in London's East End*. London: Swadhinata Trust, 2010 (also available online at http://www.swadhinata.org.uk).

Alexander, Claire. "Contested Memories: The Shahid Minar and the Struggle for Diasporic Space." *Ethnic and Racial Studies* 36 (2013): 590–610.

Banham, Reyner. "A Modern Church on Liturgical Principles." *Architectural Review* 128 (1960): 400.

Bethnal Green Trades Council (BGTC). *Blood on the Streets*. London: Stepney Books, 1979.

Bradley, Kate. *Poverty, Philanthropy and the State: Charities and the Working Classes in London, 1918–79*. Manchester: Manchester University Press, 2009.

Brubaker, Rogers. "The 'Diaspora' Diaspora," *Ethnic and Racial Studies* 28 (2005): 1–19.

Chartres, Richard. 2009. "Memorial Address." In *Father Gresham Kirkby 1916–2006. Priest of the Kingdom of God*, by Kenneth Leech, 10–16. London: Anglo-Catholic Historical Society.

Eade, J. *The Politics of Community: The Bangladeshi Community in East London*. Aldershot: Avebury, 1989.

Foucault, M. *The History of Sexuality*, Vol. 1: An Introduction. New York: Pantheon Books, 1990.

Garnett, Jane. "Religious and Intellectual Life." In *The Nineteenth Century: The Short Oxford History of the British Isles*, edited by C. Matthew, 194–227. Oxford: Oxford University Press, 2000.

Garnett, Jane and Alana Harris. "Church without Walls: Mapping the Sacred in East London." In *Rescripting Religion in the City: Migration and Religious Identity in the Modern Metropolis*, edited by Jane Garnett and Alana Harris, 115–31. Farnham: Ashgate, 2013.

Jackson, Neil. "Robert Maguire's Annual Lecture on 'Continuity and Modernity in the Holy Place,'" *Society of Architectural Historians of Great Britain Newsletter* 58 (Summer 1996): 9–10.

Johnson, Paul Christopher. "Religion and Diaspora." *Religion and Society: Advances in Research* 3 (2012): 95–114.

Keith, M. *After the Cosmopolitan? Multicultural Cities and the Future of Racism*. London and New York: Routledge, 2003.

———. "Making the Street Visible? Placing Racial Violence in Context." *New Community* 21 (1995): 551–565.

Koven, Seth. *Slumming: Sexual and Social Politics in Victorian London*. Princeton: Princeton University Press, 2004.

———. "The Whitechapel Picture Exhibitions and the Politics of Seeing." In *Museum Culture: Histories, Discourses, Spectacles*, edited by Itit Rogoff and Daniel J. Sherman, 22–48. Minneapolis: University of Minnesota Press, 1994.

Leech, Kenneth. *Doing Theology in Altab Ali Park*. London: Darton, Longman and Todd, 2006.

———. "A Personal Memoir." In *Father Gresham Kirkby 1916–2006. Priest of the Kingdom of God*, 1–9. London: Anglo-Catholic Historical Society, 2009.

———. *Through Our Long Exile: Contextual Theology and the Urban Experience*. London: Darton, Longman and Todd, 2001.

Maguire, Robert. "Church Design since 1950," *Ecclesiology Today* 27 (2002): 2–14.

———. "Meaning and Understanding." In *Towards a Church Architecture*, edited by Peter Hammond, 65–72. London: Architectural Press, 1962.

———. "Something Out of the Ordinary?" In *Architecture: Opportunities, Achievements. A Report of the Annual Conference of the Royal Institute of British Architects held at the University of Hull, 14 to 17 July 1976*, edited by Barbara Goldstein, 69–73. London: Royal Institute of British Architects, 1976.

Maguire, Robert and Keith Murray, "Anglican Church in Stepney," *Churchbuilding* 7 (Oct. 1962): 14–24.

Melhuish, Tom. "Shamiana: The Mughal Tent in the East End," *Church Building* (July/August 1998): 20–21.

Wedderburn, Sarah. "Behold, an Angel in the East." *Church Times*, August 20, 2004.

Conclusion

Symbolic Forms and the Abrahamic Religions

Sander L. Gilman

The boundaries that exist between the Abrahamic religions are real because they are symbolic and are symbolic because they are real. The essays in this volume illustrate the debates recounted in Benedict Anderson's *Imagined Communities: Reflections on the Origin and Spread of Nationalism* (1983) about the borders of the modern state. Anderson notes that these borders are where such states (and in our case read: religions) are "fully, flatly, and evenly operative over each square centimeter of a legally demarcated territory. But in the older imagining, where states were defined by centers, borders were porous and indistinct, and sovereignties faded imperceptibly into one another" (Anderson 1983, 19–22). Religions look separate even as they merge and compete, not only historically but in their physical as well as their theological interactions.

Contemporary evolutionary biology argues that such religions are one of the "groups [that] are the central mechanism for providing individuals with their identity; rather than thinking about individuals 'sacrificing' part of their identity when the become part of a group, [we should regard] individual identity as possible only in the context of secure group attachments. . . . The notion of individuals apart from groups . . . is a product of western thought, not the human experience" (Ross 1993, 76). Yet how these groups are imagined (and thus how ideas of individual autonomy are constituted) is part of the historical process as we have illustrated in this volume.

Until the eighteenth century, especially after the wars of religion in Europe, national and religious identity seemed to be fixed or at least stable: Church, Nobility, Commoners, and Peasantry shared common definitions of what religion they were and, even more clearly, what religions they were not. The anxiety about "heresy," such as about the Cathars, about the Jews, and about Islamic expansionism defined what were actually very fluid boundaries of religious belief and national identity. But even such boundaries are porous, "Medieval political speculation is imbued to the marrow with the idea of a structure of society based upon distinct orders," Johan Huizinga observes in *The Waning of the Middle Ages*:

[T]here are, first of all, the estates of the realm, but there are also the trades, the state of matrimony and that of virginity, the state of sin. At court there are the "four estates of the body and mouth": bread-masters, cup-bearers, carvers, and cooks. In the Church there are sacerdotal orders and monastic orders. Finally there are the different orders of chivalry. (Huizinga 2013, 47)

Yet these orders represented the sort of symbolic qualities of state we usually attribute to the "two bodies of the king," in Ernst Kantorowicz's sense, and the attendant symbolic values ascribed to religion in such contexts exist even into the present.

The movement toward such a modern symbolic sense of religious communities is complex and contradictory. Johann Gottfried Herder's (1744–1803) *Ideas for A Philosophy of the History of Mankind* (1784ff) in good Enlightenment tone evokes the temporality of human creations, the state as well as religion:

How transitory all human structures are . . . [the] . . . plant blossoms, and fades; your fathers have died, and moulded into dust: your temple is fallen: your tabernacles, the tables of your law are no more; language itself, that bond of mankind, becomes antiquated. (Herder 1784/1959, 38)

For this reason, he asks, "shall a political constitution, shall a system of government or religion . . . erected solely on these, endure for ever? If so, the wings of Time must be enchained." This leads Herder to criticize the stranglehold of "Tradition" which, "though in itself . . . an excellent institution of Nature, indispensable to the human race: but when it fetters the thinking faculty both in politics and education, and prevents all progress of the intellect, and all the improvement, that new times and circumstances demand, it is the true narcotic of the mind, as well to nations and sects, as to individuals." (Herder 1784/1959, 114) The conflict between what we affectively sense is the permanence of religious boundaries and practice and the temporality of the enactment of such boundaries and practices in the state lies at the heart of the debates around secularization in modernity.

It is theology, not monotheistic religious belief, that is temporal for Herder, as it is a century later for Friedrich Nietzsche, in what is without a doubt his most often cited and misunderstood passage "The Madman" from *The Gay Science* (1882):

Have you not heard of that madman who lit a lantern in the bright morning hours, ran to the marketplace and cried incessantly: "I am looking for God! I am looking for God!"
. . . "Where has God gone?" he cried. "I will tell you. We have killed him—you and I. We are all his murderers. But how have we done this? How were we able to drink up the sea? . . . Do we not hear anything yet of the noise of the gravediggers who are burying God? Do we not smell anything yet of God's putrefaction? Gods, too, decompose. God is dead. God remains dead. And we have killed him. How shall we, the murderers of all murderers, comfort ourselves? That

which was holiest and mightiest of all that the world has yet possessed has bled to death under our knives—who will wipe this blood off us?"

... Here the madman fell silent and again regarded his listeners; and they, too, were silent and stared at him in astonishment. At last he threw his lantern to the ground and it shattered and went out. "I come too early," he said then; "my time hasn't come yet. This tremendous event is still on its way, still traveling—it has not yet reached human ears. . . . This deed is still more distant from them than the most distant stars—*and yet we have done it ourselves.*"

It has also been related that on that same day the madman entered various churches and there sang a *requiem aeternam deo*. Led out and told to shut up, he is said to have retorted each time: "What are these churches now if they are not the tombs and sepulchers of God?" (Nietzsche 1882/1974, 125)

Here Nietzsche paraphrases Heinrich Heine, when in his memorial to Ludwig Börne (1840) he states that the Great God Pan is dead . . . It is the death of a living God entombed in the Temples of Religion that all these thinkers bemoan. The temporal existence of God is housed in the façade of religion. The secular state wrestles with the question of how religion and the state can or must interact. Is religion to be understood as "merely" symbolic and if so what do such symbols represent?

Karl Marx (1818–1883) argued in his *Preface and Introduction to a Critique of Political Economy* that "it is not the consciousness of men that determines their being, but on the contrary it is their social being that determines their consciousness" (Marx 1859/1970, 3). And part of that social being Marx argues as early as the 1840s is the question of religion and religious structures. State and religions are "imagined communities" in Benedict Anderson's sense as:

... an imagined political community—and imagined as both inherently limited and sovereign . . . because the members of even the smallest nation will never know most of their fellow-members, meet them, or even hear of them, yet in the minds of each lives the image of their communion. (Anderson 1983, 6)

Religion too follows this model. For Anderson:

[T]he concept [the nation] was born in an age in which Enlightenment and Revolution were destroying the legitimacy of the divinely-ordained, hierarchical dynastic realm. Coming to maturity at a stage of human history when even the most devout adherents of any universal religion were inescapably confronted with the living pluralism of such religions, and the allomorphism [direct relationship] between each faith's ontological claims and territorial stretch, nations dream of being free, and, if under God, directly so. The gage and emblem of this freedom is the sovereign state. (Anderson 1983, 6–7)

The very idea of religion in the secular state, however, retrains the sense of uniqueness in a world of secular multiplicities, and after the Enlightenment takes on self-consciously symbolic qualities.

Religion provides individuals in a secular state a symbolic identity as William Bloom, in his *Personal Identity, National Identity and International Relations* (1990) claims:

> National Identity . . . that paradigm condition in which a mass of people have made the same identification with the national symbols—have internalized the symbols of the nation—so that they may act as one psychological group when there is a threat to, or the possibility of the enhancement of, these symbols of national identity . . . (Bloom 1990, 52)
>
> The nation-state into which the infant is born as citizen is in a state of permanent competition with its international environment. Other countries are competitors in the great international game. (Bloom 1990, 74)

This "great international game" is played out within and among the Abrahamic religions in their confrontations with the secularization that characterizes modern religiously defined states (Iran, Pakistan) as well as those with state religions that do not define themselves by their religious practice (Israel, Norway), and those that abjure any religious definition but are bound historical to secularized models of religious identity (The United States, France). Indeed, the disappearance of a overarching religious identity in the older colonial states, such as Great Britain or France, seems to be paralleled by the ever greater valance of older religious beliefs, such as the abhorrence of homosexuality, in their former colonies. It is almost as if the power of colonial religions increases as the colonies become more and more independent.

The split between the older notions of a national religion as the binding power of the state and the rise of newer states, such as those in the Middle East and South Asia, in which such secular ideas are confronted with an ever greater importance of older religious models of identity are complicated by the simultaneous rise of global virtual religious communities. But even such expansions of the idea of a religious community are rooted in the symbolic. David Lyon, in his *The Steeple's Shadow: On the Myths and Realities of Secularization* (1987) noted that such postmodern social conditions are dominated by two realities. The first of these is the rise of new media technologies that provide "frames" for organizing experiencing, giving a sense of reality (while also blurring the line between the real and the image). These messages shape identity, which is now not seen as fixed, but as fragmentary and fluid. The second reality is the dominance of consumerism in society. We tend to define ourselves as consumers of symbols rather than producers of symbols.

Thus, Lyon notes that contemporary society pits the "plastic self," which makes identity as flexible as possible to experience as much as possible, against the "expressive self" that seeks authenticity and completion of the inner-narrative. As he notes, and our essays illustrate, the combination of these two dynamics cause identity to come to the foreground as a question that has no final answer. This is both a source of exhilaration (we are free to construct ourselves) and anxiety (we really do not know who we are at the deepest level).

Such a context of ambiguity leads to a rereading of religion as part of identity formation. The tradition sketched by Herder and Nietzsche has led to a dismissal of religion in the debates about cosmopolitanism in the twenty-first century. As Peter van der Veer in his volume *Imperial Encounters: Religion, Nation, and Empire* notes "perhaps the enlightened assumption is that a cosmopolitan person has to transcend religious tradition and thus be secular" (van der Veer 2001, 138). But this is certainly not the case Bruce Robbins in *Perpetual War: Cosmopolitanism from the Viewpoint of Violence* points out, which is that today, as much as in the past, religion is "certainly considered worth dying for by many" and is "at least as cosmopolitan as it is national" (Robbins 2012, 134). But it is vital to understand such a re-emergence of religion as part of identity not merely as part of a resurgence of state identification with religion as an institution but as part of Chantal Mouffe's articulation of the need in a democracy of what she has labeled "Deliberative Democracy or Agonistic Pluralism":

> Contrary to the model of "deliberative democracy," [the model of] "agonistic pluralism" that I am advocating asserts that the prime task of democratic politics is not to eliminate passions nor to relegate them to the private sphere in order to render rational consensus possible, but to mobilize those passions towards the promotion of democratic designs. Far from jeopardizing democracy, agonistic confrontation is in fact its very condition of existence. (Mouffe 1999, 456)

The essays in this volume illustrate that this irreconcilability of opposing positions as well as the potential for rational consensus illustrates the power of modernity where pluralism can be productive or destructive whether in forms of alliance or confrontation.

References

Anderson, Benedict. *Imagined Communities: Reflections on the Origin and Spread of Nationalism*. London: Verso, 1983.

Bloom, William. *Personal Identity, National Identity and International Relations*. Cambridge: Cambridge University Press, 1990.

Herder, Johann Gottfried. "Ideas Toward a Philosophy of the History of Man." In *Theories of History*, edited by Patrick L. Gardiner, 34–49. New York: Free Press, 1959.

Huizinga, Johan. *The Waning of the Middle Ages*. Garden City, NY: Doubleday & Co., 1954/2013.

Kantorowicz, Ernst. *The King's Two Bodies: A Study in Mediaeval Political Theology*. Princeton, NJ: Princeton University Press, 1957.

Lyon, David. *The Steeple's Shadow: On the Myths and Realities of Secularization*. Grand Rapids, MI: Eerdmans, 1987.

Marx, Karl. *Preface and Introduction to a Critique of Political Economy*. Moscow: Progress Publishers, 1970.

Mouffe, Chantal. "Deliberative Democracy or Agonistic Pluralism?" *Social Research* 66 (1999): 745–758.

Nietzsche, Friedrich. *The Gay Science*. Walter Kaufmann, trans. New York: Vantage Books, 1974.

Robbins, Bruce. *Perpetual War: Cosmopolitanism from the Viewpoint of Violence Perpetual War: Cosmopolitanism from the Viewpoint of Violence*. Durham, NC: Duke University Press, 2012.

Ross, Marc H. *The Management of Conflict: Interpretations and Interests in Comparative Perspective*. New Haven, CT: Yale University Press, 1993.

van der Veer, Peter. *Imperial Encounters: Religion, Nation, and Empire*. Princeton: Princeton University Press, 2001.

Index